Praise for *Beyond Duct Tape*

Everyone who has been through church planting knows that it is a family affair. It's "all hands on deck"—the church planter's wife and children are deeply involved. Yet spouses of church planters at most get a chapter in books on church planting—if they are fortunate. Here, however, Shari Thomas and Tami Resch have written and assembled an entire volume, filled with all kinds of tools, helping wives to not only cope with the intense thing that is church planting, but to grow powerfully and minister effectively. I'm grateful for their work.

Tim Keller, Redeemer Presbyterian Church, New York City
Author of *Generous Justice* and *The Reason for God*

Tami Resch is proficient at duct tape strategies learned in the trenches of life as a church planter's wife. She knows well the long hours, the disappointments, the multitasking that leave a woman feeling as if she is put together with pieces of tape. But this book is not about survival strategies. It is a tale of how long, deep draughts of God's grace have moved Tami beyond a life of patchwork pieces into the center of the battle where she has become a warrior leader for other church planting spouses. This book will challenge you. The vulnerability and openness in its pages may even frighten you. But read on! You will find great encouragement for your heart and an invitation to live a Kingdom adventure where there may be great risk but there is great reward.

Ruth Ann Batstone, mentor and counselor, World Harvest Mission

Shari Thomas is a lover of Jesus and scripture. She has worked and lived in an environment that has struggled with women's roles in leadership. Her suffering and joy have given her a heart of compassion and wisdom not only for the church planter's wife, but also the whole family. She shares the hardship of the calling and offers practical advice on how to navigate rocky terrain. If you are in the thick of it or just starting out as a church planter, this book is for you. Get out your notebook because this is not a book for lightweights.

Becky Allender, wife of a church planter for a short season

In *Beyond Duct Tape*, Shari Thomas and Tami Resch exude wisdom, passion and a deep love for pastors' wives. This is a much needed book that can guide wives of church planters to walk in step with the gospel. I was challenged and stretched as I read this book. I highly recommend it.

Scott Thomas, President of Acts 29 Network

In *Beyond Duct Tape*, Thomas and Resch provide a huge gift to those called to serve Christ in his church. They invite us to take the truths of the gospel and interweave them into our own stories, by challenging our own doubts and by calling us back to the One the True Story is about. It is a delightful collection of superb thinking and heart application of the gospel. As you read it, pray, "Lord speak to me," but be careful, he probably will!

Tom and Rachel Wood, Church Multiplication Ministries Inc.

I needed this book. Shari and Tami not only understand the unique struggles of church planting spouses, they apply gospel truth in wise and practical ways that give me hope. I am constantly sharing their insights with friends, family, and fellow church-planting spouses. God has used this material to hold my heart together through the squalls of church planting, and I am confident he can use it in your life, too.

Anne Henegar, church planting alongside her husband at Atlanta Westside Presbyterian Church

BEYOND
DUCT TAPE

HOLDING THE HEART TOGETHER
IN A LIFE OF MINISTRY

SHARI THOMAS and TAMI RESCH

parakaleo
COMING ALONGSIDE CHURCH PLANTING SPOUSES

WWW.PARAKALEO.US

Editors: Carrie Ott and Maria Garriott
Interior design: Carrie Ott
Cover design: Susie Quillen www.designeyeq.com
Photo Shots: Chris Rank www.rankstudios.com

ISBN 978-1461151296

RELIGION/SPIRITUAL

Printed in the United States of America

www.parakaleo.us

First printing August 2011

[TABLE OF CONTENTS]

What This Is and What This Isn't
by the authors

WE'RE CHURCH PLANTERS. WELL, NOT EXACTLY. We are married to church planters. Does that make us church planters? Well no, and yes, and sometimes. Confused? If you are married to a church planter or a minister, you probably know exactly what we are talking about. Like many before us and many who will follow, we have found ourselves in the complex world…

…of not being the planter, yet often taking on many of the planter roles.

…of not carrying the weight of the final decisions, yet having the weight of those same decisions deeply affect us and our families.

…of either being deeply involved in the church, or carrying most of the child raising responsibilities, or both.

…of bringing in a paycheck in order to help make ends meet or trying to still pursue our own careers.

…of living in a world where in one minute we love the ride, and in the next we'd do anything to jump off the roller coaster.

If you are new to planting, you might hope that within these pages you will find exactly what you are supposed to do and how you are supposed to do it. But if you have been in ministry for awhile, you are probably cringing at the thought of anyone trying to squeeze you and your spouse into one more ministry Barbie and Ken mold.

We have written this book to help reveal and cast off some of those molds and misconceptions. The concepts and tools found in these pages have proven helpful for both men and women in a variety of ministry contexts. However, we have purposely chosen examples and used terminology for wives in church planting. Our desire for ourselves and for you is freedom—more and more freedom!

More freedom to be who God designed us to be.

More freedom to love boldly and passionately.

More freedom to live in a way that deeply trusts God's love for us, our families, and our churches.

"FOR IT IS FOR FREEDOM Christ has set us free." (Galatians 5:1) We believe that to the extent we know and experience the freedom of the gospel, to that extent we can flourish in the world of ministry.

This is not a guide to tell you what role you should take in planting. It doesn't cover every struggle you will encounter, or guarantee your kids will thrive. And it certainly won't give you some secret weapon to alleviate the pain and suffering of ministry.

What we do in *Beyond Duct Tape* is identify the salient areas where people in this role struggle and shine. We disclose the myths spouses have discovered. We tell their stories. And we share tools and resources that have helped so many of us.

The tools selected for this book are just a few of the ones we use in training and one-on-one coaching. To get the most out of this book, consider using it as a workbook with a group of like-minded people, or with a like-minded friend. If you are new to ministry and especially to church planting, we highly recommend walking through these tools with a coach. Perhaps you are in a place where all you can do is read about the journeys of others who live in this unique calling and discover that you are not alone and that you are not crazy—even when it feels like it.

However you choose to use this book, we hope you will be pointed to the One who never leaves you to journey alone through your fear and doubt. We hope the stories of rescue will help you recognize the many ways that you, too, have been rescued—thus increasing your faith. We hope the stories of lives yet unfinished will encourage you to hope as you wait in your as-yet-unfinished stories. Ultimately, we hope all of us will be propelled forward in love: for our families, for our churches, and for the communities to which we have been called.

7

Why These Things?
by the authors

Story, Gospel, Idolatry, Calling & Identity, and Community.

We've chosen five. And we've often referred to them as Our Deeply Held Convictions. These are the five non-negotiables that must be addressed as we seek to survive and thrive in the world of church planting. They are flash points for our growth or stagnation; areas in which we can fly or flounder; core issues that not only define us, but will mark our ministry.

Of course there are many important issues we could have named here. And of course we are assuming that there are beliefs and practices you will take with you into your church planting journey whether we mention them or not, beliefs and practices such as prayer, spiritual journaling, and Sabbath rest.

So why have we chosen these particular five and placed them in this particular order?

We're glad you asked! We begin with **story**, because until we see how our story intersects with God's story, we are just playing with principles and theologies far removed from our experiences and our hearts. Our story impacts everything: how we view God, relate to others, plant a church, and raise kids.

We move on to the **gospel** because without it all we do is drag our good intentions, our self-sufficiency, our good works, our inevitable failures, and our defeating shame with us wherever we go. We've heard the gospel so many times we forget we need to hear it again and again. If the gospel is truly good news, then it is always a new, good news that brings a bright freshness each time it comes to us. No one stands on the street corner yelling, "Good news! Good news!" about news that has become outdated, unimportant, or inapplicable.

With a new awareness of our story and a deepened appreciation of the gospel, we gain the desire and the courage to face the issue of **idolatry**. Here is where we delve even deeper into how good the good news really is when it is brought to bear on the ways we've learned to build, settle for, and maintain our lesser gods.

Having obtained a deeper understanding of the gospel and our story, and having taken a sobering look at our insatiable need to make our life work and our adept idol-making skills, we find our hearts humbled, ready, and emboldened to hear more clearly from God who *he* says we are: our **identity**; and how he longs for you and me to join him in a particular way as he redeems all things: our **calling**.

And where else to end but in **community**, where we live and breathe and grapple with all these things? Without each other, our ever-evolving stories remain disjointed, unsolvable mysteries. Without each other we seldom find, grasp, or continue to believe the radical implications of the gospel. In community, as broken as it is, we have the greatest chance of revealing and dethroning our lesser gods. And it is in community that we find the courage and clarity to embrace and inhabit our identity and callings.

We have delved into, wrestled with, and become intimately acquainted with each of these five convictions we bring to you. Over and over we find them to be inexhaustible and ever new. We invite you to take your own swan dive into the nuances, intricacies, and wonders of each. And we cheer you on as you discover the many bridges, paths, and tunnels that link them to each other. Welcome!

STORY

WHAT IS MINE ?

WHY DOES IT MATTER ?

God is manifest in the ordinary, in the actual, in
the daily, in the now, in the concrete incarnations
of life. That is why I say it is our experiences that
transform us if we are willing to experience our
experiences all the way through.   RICHARD ROHR

10

The Myths of Story
by Shari Thomas

"I don't see what the big deal is about looking at our pasts. Come on, God forgives. It's time we do too."

"Looking at your past just promotes narcissistic navel gazing."

"I'm raising two toddlers. A third child is on the way. We are in the first year of our church plant, and you're asking me to take time to look at my story! Are you serious?!"

SO WHY THE AUDACITY TO suggest looking at your past during this intense stage of life? How could this be an ideal time to do it? Perhaps it's not. But maybe, just maybe, the intensity of this time of life is bringing out a side of you that is a bit unfamiliar. What of those nagging thoughts about your faith that surface in the middle of the night? The ones you thought were firmly settled? What of your attitude toward people in your core group or in your church that surprise you? Do brushes with conflict draw others deeper into relationship with you or encourage them to keep a safe distance? Or do people find you so nice that you don't have any conflicts at all? Do you feel compelled to take on ministries just because there is no one else to do it?

Could your story and how you view your world impact these situations? We think the answer is yes.

You'll find further teaching in this manual on forgiveness, repentance, identity, and the like. However, we are convinced that merely applying principles and biblical teaching to these issues without any regard for the story God has placed you in leaves the surface of these issues barely scratched.

Out of our unique stories emerge

> *If we do not transform our pain, we will most assuredly transmit it.*
> —*Richard Rohr,* Things Hidden: Scripture as Spirituality

our styles of relating, our philosophies about boundaries, and our posture toward pain. These are just a few of the issues that deeply affect our relationships, and thus our churches. So often we attempt to deal with these issues by just doing what we think needs to be done or should be done, but we never look at how or why we think the way we do about our relationships and what they require. Yes, we all know that

trying to measure up to the inordinate standards we hold for ourselves, or that others hold for us, is a living death. We know this living death is never espoused in scripture, and we certainly don't want to engender it in our churches, yet how often do we continue to live and move in just this way?

We believe that free grace penetrates our hearts in the here and now only to the depth that we allow it to simultaneously penetrate our past histories, pains, and woundings. Allowing ourselves to see and experience the negative aspect of our lives along with the positive keeps us from avoiding, denying, and compartmentalizing the truth. By seeing our lives as they really are (or were), we see that the God of the universe has invited us to know the real him in the reality of our lives. Sadly, when we deny the truth of our own lives, we ask other people to do the same with theirs. We can only invite others into their lives as far as we have gone into ours. When we truly experience a God who can handle the ugliness and brokenness of our lives,

> *Stories tell me not only who I am but also who you are and what we are together. In fact, without you and your story I cannot know myself and my story. No one's story exists alone. Each is tangled up in countless others. Pull a thread in my story and feel the tremor half a world and two millennia away.*
> —*Daniel Taylor,* The Healing Power of Stories

story

our anger, and our shame, as well as our delight, our glory, and our hope, then we can invite others to know this same God.

It is our belief that the more we know and become familiar with our own stories, developing self-awareness and healthy critical thinking, the more we have the capacity to know God and his story. When we truly see our pasts for what they are, then we can begin to understand how we have sought to bring peace into our lives apart from relying on Christ. We begin to see where we have created idols to give us a false sense of hope and comfort. We begin to see how we relate to others apart from relying on Christ.

The more we open the doors to our past, the more freedom we encounter. It is this freedom that draws others to the life-giving hope we possess.

So, more than helpful tips on ministry, we need this God to invade our stories and our lives—past, present, and future. As we live out of our own stories, we discover we are uniquely created for this life to which we have been called. We do possess the gifts, the abilities, and the power of the Spirit that enables us to live this life. We begin to see that ministry is not something we do, but something we are. The power of comparison and envy of others begins to lose its grip. We begin to see and slowly believe that our unique story, which formed who we are, is much needed in our family, in our church, and in our community.

Do you know your own story?

Let each generation tell its children of your mighty acts; let them proclaim your power. I will meditate on your majestic, glorious splendor and your wonderful miracles. Your awe-inspiring deeds will be on every tongue; I will proclaim your greatness. Everyone will share the story of your wonderful goodness; they will sing with joy of your righteousness.
—Psalm 145:4-7 (NLT)

Jesus shines the light of the gospel on us both to expose our brokenness and to bring us to brokenness. I guess we should call this "gospel brokenness," because only the gospel of God's grace can enable us to be completely honest about our stuff without falling into toxic shame or self-contempt. And only the gospel can humble us, soften us, and give us the power to repent - or at least, not run away or rant. When followers of Jesus walk openly in this kind of brokenness—gospel brokenness—angels in heaven rejoice, and people without faith, or those with much cynicism about Christians, are likely to reconsider who Jesus is. Write this down: no greater beauty can be found at any point or any place in God's story than the times when God's people manifest this gospel brokenness—for that is where God's glory is revealed most clearly.

—Scotty Smith, Restoring Broken Things

God's Story, My Story
by Shari Thomas

I GREW UP IN A FAMILY OF STORYTELLERS, and many of the stories my family told time and time again were from the Bible. One of the stories I heard was about two undisciplined sons who died for their folly and their fat, priestly father who obviously fathered poorly and did not care well for his people. Upon learning of his sons' death, he fell over dead himself. I thought to myself, "Lesson One: Don't be foolish! Lesson Two: When I have kids, I better teach them well, or else! Lesson Three: Don't get fat!"

Well-meaning teachers wagged their fingers, "Do better, be better, or else you'll end up like that." Quite frankly, I was rather intrigued by many of these stories. What would it take to be a Delilah who maybe didn't win the *heart* of Samson, but got the most sought after man in her bed? Maybe I could learn something.

Lost in the many dos and don'ts, the tales of intrigue and deception, the stories of heroism and folly, I just never got the big picture. Somehow the stories all ended with Jesus being the answer, but the questions seemed measly and were ones I really didn't want to ask. When I asked my real questions, especially at church, I was met with stares and the room would go silent. I felt a deep sense of shame wash over me that I even had the questions I did.

Yet I knew there was something I was supposed to learn. Finally I boiled it down to this: Fear God above all else. I mean, fear, as in the fear that nothing could be worse then God finding you out, for he could see what even mothers couldn't see. The way to get God really good and mad at you was to sin. In the stories I had heard,

people were struck dead when they lied. If God could catch those lies, he could see through anything I did. For me, fearing God meant fearing sin above all else. In my child's mind, this meant managing all my small sins which would of course help me keep my distance from any of the big ones— the ones that would really upset him. Or, perhaps I could merely kill any desire or longing that might eventually get me into trouble. Then I wouldn't even be tempted to sin! Yes, that was the answer. In the Christian world I lived in, this wasn't hard to do. Hanging around many of the Christians I knew, not to mention attending church services, could kill the joy of the happiest person. Desire? Ever sit through a missionary slide show? My deepest desire was figuring out how to get the dour missionary to end the slide show as quickly as possible! And this was how we entertained ourselves at Christmas parties! In my world there wasn't really much time, inclination, or motivation to sin, at least not the way I was taught to define sin.

TRUE DESIRE WAS KEPT SAFELY AT BAY. And sin was made manageable. All was well with my world, and I hadn't yet reached my twenties.

Surely, among our deepest regrets will be that we have managed to somehow lead such tremendously boring lives!

It wasn't until I sat in a college classroom listening to a small, meek man tell us, in almost a whisper, the BIG picture of the Story of God, that something—was it desire? longing?—began to stir inside me.

13

I had grown accustomed to the tossed salad approach to the Bible—picking out the good stories for role model material and discarding the bad as unfortunate waywardness. Instead, this man served up the whole meal. I began to see something new. In his classes, Buck Hatch built a framework for the gospel story which pieced together the many "discarded" stories I had wrestled with into a workable whole.

Twenty-plus years later, with the help of another friend, Elizabeth Turnage, I began to see the place my own story had in the gospel story. From her, I discovered the very precious gift my story contained. She sent me headlong into the priceless journey of telling my story purposefully, honestly, and honorably.

I learned my story began with the first of all stories, in the garden. It is a story of beauty, and I learned we were created for glory, for joy, for delight, for desire. We are glorious creatures. But it is also a story of tragedy. We are fallen and we live in a broken world. This was not merely a story of sin, but a story of sinners. Sinners. Even when we are looking our best, when our teeth are shiny-white and straightened, when we finally lose that last ten pounds, when the expensive bra hides what sags—even then we find how often we mimic the "us" we *want* to be, hiding who we truly *are*. How often are we one small step away from stubbing the polish off yellowing toenails? How often are we one small slip of a word or deed away from exposing the rotting decay below the glossy front we present to the world? This is the tragedy.

But the Story tells us we are loved anyway. Even when we don't know our own misfortune, God does. Even in our shiny pretending, he cherishes us, forgives us, and bleeds for us. It's like a *true* fairy tale. One where, when all hope seems gone, a rescuer indeed comes. And he comes again and again, in the many tiny rescues of our lives, as well as the One Big Rescue when his life was given to save all of us he dearly loves. It is a fairy tale in that it seems too good to be true, yet there really is a happy ending.

But it's not only about the ending.

Extraordinary things happen to us and in us and through us, before the end! We find that in spite of ourselves, we rise to the occasion, we manage not only to survive, but to shine. How is that possible?

It's the gospel.

It's a fairy tale.

It's true.

We find our tragedies are redeemed and we are given a new name, a new family. Our frozen hearts are thawed, and we are invited to join in writing the rest of our story.

Ah, so *this* is where I begin to fit in with David and Esther, Moses and Sarah, Samson and Rahab. They aren't Sunday school stories anymore. They are raw, beautiful, horrible stories—real flesh and blood stories, and mine is among them. We are all part of the Larger Story. All of our tragedies, hopes, comedies, and fairy tales blend together, weaving into the One Great Story.

The Story of Redemption.

In his book *Telling Secrets*, Frederick Buechner writes,

Maybe nothing is more important than that we keep track, you and I, of our stories; who we are and where we have come from and the people we have met along the way. It is precisely through these stories, in all their particularity, as I have long believed and often said, that God makes himself known to each of us most powerfully and personally. If this is true, to lose track of our stories is to be profoundly impoverished not only humanly but also spiritually. The God of biblical faith is a God who began history in the first place. He is also a God who moment by moment, day by day, continues to act in history. He acts in the history that gets written down in the New York Times in the same way he acts in my history and your history, which may not get written down anywhere except in the few lines that will be allotted to us on some obituary page. The Exodus, the Covenant, the Entry into the Promised Land—such mighty acts of God appear in Scripture, but are no less mighty than the acts of God as they appear in our own lives.

What is your part of the story?

Do you hide? Do you alter your story? Do you tell

a better story of yourself than is true? David and Esther, Moses and Sarah, Samson and Rahab did not. Are you tempted to squeeze your story into a preconceived idea of what you think others want you to be—one that would serve as a good role model? Maybe you try to hide some pieces of your story in hopes that they didn't really happen. Sadly, this temptation is often greatest for those of us in the church, and especially for those of us in professional ministry. I mean, after all, we truly want our churches to succeed. If we need to hide our real sins, or squelch who we really are, shouldn't we do it for the sake of the Church? Or if nothing else, for self preservation? You may have been deeply hurt in ministry and, quite frankly, may have good reason not to open up to others. Why should you take the risk?

The only truly powerful personal story is the true story.
~Leanne Downing

It is for freedom Christ has set us free.
~The Apostle Paul

This freedom liberates us from being conformed to the image of the world (those nagging inner voices that tell us we need to hide who we really are to please others), and reminds us of our true identity in Christ. Yes, wisdom dictates that we don't share every aspect of our story with everyone. But we are free to be vulnerable because it is Christ who defines us. Often in church leadership we feel we need to be cautious with what we say and how much we share of ourselves. It is vitally important we create environments and communities where we can share our stories as we grow and thrive. Telling our stories is one of the most caring and liberating things we can do for each other.

Remembering the bad parts of our story may be painful and provoke deep questions about the meaning of our lives and the meaning of what God has for us. But remembering reminds us, and others, of what Christ has really done for us. Remembering inspires faith and encourages us to dream of the redemption yet to come while we are yet in the middle of painful unfinished stories. Re-

membering draws us to hope in our One True Hope. As we remember with others, we are all reminded how our lives and stories are part of the Great Story God is writing. It is in this Great Story we find the courage to love each other and God with abandon!

This is true freedom!

I encourage you to look for others with whom you can share your stories—stories from the past and stories of the present. And I encourage you to dream of how God will form your stories of the future. The tools given here will help you learn to share your own stories truthfully and with kindness to yourself. We hope you find great courage to tell your story—it's one of the most meaningful and powerful ways to recount the marvelous deeds God has done.

God leads us step by step, from event to event. Only afterwards, as we look back over the way we have come and reconsider certain important moments in our lives in the light of all that has followed them, or when we survey the whole progress of our lives, do we experience the feeling of having been led without knowing it, the feeling that God has mysteriously guided us. Time has to elapse to enable us to see it.

—Paul Tournier, Reflections

TOOLS on STORY

17

story

Finding Your Place in God's Cosmic Story
by Shari Thomas

Why Use This Tool?
- To develop a framework for a biblical worldview
- To answer the questions, How did it all start? What went wrong? How is going to get fixed? How will it end?
- To identify how your life story reflects God's cosmic story

The overarching story conveyed in the Bible is one of grace. Often we refer to the Bible in the categories of: Creation, Fall, Redemption, and Restoration.

Creation in all its glory can be characterized as a time of peace, or life as it was meant to be. The world was perfect. The most beautiful day we have ever seen gives us merely a glimpse of what nature was created to be. I often wonder, did the trees walk, did they talk? When they shed their leaves in the Garden, did they burst into a show of flaming colors combined with song in their native tongue? Surely our greatest imaginings do not come close to guessing the glorious possibilities of an unspoiled creation. We know that the world we live in today—and all that we see around us—is nothing compared to what it was created to be. And what of us humans? What were we like when we were without sin? We who were designed with dignity and in the image of God himself often have little idea what immortal beings of glory we were meant to be, and can be.... and one day will be! I am convinced that when we look at God's story and our own stories we begin to get a glorious view of what he is calling us to be now, and where and how we can join him in bringing in his Kingdom.

When sin entered because of the Fall, this shalom—everything in perfect wholeness—was shattered. The beauty of nature was marred and broken. Since then, life has not functioned as it was meant to. Even when I climb the snow-peaked ridges of the Olympic Pennisula and gasp at the beauty, it's only a small picture of how great it once was. Humans, while still bearing God's image and created with dignity, are not now what we were meant to be. When I watch a volleyball game and see a girl in perfect form spike the ball exactly where she wants, I wonder how high she would be able to jump if she was not affected by the Fall? Can you even imagine or guess at what it could have been? Often, when I snuggle up to one of my children and touch their soft, sweet necks, I marvel at the smoothness of their skin. And yet I know that what I see is nothing close to what they, in physical form (let alone emotional or spiritual), were meant to be. At its best, the human race is in a state of decay. If you don't believe me, go look in the mirror. Even when we shine as our very best selves—in times of great personal accomplishment and moments of redeeming sacrificial love—we still show signs of decay. We live and move in the Fall.

But what about redemption? In the Garden, even when the curse was spoken over mankind, God sowed the seeds of redemption. Almost hidden, yet right there in Genesis 3:15, we find the first reference to the offspring of woman—Jesus—who will crush Satan's head. A Redeemer is coming who will right all wrongs, who will save us, restore us, heal us. We experience bits and glimpses of this now. We can already see in some aspects of our stories where Christ has come and begun to make all things new. It's here already, but not yet complete as it will one day be. We all have stories where we've been rescued by Christ. Sometimes we can see them clearly; at other times we feel as if we are gazing into a muddy lake, unable to see anything. But it's there. Even when we don't see it fully, or clearly, we know that one day all things will be restored.

Another name for the story of grace is *the progress of redemption*. We see that the purpose of the Bible is to show that history moves progressively toward a goal, toward completion, toward the day when all things will be made new. This is what we often forget and yet what all of scripture points to—the restoration—when Christ

story

will return and restore all things to their rightful place—to wholeness and complete perfection. So even though redemption comes now, it comes only partially. One day it will come fully and completely.

While this larger arc and story are evident in history as a whole, we also see the many small stories of the Bible that form the larger story. Each Bible story contains signposts for redemption. And as we study them, we find they contain (in smaller versions) mirrors of creation, fall, redemption, and the signs of what will one day be restoration. The stories of Esther, Moses, Samson, Rahab, David, and Elijah all contain images of smaller redemptions while at the same time pointing to *the* Redemption, when our Redeemer will come and bring redemption to the entire world and to each and all our stories (restoration). Their stories point to this Redeemer and are a chapter in the greater story of redemption.

While our stories may not get written down in history books or mentioned in the news, they also reflect what we see in scripture: Creation, Fall, Redemption, and Restoration. And just like the heroes of old, Noah and Lydia, Deborah and Paul, we each play a role on the various stages of our lives in this grand play of redemption. Yet, unlike a theatrical production, our roles are not tediously scripted for us. Oh yes, we have a sovereign God, but he invites us to join him in this great story of redemption. Come into the play; enter into the drama of the history of the world, and join him in bringing redemption! What is your part? What has your story been up to this point? Where do you see him bringing redemption in your life and where is he inviting you to join him in bringing redemption to others?

It is helpful to think of your life in the categories mentioned on "The Progress of Redemption" chart on page 28.

Creation in your story is not just when you were conceived or born; think metaphorically. Just as life in the garden was without brokenness, do you remember a time in your life characterized by shalom or peace?

Fall: When did you first become aware of peace being shattered? How did you then seek to restore peace on your own? (This will give you a hint of where you tend toward idolatries.)

Have you experienced **Redemption**? Have you come to see where Christ comes in and saves, not just eternally, but in the here and now? How is peace partially restored in the here and now in your life?

Consummation: What do you envision your life will look like when peace is one day fully restored?

Try looking at the smaller stories of your life in the same structure of these four categories: Creation, Fall, Redemption, Restoration.

Here are some examples:

Adam and Eve
They are the only two people in history who have known creation and life in complete perfection. Their first encounter with the Fall, their fall, was more brutal than we can imagine, as they *immediately* felt and knew that life was now terribly broken. The first recorded realization of shame flowed from the burning knowledge of being seen, or known, with all their sin. And the first recorded reaction to shame was hiding. Their response to shattered peace was also to shift blame. Hint: Look for how we do the same in our stories. The curse, while a result of the Fall, also brought a sign of redemption in seed form for them and for future humanity. The curse not only *hindered* Adam and Eve from getting everything they desired, it *protected* them from getting everything they desired—just as it protects us from getting everything we desire. If, with a fallen nature, we could get all we long

for by our own efforts, we would completely devour and destroy ourselves along with everyone and everything in our path. So while the curse *is* a curse, it is also a kindness of God that already brings partial redemption (as a way to keep us from devouring ourselves). The curse also promises future redemption (through Christ, born of a woman) and ultimately complete redemption (consummation, which will restore all things).

Esther

We don't have any record of Esther knowing life the way God originally designed it to be (shalom). We enter her story at the cusp of destruction for her and her entire nation. She is already an orphan, so we don't know if she ever knew her parents. She is living in captivity. She has had plenty of experience with life not being how it should have been. Her ascent to the throne could have been her attempt to save herself and opt for a life better than the one slavery offered her. We could so easily justify Esther's actions. Her longings for a better life are ones we all share. Yet Mordecai, her cousin and guardian, confronts her. Esther's repentance from seeking to save only herself is clearly portrayed when she risks her life to save her nation. In her story, we see her beautifully waiting on her God to bring redemption, which comes not only for her, but for her nation through her. Not only do they find rescue, but Esther becomes a prototype of the great Rescuer who would one day come. Redemption, clearly seen in Esther's story for herself and others, also points to that future day when salvation will come for many through one.

Cindy

She has early memories of a cohesive family unit with two parents and two siblings. But after her parents divorced, she longed to keep her world from further falling apart. She found that making her mother happy was the best way to achieve this. By the age of nine, she was keeping the home clean, the family fed, and covering for her father's multiple affairs. It wasn't until after she became a Christian that she realized Christ had become merely one more person she worked very hard to please. She began to understand her story and recognize her legitimate longings to be loved as well as her valid fear of betrayal and abandonment. Cindy began to grieve over how she had been sinned against and how she, in turn, used kindness and favors to manipulate others into not abandoning or betraying her. She began to repent of this twisted form of kindness. Redemption is coming into her story as God is using her redeemed gift of kindness to draw many to her. What used to be only a strategy to keep Cindy's life free of conflict has become a passion to use her gentle ways and soft words—filled with truth—to set others free. She occasionally catches glimpses of that future day and what a completed Cindy will look like as she rests completely in the one who will never abandon her.

Curt and Charlotte

Curt and Charlotte's first year and a half at Grace Hill was characterized by unity of vision, selfless sacrifice, and very little conflict. Gossip was almost non-existent among the body. But when they enrolled their son in the neighborhood public school, the church body began to unravel. Because Curt and Charlotte were homeschooling when they planted Grace Hill, many assumed that they would make homeschooling a hallmark of the church. Curt and Charlotte were unprepared for the biting and devouring that ensued as families drew battle lines on school choice. Within two weeks, six families left the church, unwilling even to speak to Curt about their concerns. They were tempted to say "Good riddance!" But God had been showing them both how often they too placed their own choices, ideologies, and reputations as their primary source of identity and worth. They longed for change in themselves, their church, and those who left. Instead of succumbing to the reflex of pleasing people at any cost, they refrained from removing their son from the school. As Charlotte reflected on this, she was amazed to see how much God was changing her heart. The painful hemorrhaging of their church body plunged both of them deeper into the implications of the gospel and their identity individually and corporately. They are sad; but they are also excited to see how God will knit diverse people together in love when men and women from every tribe, nation, and schooling choice will worship in Spirit and truth.

 story

God's Story: Art and Narrative

The Art of God's Story
by David Arms

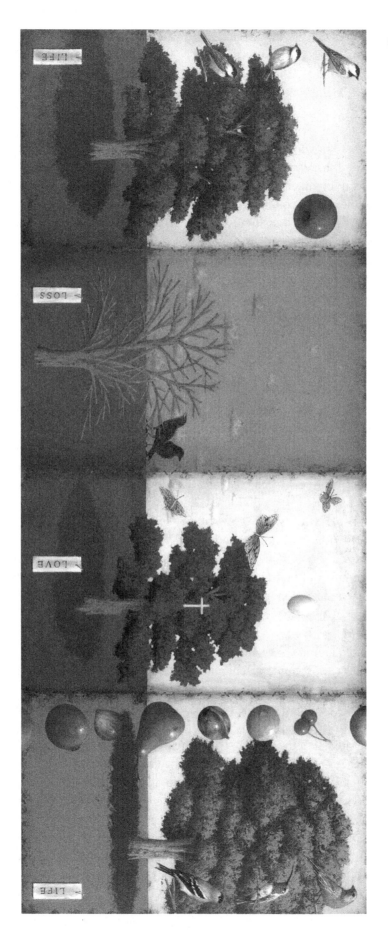

Scotty Smith and David Arms have graciously granted us permission to reproduce this beautiful painting, "God's Story," by David Arms. Because of printing constraints, we were unable to bring it to you in color. You may view the original painting at www.christcommunity.org/Home/OurVisionValues/GodsStory.aspx. Please do not copy or reproduce this artwork without consent of Scotty Smith at www.ChristCommunity.org.

story

The Narrative of God's Story
by Scotty Smith

Why Use This Tool?
- To gain an artistic perception of God's beautiful story
- To meditate on the centrality of Jesus in the entire biblical narrative
- To expand our biblical worldview

September 2007

In October 2003, David Arms and I met at the Green Hills Starbucks to collaborate over coffee. I had a gnawing longing, and I was convinced David had the art and the heart to make this longing a reality. I had just one not-so-simple request. I ached for someone to capture on canvas the Story from which all stories come… God's Story, as it progressively unfolds in the Bible, in history, and in broken hearts.

To say I was stunned when I walked into David's studio and saw the completed piece for the first time would not do justice to what I felt. Overwhelmed by beauty, I rejoiced in David's capacity to capture the glory of the most wonder-full story in the world. But as I continue to study the painting as a whole, and every little detail prayed and brushed onto the canvas, I experience the full range of emotions God's Story calls forth in the hearts of those who enter it. Both David and I hope this will be your experience as well.

God's Story comes to us as a redemptive drama in four parts:

Creation - when everything was as God meant it to be.

Fall - the tragic intrusion of sin and death, resulting in the pervasive brokenness of all people and everything God has made.

Redemption - God's astonishing promise to redeem his fallen image bearers and creation through the grace-full work of his Son, Jesus Christ.

Consummation - the magnificent fulfillment of God's plan to gather and cherish a people forever, and to live with them in a more-than-restored world, called "the new heaven and new earth."

Each panel of the painting presents one of the four interrelated parts of God's Story, and each is replete with well-chosen symbols. First you notice that a tree is the predominant image in each panel; each tree is tagged with an identifying word: life, loss, love, and again, life. Why was a tree chosen as the best symbol to tell God's Story? When God first created mankind, he placed Adam and Eve in a garden paradise called Eden. In the middle of the

Garden was the tree of life, a clear statement and celebration of the fact that God is so very good and generous. It is from God that we receive life and it is from him that all blessings flow. However, the tree of life wasn't placed in the center of the Garden just as a reminder of the goodness of God, but also of the "godness" of God. God is God, and we are not! The tree of life calls us to great gratitude and great humility.

First Panel

Depicting Creation, we see the tree of life standing tall and verdant. To the left David has painted three black-capped chickadees, whose cheerful disposition and life-giving call represent Adam and Eve, and all of creation, singing God's praise. The pristine wonder of the beauty, truth, and goodness of the first heaven and first earth compelled such a full-hearted, full-voiced response. The prominent, bright red apple in the upper right corner represents both God's gracious provision and the loving prohibition he placed on Adam and Eve. As his trusted stewards and beloved image bearers, the first man and first woman were free to eat from the fruit of any tree in the Garden of Eden—except the fruit of the tree of the knowledge of good and evil.

Though the Bible never says the fruit of this tree was an apple, this notion became well-established legend. Whatever the fruit, death was the promised consequence for violating God's boundary and clear warning. Listening to the enticing lies of the serpent, Eve and Adam chose to disregard God's will, and the result was catastrophic. Sin and death entered their hearts and every sphere of God's creation. As a result of the Fall, nothing remained as it was meant to be. Everything and everyone was broken. The first couple, who had lived in shameless nakedness before God and one another, was now filled with fearful brokenness, perpetual hiddenness, and blaming spitefulness.

Second Panel

The haunting ashen hues underscore the polluting, alienating, and destructive effects of sin. To depict the tragedy of the Fall, David placed a starkly barren "tree of loss" (note the tag) beneath the level of the tree of life in the first panel. Creation's clear sky is gone, and now the heavens are heavy with dark clouds. The grating screech of two ravens, perched on the horizon, overtakes the invigorating song of the chickadees. One of these "life-swallowing" scavengers looks back at the Creation glory lost in the Fall. The other looks ahead, suggesting that the Fall will not be the final chapter in God's story.

Ravens appear in the Biblical narrative and in the history of literature in two distinct ways. These ominous black birds are often used as a symbol of death and God's judgment (Isaiah 34), but ravens also appear in God's Story as a sign of provision in times of need. The prophet Elijah was miraculously fed by ravens in the wilderness (I Kings 17:1-6). Jesus called his anxious followers to see in the ravens an example of God's faithfulness to care for them, for we are of much greater worth than birds (Luke 12:22-24). The raven looking to the right draws our attention to the third frame.

Third Panel

The same God who brings great judgment also promised to bring an even greater Redemption to the world. In the third panel we see the foundation and first-fruits of this Redemption. Higher in elevation than the tree of loss, the "tree of love" emerges in the visual narrative. This tree is a compelling declaration of God's irreversible commitment to make all things new through the work of his Son, Jesus Christ. God will not leave his beloved creation and creatures enslaved to sin and death and the comprehensive damage of the Fall. He took upon himself the hard and heart work of Redemption.

This incomparable act of mercy and grace explains the presence of an empty cross at the center of the tree of love. God loved the world so much he gave his only begotten Son, and the Son willingly paid with the currency of his life. "Christ redeemed us from the curse of the Law by becoming a curse for us, for it is written: 'Cursed is everyone who is hung on a tree.'" (Gal. 3:13). Jesus willingly took the judgment we deserve for not loving God and our neighbors as the Law demands. The cross is empty because Jesus has done everything necessary to reconcile unloving and lawless people, like me, to God. His death, so grand in its implications, also secured the ultimate renewal of all things.

God did not send Jesus to die on the cross as our substitute as an afterthought; Genesis 3:15 tells us that he planned this Redemption from the beginning. As God's Story unfolds in the Bible it becomes more clear that the Messiah, the promised Deliverer, would bring salvation, not as a great political leader, or as a powerful king, or as

24

a religious revolutionary. Rather, he would be revealed as God's suffering Servant, who would lay down his own life as a sacrifice for the sins of those he came to deliver. Isaiah, one of Israel's prophets, foretold the Messiah's great humility and unparalleled sacrifice in these words:

> *He was despised and rejected by men, a man of sorrows, and familiar with suffering. Like one from whom men hide their faces he was despised, and we esteemed him not. Surely he took up our infirmities and carried our sorrows, yet we considered him stricken by God, smitten by him, and afflicted. But he was pierced for our transgressions, he was crushed for our iniquities; the punishment that brought us peace was upon him, and by his wounds we are healed. We all, like sheep, have gone astray, each of us has turned to his own way; and the Lord has laid on him the iniquity of us all* (Isaiah 53:3-6).

Indeed, what wondrous love is this!

The New Testament unambiguously declares that Jesus Christ is the promised Messiah. His death on the cross fulfills the promise and hope of Isaiah, and all the prophets. Jesus is the main character in the entire story God is telling, and it is by the sacrifice of his blood that we are made whole and that creation will be healed one Day. Notice that David has painted a scarlet thread which binds each of the four panels to one another, emphasizing that the unparalleled sacrifice Jesus made for us is central to the whole story. The scarlet-thread binding also reminds us that God is telling one big story, not four different stories. We cannot possibly understand any one aspect of God's Story apart from engaging with the whole glorious drama. Many distortions of the Christian faith result from a failure to do so.

In playful orbit around the tree of love we see three butterflies. These beautiful creatures represent the emergence of new life from death. Through Jesus' resurrection from death, new-creation life is emerging in the lives of those who know him, and in every sphere in which he brings his kingdom reign to bear. Those whom Jesus sets free are free indeed, but none of his followers are as free as they will be one day. This reality is captured by the other central image in the third panel. Positioned above the tree of life is a single egg. As a symbol, the egg holds forth the promise of present life and of greater life to come.

Resurrection life in Jesus is a life of the "already and not yet." The clouds filling the fallen sky are now lifting in the third panel, but they are not completely gone. Believers already enjoy a measureless trove of treasure in Christ, but not yet do they savor the fullness. As God's image bearers, echoes of the glory of Eden reverberate in our hearts. We know there was a time when everything was right and nothing was broken.

And as those who enjoy the first-fruits of Redemption, our yearning for what is ahead intensifies. A growing tension between sadness and hope is a mark of our journey home. We "groan inwardly and wait expectantly" because we are pregnant with glory, and birth pains abound. David captures this gradual and groaning ascent home by positioning the tree of love higher in elevation than the tree of loss, but not as high as the tree in the last panel, where once again, we meet the tree of life.

Fourth Panel

The fourth panel attempts and approaches the impossible: to visually capture Consummation—the completion and eternal wonder of God's Story, the full beauty and radical implications of the Redemption promised and provided in Jesus Christ. This is why David had to allow the elements in this final panel to spill beyond its borders.

The consummate fulfillment of all of God's promises cannot be contained in one frame! "No eye has seen, no ear has heard, neither has it even entered into the imagination of man… the things that God has prepared for those who love him!" (1 Cor. 2:9)

In this last panel, David has painted the tree of life much larger than in the first panel and has placed it noticeably higher as well. This powerful image refers to a deep and profound biblical reality. In the last chapter of the Bible, Revelation 22, we encounter the reappearance of the tree of life, but it's hardly recognizable as the same tree described in Genesis 2. The message is clear. The Consummation of God's Story is much grander than its beginning in Creation! In God's Story, the movement is not back toward the Garden of Eden but forward and toward the new heaven and new earth. The Garden of Eden was just a preview of coming attractions! The beauty of the sky in the new Creation world will far surpass that of the first Creation world. This is why the placid blue of the first panel has become a deeper and richer blue in the fourth panel.

A cornucopia of lush fruit also seizes our attention in this panel. Why so much and such grand fruit? The Scriptures promise that the tree of life will offer citizens of the new heaven and new earth a different crop of fruit each month, and the leaves of this life-giving tree won't just provide shade, but "healing of the nations." Indeed, the tree of life, as described in Revelation 22, represents the fulfillment of God's covenant to redeem a people for himself and to restore his broken creation. The sheer enormity and diversity of fruit in the fourth panel invite us to consider the abundance, beauty, and adventure God's people will enjoy forever and ever in the new heaven and new earth.

But who are the people God so graciously redeems? Who will eternally enjoy full access to the presence and presents of the tree of life, and life in the never-to-be-broken-again world? According to the promises of Redemption, God is reconciling to himself, and to one another, a family from every single race, tribe, tongue and people group… from every period of history. War, tribalism, racism, and pettiness will be gone forever, along with death, mourning, crying, and pain!

Conclusion

Can you imagine such a rich tapestry of redeemed lives loving each other perfectly and living in unbroken community forever? David has done so by painting three birds you've never seen perched or flying together… a painted bunting, a hummingbird, and a goldfinch. The utter brilliance of their feathers signifies the glory each of God's sons and daughters will manifest when we are finally and fully freed from every semblance of sin, and every effect of the Fall.

This is God's Story. Even as Jesus is the main character in God's Story, each of us is freely invited to find our place in this grand narrative of hope. What a privilege, what an honor, what a calling—to live as a character in and a carrier of God's Story.

By Scotty Smith. Used by permission of the author.

The Progress of Redemption Chart
by Shari Thomas

Artwork by David Arms

Creation	Fall	Redemption	Restoration
Good Life	*Aching Loss*	*Restoring Love*	*Full and Complete Life*
When all was right and perfect in the world/When everything in life felt as if it was as good as God meant it to be	The tragic intrusion of sin and death	God's astonishing promise that he will redeem all things through Jesus Christ. Resurrection life in Jesus is a life of the "now, but not yet."	The magnificent fulfillment of God's plan to gather, cherish, and live with his people, fully healed and deeply loving each other in unbroken community forever
Times in our lives when all felt good and right	I was awakened to the nightmare of a broken world infecting every aspect of our lives.	Sadness for the loss of what should have been, yet hope for what will be	A growing and compelling vision for what will be one day when Christ makes all things new
MINI-STORIES	**MINI-STORIES**	**MINI-STORIES**	**MINI-STORIES**
Riding in the car to my grandparents every summer with my family	*After the divorce* of my parents, the eagerly anticipated summer trips only served as reminders of the great ache in my soul for what had once been.	*I still experience* sadness for the loss of what I would have had. But redemption in mine and my father's story is seen in his recovery from alcoholism and him actively pursuing me.	*I will be healed* of the pain of my mother leaving. In that new heaven and earth I envision restored family relationships and our home. This vision for the future fills me with hope to courageously love my broken family now.
Getting that longed-for, shiny, new bike	*Being taunted with* the news that my new bike was really an older sibling's hand-me-down	*Experiencing an entirely* different life with Jesus in a community that shares and gives freely! My family continues to use favoritism and gift-giving in harmful ways, but others in my community model a hope for redemption when I'm unable to envision it.	Delighting and basking in Jesus' love completely, and knowing that the trick, taunt, and disappointments of life will one day have no hold over me

We are indebted to Elizabeth Turnage at Living Story for her brilliant work connecting the story of scripture to our stories of God's grace.

s t o r y

The Progress of Redemption:
Your Story Through the Lens of God's Story
by Tami Resch and Shari Thomas

Why Use This Tool?
- To understand the broader picture of God's Story
- To see where your life fits in this broader story
- To learn to love, rather than to despise, your story
- To remind your heart to hold out hope for the unfinished pieces of your story

When you look at your life, what do you see? How do you make sense of the world around you? Of the thoughts inside you? How is your story unique? How is your story similar to all other stories in the world? How did it all start? What went wrong? How is it going to get fixed? How will it end?

We approach the questions of life with certain presuppositions—filters through which we evaluate and categorize our world in an attempt to bring clarity, order, and understanding. The lens through which you choose to look determines how you process and how you respond to the world inside and around you.

Is the world all evil? Is it all good? Will it all disintegrate? Will it last forever? Am I all evil? Am I all good? Will I disintegrate? Will I last forever? Is this my only life? Must I strive to get all I can out of it? Or is this my short life? Is there eternal life?

How you answer these and other questions is directly related to your lens. We invite you to view life through the lens of GOD'S STORY. This panoramic BIG PICTURE lens reveals God's pursuit of *our* redemption as well as his pursuit of cosmic redemption.

You may be familiar with an understanding of the Bible referred to as the progress of redemption, or the unfolding of God's redemptive plan. In this understanding, the progress of redemption is revealed in four acts: Creation, Fall, Redemption, and Restoration. As we study further, we see this overarching view of scripture played out in each of the smaller stories in the Bible as well. But it doesn't end there! We see these themes in our own lives, in the big events as well as the mini-events that form our life story. When we view our life through this lens, we begin to catch a glimpse of what God may have intended in our story. We see a cosmic purpose and how we are part of that purpose. Our lives begin to make sense. We hold out hope for the broken and *as yet unredeemed* pieces of our lives. We begin to work for and offer hope to others, to our communities, and to our world for that day when Christ will make all things new.

Creation – Life/Beauty

When was the last time you felt that *all was right with the world*? Describe what made it feel *right*. Reflect on your story past and present, and ponder the times when you sensed, *life is now as it was meant to be!* What are some of the themes you discover? How long did the beauty, peace, joy, order, intimacy, or any other themes last?

The Bible offers a paradigm that accounts for the beauty and order of the world.

SCRIPTURE: Genesis 1-2 and other passages tell of the perfection of God's created world and of the naked and unashamed intimacy between man and woman and their Creator God.

SO WHAT? Listen to your innate longings to be known and valued, to have unity, intimacy, and harmony with God and humankind. Consider how God intended life to be. Continue to hold these longings in your heart, bringing them to your Heavenly Father in prayer. Ask God for eyes to see how Christ has made a way for these longings to be realized partially in this life and fully in the next. Repent when you see your heart demand that God, yourself, and others fulfill these longings according to your design and timetable. Celebrate when you see and experience tastes of *And it was good*. And *It was very good.*

Fall – Loss/Brokenness

In your story, when did you first become aware of life being broken? Think of a time when you failed, or others failed you, or circumstances thwarted your longings to be loved, safe, known, or valued. Where are you seeing disintegration, decay, and death in your current story?

The Bible offers a paradigm that accounts for death, separation, idolatry, suffering, and evil.

SCRIPTURE: Genesis 3 informs us about the Enemy of our soul and the Enemy of God. The rest of Scripture reveals Satan's sabotage and counterfeit schemes against God's redemption until his defeat in Revelation 20:10. *And the devil, who deceived them, was thrown into the lake of burning sulfur… [he] will be tormented day and night forever and ever.*

SO WHAT? This is not the way it was supposed to be! Evil perverted and permeated all of creation and all of mankind. Mankind and creation groan with pain at the loss of intimacy with God, the loss of life as it was created to be, and the loss of humanity as we were created to be. We suffer death, decay, hatred, pain, indifference, heartache, loss, and injustice. In this broken world we should not be surprised by terrorism, murder, and genocide, yet we should rage against the brokenness and decay in our world, our churches, and our personal lives. We can join with the Spirit, the Bride of Christ, and all others to see justice and restoration.

Redemption – Love/Liberty

Where are you waiting for rescue? Where are you waiting for redemption? How do you define rescue/redemption? Have you placed demands on God to rescue and redeem according to your definition? What might it look like to wait for God's rescue and redemption in this season of your story? How is Christ the hero of your story? What might it look like for you to trust Christ to be the Redeemer and Savior of your story, your church's story, and the world's story?

The Bible offers a paradigm that accounts for restoration, liberty, and the reconciliation of broken things and broken people.

SCRIPTURE: Although Ephesians 1 tells us that God foreknew/fore-loved us in pre-creation eternity, none of us in the 21st century have literally lived in the Creation or Restoration parts of God's cosmic story—*yet*! We all live in *the radical-in-betweenness*, that time period between Redemption and Restoration. We experience the reality of sin in our lives and in the world, but we also experience the "now, and not yet" of Christ's redemption applied in our lives. No wonder Paul cries out in Romans 7:

> So I find this law at work: When I want to do good, evil is right there with me. For in my inner being I delight in God's law; but I see another law at work in the members of my body, waging war against the law of my mind and making me a prisoner of the law of sin at work within my members. What a wretched man am I! Who will rescue me from this body of death? Thanks be to God through Jesus Christ our Lord!

Until Christ returns as Lord, King, and Bridegroom we remain in the battle against evil within and evil without. But we are not left alone. God has given us his Spirit to partner with us as he transforms our hearts, our relation-

story

ships, and our world.

SO WHAT? Even the redeemed remain in a broken world that will show only glimpses of our final redemption and rest. We are *simul iustus et peccator* (simultaneously justified and sinners). Should we be surprised when we sin? When our spouses sin? Our kids? Our pastors? Our church leaders? Our government leaders? We can grieve and repent of our personal and corporate sin against God. We can celebrate glimpses of wholeness, justice, and redemption. We can look for the scarlet thread of redemption—the promised and accomplished spilled blood of Jesus, the Rescuer—woven through each panel of God's Story.

Restoration – Life/Glory

How will your longings to be loved, safe, known, or valued be fulfilled when you are at last face-to-face with God? How might the knowledge of your secured future impact your present uncertainty? What could hope look like for you in the current chapter of your life story?

The Bible offers a paradigm that accounts for our innate longing for life to be restored and made new.

SCRIPTURE: Revelation 21:1-5

> Then I saw a new heaven and a new earth, for the first heaven and the first earth had passed away, and there was no longer any sea. I saw the Holy City, the new Jerusalem, coming down out of heaven from God, prepared as a bride beautifully dressed for her husband. And I heard a loud voice from the throne saying, "Now the dwelling of God is with men, and he will live with them. They will be his people, and God himself will be with them and be their God. He will wipe every tear from their eyes. There will be no more death or mourning or crying or pain, for the old order of things has passed away." He who was seated on the throne said, "I am making everything new!" Then he said, "Write this down, for these words are trustworthy and true."

SO WHAT? Hold on! We cling to Christ and the hope he offers so that we may be encouraged and have God's promised salvation as an anchor for our soul, firm and secure (Heb. 6: 18-19) *Look up!* Jesus will come again and usher his bride to the most royal of weddings. You are a story—a story to be told. Do not despise your story. What men and women of the Bible have unblemished stories? God is **not** shocked by our stories. Instead, he redeems them. He tells them. He even started the New Testament section of his Story of redemption with a list of Jesus' relatives that included a woman who tricked her father-in-law to sleep with her in order to bear his child; a prostitute; a Gentile foreigner; and an adulteress! He invites us to tell our stories.

Looking through the lens of God's story, we can re-member, re-think, re-write, and re-tell our stories—not to put a spin on them, but to show the grace and glory of a redeeming God.

The Art of Storytelling

In our Parakaleo* network meetings and coaching relationships, we spend time telling stories of our past and our present. We focus on stories in our local networks because leaders in ministry tend to live behind masks. We desperately need each other to identify the lies we believe.

Jesus Christ and his gospel of grace changes everything. Everything is turned upside down and inside out and everything is made true and new—even our stories and how we see them. The gospel is the grid and lens through which we can look at our lives. Throughout the Old Testament, God invites his children to remember. Remembering the stories of His faithfulness instilled courage and faith in God's children in the midst of their chaotic world. Telling the stories of God's faithfulness to each other and to their descendants was common practice as a means of comfort and future hope. Think of the Exodus of the Israelites from Egypt. Told again and again—in different circumstances and in different times—this story brought, and still brings, courage, comfort, and future hope to the hearts of the ones telling the story and the ones hearing it.

Think about the story of your life. Think of the mini-stories that make up your larger story. The circumstances and emotions of these stories remain the same, like that of the Exodus, but the lens of the gospel enables us to see our story from a different vantage point. What we want to do is re-member, re-think, re-write, and re-tell our old stories through the grid of God's progress of redemption (creation-fall-redemption-restoration) so that we may instill courage, comfort, and future hope to our own hearts and to the hearts of others.

Re-Membering Our Stories
Adding a hyphen to the word remember gives us a different action than merely recalling something that happened. We see that a "member," a part of us, has been cut off or separated. The opposite of re-member would be to dis-member, which is often what we do with our stories. Fear, shame, and pain prompt us to cut our stories off from our memory, our lives, and our hearts. To re-member a story is to once again let that story become a part of our lives, our formation, and the story God is writing for us.

Re-Thinking Our Stories
When we say we "re-think" our stories, we don't mean that everything in our past must be scrutinized and/or doubted and proven. What we mean is that seeing and re-thinking our lives through the grid and lens of the gospel gives our stories new meanings and takes them in new directions. We find rescue we never recognized and hurts we have yet to grieve. We often find a greater hope, a greater purpose, and a greater beauty in the long arc of our story.

Re-Writing Our Stories
It is very helpful as you are re-membering and re-thinking your stories to also be re-writing or writing them for the first time. Writing, as opposed to just thinking, uncovers deeper levels of understanding and connects different dots. To have significant stories of your life written down allows you to concisely share them with others, and it gives you a record of the rescues and redemptions of your life.

Re-Telling Our Stories
Tell your stories again and again! Let your stories be a way for others to see where you've been, what you've suffered, and what God has done. Stories of betrayal, stories of rescue, stories of harm, stories of delight—*each* of our stories are pieces of ourselves we share with others. They are substantial gifts we give to the people in our world. Every time we re-tell a story, we infuse it with a new essence by the very circumstances in which it is told, who it is told to, and how it is told. Our stories are limitless. Some relay our grief and loss, and our deep longing for the way things were created to be. Some may show how we still wait for redemption, while others show us redemption glimpses. Still others point the listener to Christ as the hero and rescuer.

Storytelling is a powerful way to instill courage, comfort, and future hope. Taking your stories through this process will bring insight to you and a precious gift to the *hearers* in your world.

*Founded by the authors, **Parakaleo** is a ministry that comes alongside church planting spouses and couples.*

story

Discovering Your Story
by Carrie Ott

Why Use This Tool?
- to gain an entry point into story discovery
- to begin a process that helps us recall and collect our stories
- to be inspired to write our stories
- to understand the rewards and unique impact story sharing has on our relationships

The first time I heard others talk about "telling their story" or "writing their story" I was absolutely daunted by the imagined task of sitting down and, beginning with my earliest toddler memories, writing chronologically through each year of my life, recounting every person, place or thing I had encountered up to the present moment.

And, of course I was sure I would have to come up with all sorts of "ahas" and deep spiritual insights along the way regarding myself, my parents, generational sin, pillars of idolatry, and gene pool tendencies. Not only did it seem impossible, it seemed like downright drudgery. And I'm a writer!

Thankfully, discovering, telling, and—yes—even writing your story doesn't have to be anything like that. I have spent the past ten years discovering and telling my own story, and for several years I have helped others discover and tell theirs. Story discovery and storytelling is a journey that not only transforms your present, it places your past in an entirely different light as you grapple with the world's brokenness, God's sovereignty, and a new framework of hope: redemption already accomplished and redemption yet to come.

The purpose of this article is two-fold: to encourage you to begin the initial steps of story discovery, and to inspire you to continue in journey toward writing your story and sharing your story. This process of story discovery has proven to be helpful, attainable, and encouraging to those wishing to begin recalling and collecting their stories.

But first, some definitions.

Defining Your *Story* and Your *Stories*

We all have a *story*, and we all have *stories*.

Our Larger Story. Each of us has a larger *story*—the overarching, chronological story of our unique life, e.g., *I am beginning to see God's long and faithful movement in my story.*

We don't nail down our larger story in an afternoon. We spend our lives living in and moving towards a deeper understanding and growing clarity about our story, complete with all its twists and turns and mysteries and surprises. The fact that our story keeps happening and evolving as we inhabit it means that we grapple with a living, changing, organic thing. Our larger story invites us to see what God has done and is doing in our past, our present, and our future. It's good to remember that our larger story will not be entirely clear or understood until eternity!

Our Many Small Stories. And we each have our many small *stories*: all the bits, pieces, slices, images, fragments, memories, scenes—all the moments and clumps of moments that form and are unique to my larger story— to your larger story, e.g., *I remembered something about the story of that summer vacation when I was seven that intrigues me.*

Story Discovery: *A Place to Begin*

How and Where to Begin

When we long to delve into, understand, or perhaps see our larger story for the first time, it is with our innumerable small stories that we begin. Because childhood is the beginning of everyone's story, it is especially helpful to start there, ages 0-18. The beauty of beginning with childhood is that our task is not to construct or build our larger story, but rather to recall and collect our small stories, allowing God to show us how they fit together.

Story discovery is a lot like working a jigsaw puzzle—except you don't have that cardboard box top with the picture of where you are headed. When you work a puzzle, do you begin by sorting and fitting all the edge pieces? Or do you gather pieces that share interesting textures or colors and work from there? Though I'm a die-hard edge worker, I'll start working pieces with words or text as soon as I see them. The beauty of working a puzzle is that you really can begin wherever you like. And it's the same with story discovery. The trick is to begin!

When even the thought of gathering or collecting our small stories is daunting, it is helpful to remember that what we are collecting is specific memories and specific scenes. Again, our job here is not to build or construct, but to recall and collect.

Using a Story Well

A story well is a place (a journal, a box of 3x5 cards, a computer document, a spiral notebook) where you keep lists and prompts to help you recall memories, and where you actually *jot down* the memories and scenes from your childhood that come to you.

The Lists in Your Story Well

Your story well lists will grow with varying levels of specificity. By using titled lists, you focus and prompt your mind to recall a particular area of memory. Because we all have unique entry points and varying levels of accessibility to our memories, our story wells will be unique to each of us. Start where you are, and be as specific or broad with your list titles as you want or need to be. Start with the simple definition of a noun—a person, place, or thing—and you'll find a plethora of ways to begin lists that prompt your ability to recall.

If you haven't thought of your childhood in years, you may need to start with broad lists such as: *Places I Lived; My Best Friends; People in My Childhood.*

If your memories are pretty accessible and flow quickly, be as specific as you like, such as: *Things I Was Sure I'd Be When I Grew Up; Trips We Made With Cousins; People Who Taught Me Stuff; Everything I Ever Ate in My Grandma's Kitchen; Relatives I Didn't Know What To Do With and Why.* Obviously, you can have fun with your list titles. The more fun, poignant, and specific they are, the more helpful they will be.

As I begin this paragraph, a list title comes to mind I've never used before: *Cars Our Family Owned.* And the first car I think of is the old green Volkswagen van with the white roof that my mom and dad and older brother and I traveled around the country in several summers in a row when my parents were raising support for ministry. My folks pulled out all the passenger seats except for the one in the far back, installed padding and carpet on the van's floor, and since there were no seatbelt laws (and not much thought about seatbelts to begin with) my brother and I spent the summer traveling in a carpeted playroom on wheels, complete with our favorite toys, books to read, pallets to naps on, and coolers of food for snacking. Traveling was a fantastic adventure!

This one car memory immediately acts as a magnet to other childhood memories: the companionship my brother

story

and I shared, favorite toys, my mom's cooking and magician-like ability to produce on-the-road food, people we knew all over the country, and other trips I took when I was older. Remembering how much I loved to lie on my van pallet, hearing the rumble of the road beneath me and watching the clouds go by in several states, reminds me how much and how often as a child I loved to sit or lie and just think on life.

This is how memories—and stories—work: one memory leads to another, and another, and another. And with a story well, you can quickly and succinctly collect your memories and get them jotted down. When you return to them another time, they are there waiting to be picked up, mused upon, and turned round and round.

Spending focused time working on your lists—your story well—tells your heart and your mind that you are going to pay attention. You will be surprised how memories reveal themselves. Suddenly, everyday activities throw open a window to snippets, scenes, and stories you haven't thought of in years. When the memories come, jot them down in your story well if it's handy, or it it's not, use a paper napkin, a scrap of paper—anything you can find so you can add them to your story well later.

Jotting Down vs. Writing Fully
You will have plenty of time to write out your stories as detailed and complete as you like. But a story well is most helpful when it is used as *jotted* lists of memories. Of course you can jot down as many details as you like, but we are often tempted to think we'll lose specific details of a memory when it first comes to us if we don't immediately record it in all its fullness. True, this definitely happens with age (which is another good reason to work on your stories now), but the beauty of recall is that sights, sounds, and textures stay more attached to our memories than we imagine.

Using Memory Hooks
Since our goal with story collecting is to jot down our memories, we use memory hooks. A memory hook is a phrase that gives you enough information to recall your memory later, but not so much information that you become overwhelmed by the task of recording it in your story well.

For instance, I have this memory hook in my story well: *Playing Swiss Family Robinson with Chip*. Jotted down, this phrase gives me everything I need to hook the memory so I can come back to it when I can spend more time there. At this point, I don't have to write and write about the summer fun my brother Chip and I had with my grandparents boating on the Tennessee River; the small islands my grandparents would motor to so my brother and I could pretend we were shipwrecked on a deserted island; the sound of the river lapping against the hull of the boat, anchored in the shade afforded by the dense trees leaning out from the riverbank; the obvious happiness—no, *delight*—on my grandparents' faces as they watched us play all afternoon; the cold swims between boat and island and the soggy weight of the orange life preserver on my shoulders; the gritty Tennessee riverbank under my feet and between my toes; the "food" my brother and I foraged—sunbleached river clam shells hooked over a spit built of twigs, and our imaginary fire of piled sticks; and of course Grandma's ham sandwiches and fizzy root beer pulled from the ice cooler, an irresistible respite from island food even as it required yet one more cold swim from island to boat. When I jot *Playing Swiss Family Robinson with Chip* in my story well, I make a placeholder for all these emotional and sensory details of the memory I will return to another time.

In addition to being a useful and efficient shorthand to use in your story well, memory hooks also provide two things vital to your story journey: kindness and privacy.

There's just something about writing it down. Putting memories to paper with pen, pencil, or keyboard becomes an act of committing the memory to the reality of our heart and our experience. This is a joyful experience when we are recalling and listing fun and pleasant memories, but quite unnerving when we write—even jot down—sad, painful, and shameful memories. We become reticent to translate our painful memory to the physical reality of words on paper because this undoubtedly makes the memory more real and opens our hearts wider to its pain.

So give yourself kindness. Jotting a memory hook allows you to gather or collect the memory without forcing you to delve into all the details and the full impact of that memory the moment you recall it. By jotting down your memory, as opposed to immediately and fully writing it out, you give your heart the gentle kindness it deserves and requires in this journey. Not only does this give you strength and the elasticity you need for the long haul, I believe it sends a message to your heart that you are going to be kind to yourself, and, when gently invited, your heart tends to offer more of its memories to you.

And give yourself privacy. I encourage you to keep your story well in a place that ensures the level of privacy that you need in order to feel comfortable with the story discovery process. Remember that, here again, the act of writing words is powerful, and thus will affect your *sense* of privacy. Even when you know your words and lists are secure and private, padlocked, or password protected, writing down a painful or shameful memory can suddenly leave you feeling vulnerable, exposed, and as if your words are sure to be on the Internet by day's end. By jotting your memory hooks, you gain a measure of privacy as you record enough of the memory to know what you are referring to, but not so much that you feel exposed to the point you begin to avoid gathering painful memories into your story well.

A NOTE OF CAUTION:
Childhood memories run the gamut from fun to frightening, confirming to confusing, joyful to heartbreaking. The further we delve into our stories, the more the memories bubble up; and these memories come wrapped in all sorts of emotion. If you find yourself overwhelmed by traumatic memories that surface, or by the pain, anger, or shame that accompanies your memories, speak to a close and like-minded friend and ***get the help of a professional***. If memories come to you that are shocking or that you have never recalled before, again, ***get the help of a professional***.

Story Writing: *Giving Your Stories a Home*

Once you begin to jot down and collect your stories, you will find yourself intrigued with or mulling over certain stories more than others. What's next? It's time to give that story a place to live in more of its fullness. By the way, you don't have to wait for a full, complete, and volume-thick story well to begin writing your stories. You can start writing as soon as you like. But at some point, start writing! I know, I know, many of you are thinking, *Easy enough for you to say, you like to write!*

Yes, but I have listened to enough people swear they *hate* writing and that they will never, ever be able to write down one of their childhood stories, only to watch these same people turn around and write the most amazing, heartfelt, articulate, and well-told stories. I've watched person after person be shocked by their ability to write their stories, and by the meaning and value they find in their recorded stories.

If you come to writing with the presupposition that you need to produce amazing sentences, and are consequently filled with dread, then back up. Return to your story well and write that particular story title/memory hook at the top of a blank page and start jotting down words and phrases that come to you. Work through all your senses (sight, sound, smell, taste, touch). Start by writing a few words and more words will follow.

The writer E.L. Doctorow said, "Writing is like driving at night in the fog. You can only see as far as your headlights, but you can make the whole trip that way."

The important thing is to *start writing*. What happens to the mind and the heart in the writing process happens nowhere else. Take your stories to the next level and give them a permanent place to live: the page. It matters what happened to *you*, and it matters that what happened to you *happened*. Writing down your stories is a palpable and profound way to agree with this truth.

My experience has been that the best place to jump into writing memory stories is with a story group, or a like-minded friend. Of course you can write your stories without a group, but without a group you are less apt to share them. And story sharing is the place where your story journey begins to come full circle. "Your awe-inspiring deeds will be on every tongue; I will proclaim your greatness. Everyone will share the story of your wonderful goodness; they will sing with joy about your righteousness." (Psalm 145:6-7 NLT)

Writing with others gives us the nudge and energy to write. When two or more people decide to hold hands and jump into the deep end of the writing pool, everyone gains courage. When we realize, as members of a group, that we truly have an audience waiting to hear our stories and know our hearts more deeply, we become emboldened with a desire to write our story in a way that clearly marks and truthfully tells where we've been, what we've seen, what we've suffered, and what we've survived.

And with a story group or story friend we can move immediately from the writing down stage to the sharing stage of story.

A NOTE OF RECOMMENDATION: I highly recommend the book *To Be Told*, by Dan Allender, and the workbook of the same name by Dan Allender and Lisa Fann. These two books provide all the guidance you need to begin and to continue telling your story with a group or another person.

Story Sharing: *Giving Your Stories a Voice*

There are so many things I could try to explain about sharing stories. But instead I am going to tell you some stories. We're going to pretend for a few minutes. We're going to pretend that you and I are friends, that our lives intersect regularly and that over time we've heard many of each other's stories. Are you game?

Our friendship began when we met and participated in a story group together. Of course, in that setting we learned a lot about each other in a short period of time and we ended up becoming good friends. Story group concluded several years ago, but discovering our small stories and seeing more of our larger story has remained an important part of your and my life. Story sharing has been deeply woven into the fabric of our friendship.

One of the first stories you heard me tell was about myself as a fourth-grader making my first Christmas ornament at a neighbor's house, how I discovered the artist inside me, and that I've kept that ornament all these years. Last Christmas you were over and you asked if you could see that 36-year-old bread dough snowman. There he was, hanging on my tree, and I couldn't believe you remembered! What a treat to show him to you. And then you told me what the artist part of me means to you and how you were so glad I found that side of myself so long ago.

On your birthday a few years ago, I surprised you with a story feast. I had everyone come prepared to tell a story about you and what they see in you. You never thought yourself especially courageous until almost every single story shared reflected something specific about your courage. You saw yourself through our eyes—the ones who know you best. Sometimes, when you forget your courageous heart, I am bold to remind you that I know it is real and that those closest to you have been witness to it.

Recently, I told you about a fight my husband and I had, and how a perfectly ordinary question from him absolutely leveled me. I still couldn't understand why I reacted in a way that seemed so completely over reactive. I was feeling such contempt for myself and my sensitivity. You immediately made the connection to a story you knew about me. I could look at me through your understanding of me, and seeing myself through your compassion, I was able to let go of my self-contempt and accept your tenderness toward my heart. Added bonus: mystery solved for my husband, too!

One Father's Day, after church and over Cuban food, we initiated your family into our family's Tell-Your-Dad-What-You-Love-About-Him Father's Day tradition. We expanded it a bit, and my husband and I told your husband something we each loved about the way he fathers your oldest child. You and I are fortunate because our husbands have had their own experiences and journeys with story sharing. Not only was your husband delighted to hear what we had to say to him, he immediately saw this particular movement toward your child as beautiful redemption born out of particular pain in his childhood. He has told me since that each time he relates in that particular way he is reminded how beautiful redemption is.

Here is where we leave our pretend scenario. What did you think? Did it seem too good to be true? Did you find yourself feeling cynical? Or did you find yourself longing to know and be known in such a way?

I have had the privilege of being part of several story groups, and each of the stories I recounted to you were true moments of friendship I have shared with those with whom I have traveled in the world of story sharing. A wise friend once told me, *When it comes to what God is doing, if it's too good to be true, then you know it **is** true*. Another friend of mine says, *God is a we, not an I*. God desires us to live in deep *too good so it is true* relationship with each other. Story sharing is one way we experience that.

Is it all sunshine and roses? Absolutely not. When we know each other's deepest fears, most tender and raw stories, we become incredibly vulnerable to each other. We can be careless with each other's stories and easily wound and be wounded. We often forget where the other comes from and demand behavior that precludes us having lived the lives we've lived. Story sharing in a fallen world is fallen too.

But the risks, the wounds, and the vulnerability can become places of deep redemption and intimacy with each other and deep places of comfort and trust with God. Story sharing is worth the risk it entails.

You share your stories with me, and I wrestle with God's seeming absence, obvious rescue, and everything in between—*with you*—in your stories. Because you have shared your stories with me, not only is my life impacted, my heart is invited to move toward you with compassion, affection, appreciation, and deeper understanding.

I share my stories with you, and you offer me empathy, understanding, and a measure of healing I did not experience when I lived through my stories. You can see, often before I can, that God was working steadily and stealthily on my behalf. Because I have shared my stories with you, you recognize and name the harm I have grown accustomed to and tend to minimize or brush off. My stories become richer and more clear to me because your eyes are on them.

story

You share your stories with me, and I am able to name and celebrate the YOU God made you to be because I can relate your *then* stories to your *now* stories, the *then* you to the *now* you.

We share our stories with each other and gain context about our, as well as each other's, relationships, dreams, pains, and joys.

I share my stories with you and I am seen. I am heard. I am not alone.

You share your stories with me and you are seen. You are heard. You are not alone.

Sharing our stories lets us share our hearts, our lives, and the God we both long to know.

Story Discovery: Practical Helps and Prompts
by Carrie Ott

Why Use This Tool?
- to discover how to make your story discovery experience unique to you
- to be inspired by the innumerable and varied ways you can step into story discovery and story recording
- to begin a story well with prompts you didn't have to think up

The sky's the limit when it comes to the varied ways you can discover, record, and write your story. Every chance you get, bring who you are to the process. Do you love the visual? Think about incorporating art into your stories. Are you especially organized and methodical? Put some thought into how you want to organize your story well so you will come back to it again and again. Do you enjoy reading a particular genre of literature? Think about writing some of your stories in that form. Whoever you are, and whatever particular bents and quirks are yours, bring all that to your journey with story.

Using Art and the Visual
You don't have to be adept in particular art techniques to use art in your story. I recommend getting a good size art journal (or plain journal, or any book you want to re-purpose to use as a journal). You may want to keep your story well, as well as your story art pieces, in this journal. If you don't want to work in a journal, keep your art together (unless you want to put it up all around you!) so you can see the body of story work you are creating.

Draw like a kid again. Grab some crayons or big fat markers and draw stick figures of family members, kids in the neighborhoods you grew up in, or different aged versions of yourself. Drawing with crayons as if you were a kid again can be a great way to access memories your adult brain may pass over.

Sketch a quick floorplan of a particular house you lived or spent time in. Jot down memory hooks on the floor plan as they come to you. Or draw a bird's eye view of your favorite room or backyard as you remember it. Add in all the details you can think of. Draw a map of the/a neighborhood you grew up in and the surrounding places you frequented.

Make a magazine collage. Gather magazines you can cut up. Set a timer for 10 minutes and go page by page through the magazine ripping out images you feel drawn to that relate to your story. Glue them into your art journal or onto a piece of paper. Jot memories, thoughts and whatever else comes to you around, or across the images.

Use family photographs. If you have access to photos of your childhood, copy, scan, or print them out. Glue a particular photo or group of photos into your art journal and jot down memories or write around or on the photo. Try writing the story of a particular photo. You can also make a story well using only photos, i.e., *My Favorite People* or *Places I Visited* or *This Was Me*.

Make a pictoral scrapbook of your life using each year as the heading of that page. Start with historical events of the year, movies released, popular music, and anything else you can think of. Use an image search engine to find and print images related to that year. You'll be amazed at the visual impact these familiar images have on your memory recall. Then add what you were up to that year in your life. Use as many photos of yourself and your life as you have related to that year.

If you enjoy the visual and the artistic, search the Internet for *art journaling* or *visual journaling* for more ideas.

story

Using Other Ways of Writing

Besides using first person narrative ("When I was a kid, I..."), experiment with other ways of writing your story. Write as the all-knowing narrator, and your child self as one of the players in the story. ("The little girl loved to climb the tree and sit unnoticed in the yard.")

Write a letter to your child self from your adult self. Several years ago I became a pen pal to my little girl self regarding several memories. Yes, "we" wrote back and forth to each other. Since I could establish the rules of our pen pal universe, I decided she didn't know I was the grown-up her, but she did know I was trustworthy and for her. Because as children we often blame ourselves for so much that happens in our childhood, we often carry contempt for our child self into our adulthood. Writing to the child you were gives you the opportunity to express compassion, empathy, and understanding you might not otherwise feel. I found an entirely new affection and compassion for the little girl I was after this season of writing.

Begin an encyclopedia or dictionary of you. Label the pages alphabetically and begin jotting down whatever comes to you. Ex: ***B, banana bread:*** *what I baked every Christmas with Grandma.* ***Boone, Daniel:*** *what Chip and I watched on TV with Grandy;* ***beagle:*** *our dog Nina when we lived in Dallas.* This is a great way to jump into recalling and writing your story because it doesn't even require complete sentences!

Begin a diary of the past. Record entries from your childhood perspective about specific events as if they are happening in real time. Don't get sidelined by date accuracy; make them up, leave them off, or ballpark them.

Write a How To Manual with entries that apply to your childhood. *How to Have Fun With Your Brother After School* or *How to Get Your Mother Really Angry During Dinner* or *How to Survive Fourth Grade in A New Town* or *How to Practice (Or Not Practice) The Piano.* Of course the material is all about you and how you lived and coped and learned about life. These stories can be hilarious or heartbreaking. Let the story tell itself.

Be a poet. Write a limerick, a haiku, or narrative verse about your childhood. I highly recommend *Love That Dog*, by Sharon Creech. You'll be inspired by how simply and beautifully a story from your childhood can be expressed in poetic form.

Using What You Read

Do you enjoy reading science fiction? Write one of your childhood stories with the universe bending power of sci-fi. Your desires, wishes, and heartbreaks will ring true even when you apply the backdrop of the fantastic. Do you collect recipes? Use the form of a recipe or cookbook entry to tell one of your stories. Do biographies fascinate you? Write some of your childhood stories as if you are famous and someone else is writing your biography. I can't think of a writing genre that wouldn't prove helpful in discovering and telling our stories. If something intrigues you, go for it!

Using the Writings of Others

There's nothing like a good memoir to get you thinking about your own life and experiences. Three of my favorite memoirs of childhood are: *An American Childhood*, by Annie Dillard; *Don't Let's Go to The Dogs Tonight* by Alexandra Fuller; *The Liar's Club* by Mary Karr. If writing your story in depth intrigues you, I highly recommend *Inventing the Truth: The Art and Craft of Memoir*, edited by William Zinsser. In the book, ten phenomenal authors write about their journey discovering and writing their stories.

Story Well Prompts

The simple definition of a noun (person, place, or thing) is always a great place to begin. Remember, a story prompt is not a fill-in-the-blank correct or incorrect answer. If *People Who Taught Me Stuff* makes you think of snuggling with your dog, write it down! If *Vacations I Went On* reminds you of a movie you saw when you had the flu, write it down. Every memory is a story; every memory you recall is worth recording.

PEOPLE
Kids I Grew Up With
Neighbors I Had
My Best Friends Through The Years
People I Did Not Like
Enemies at School
My Favorite People
My Family
My Extended Family
Favorite Teachers
People Who Were Famous When I Was Young
People I Was Not Allowed to Like
People Who Taught Me Stuff

PLACES
Houses I Lived In
Vacation Spots
Where We Shopped
Where We Went To Church
Where I Loved To Go
My Bedroom
My View From Where I Sat in The Car
Rooms in My House
Countries, States, Cities I Lived In
Countries, States, Cities I Visited
When It Was Christmas at My House
The School Lunchroom

THINGS
Pets I Loved
Pets I Didn't Love
Pets I Never Had
A Few of My Favorite Things
Hobbies I Adored
Sports I Played
Lessons I Took
Bicycles I Owned
Favorite Things to Do Inside
Favorite Things to Do Outside

THINGS (continued)
What the Weather Was Like in My Neighborhood
Cars We Owned
My Favorite Movies
Music I Liked
Things I Had Alot Of
Things I Collected
Things I Saved My Money For
What Made Me Laugh
What Made Me Mad
Things That Made Me Happy
I Was Never Afraid Of...
If I Ever Worried
Things My Parents Never Knew
What I Watched on TV

DON'T FORGET THE SENSES
(sight, sound, smell, taste, touch)
Things That Were Blue (or other colors)
What Things Looked Like
Things That Were Loud
Things That Smelled Really Good
My Favorite Dinner
Snacks I Loved
Scratchy Things in My House

OTHER PROMPTS
What I Was Sure I Would Be When I Grew Up
Things That Went Bump in The Night
Secrets I Knew
What I Was Told
What Was Never Allowed
Things I Dreamt At Night
If I Could Ever
What We All Knew
Those Were The Rules
The Most Important Thing
When I Felt Sad I...
What Everyone Else Knew/Had/Forgot

Copyright 2011 by Carrie Ott. Used by permission of the author.

story

Story Resources

Far As the Curse Is Found, Michael Williams
Glittering Images; Glamorous Powers; Ultimate Prizes; Scandalous Risks; Mystical Paths, Susan Howatch
A Grace Disguised, Gerald L. Sittser
The Hidden Hope in Lament, Dan Allender; www.leaderu.com/marshill/mhr01/lament1.html
The Healing Power of Stories, Daniel Taylor
Jayber Crow, Wendell Berry
The Jesus Storybook Bible: Every Story Whispers His Name, Sally Lloyd-Jones
Lament for a Son, Nicholas Wolterstorff
Learning God's Story of Grace, Elizabeth Reynolds Turnage
Making Sense Out of Suffering, Peter Kreeft
On the Threshold of Hope, Diane Langberg
Pilgrim's Progress (modern translation with study questions), John Bunyan, ed. by Musselman; www.lulu.com
Telling Secrets, Frederick Buechner
The Message of Job, David John Atkinson
To Be Told, Dan B. Allender
To Be Told Workbook, Dan B. Allender and Lisa K. Fann
Total Truth, Nancy Pearcey
When God Interrupts, Craig Barnes
The Wounded Heart, Dan B. Allender
The Wounded Heart Companion Workbook, Dan B. Allender

Ways to Further Explore Your Story:

Journey Groups; www.ohmin.org
A small group experience led by Open Hearts Ministry; designed for dealing with the wounds of our pasts.

Living Story Retreats, by Elizabeth Turnage; www.livingstorygrace.com
A website filled with helpful questions, resources, stories, guides for telling your own story, and ideas for leading stories feasts.

Parakaleo Training Retreats; www.parakaleo.us
A small group experience led by Parakaleo and designed to help a planting spouse see how her story intersects with her church planting experience.

The Story Workshop, by Dan Allende; www.thepathlesschosen.com/seminar_info.html

THE GOSPEL

WHAT IS IT ?

HOW DOES IT MATTER IN

THE HERE AND NOW ?

Have not our suspicious hearts darkened
this book of light? Do we not often read it
as the proclamation of a command to do,
instead of a declaration of what the love
of God has done?   HORATIO BONAR

44

The Myth of the Gospel
by Shari Thomas

"The gospel is for salvation. But it doesn't really apply to my everyday life."

'The gospel is good news, but it's really better news for those who aren't in ministry. Everyone expects us to live by a higher standard of righteousness."

"The Gospel! That's just what we need! Some good old-fashioned fire and brimstone messages to get us into shape."

"Belief in the gospel of grace frees me from obedience. Since I am not saved by my merit, I don't have to obey."

THE GOSPEL. We've heard the word hundreds of times, yet how often have we heard it misused (and misused it ourselves), or so blithely spoken of that we fail to grasp its true and full meaning? What a challenge to unpack a word that encompasses the vast love of God expressed through the sacrificial work of Jesus.

Romans 3:22 says "this righteousness from God comes through faith."

We are made right with God by placing our faith in Jesus Christ and thus we are *justified*—just as if we had never sinned. Our record is wiped clean; we are forgiven. But if we stop there, all we get is a blank slate—and God gives us so much more! Not only does Christ remove the record of our

sin, he also **credits** our record with Christ's righteousness. It is a righteousness outside ourselves that fills our empty account.

Colossians 2:6 says, "just as you received Christ Jesus as Lord [by faith], continue to live in him." And Galatians 3:3 states, "You foolish Galatians, who has bewitched you... after beginning with the Spirit are you now trying to attain your goal by human effort?"

In other words, the way we come to Christ in the first place (by faith) is the way we are to live out the rest of our lives in Christ (by faith). We are justified by faith in Christ's finished work on the cross, and we are sanctified daily by that same faith in Christ's finished work. This is why we cannot stress enough that Christians need the gospel as much as non-Christians.

Here's another way to explain it. THE BAD NEWS: Everything in this world is breaking down. We, too, are much more broken and wounded than we realize or care to admit. THE GOOD NEWS: God, through the person and work of Jesus, is restoring both the world and his people to their original beauty and glory apart from any of their merit—past, present, or future.

In these pages you will read about the bad news; we will certainly encourage you to face your brokenness. But we will also remind you of the good

news! We will encourage you to look and see what Christ has done and is doing for you. The Gospel truly is for your everyday life.

It is our deeply held conviction that believing the truth of the gospel affects us to the very core of our being. The same power that raised Christ from the dead is the same power that is working in us now. Thank God it is not our efforts that change us! We don't get extra brownie points for doing good work for God, for being a pastor's wife, a super-good citizen, or a great mom.

In this section, you will find stories of how we have wrestled with this truth, tools to help you uncover what you believe about the gospel, and resources to help you gain a deeper understanding of this good news.

Is it not wonderful news to believe that salvation lies outside ourselves?
—Martin Luther

The Gospel For Everyone But Pastors
by John Thomas

I WAS DREADING THE WEEK. I walked into the room full of squeaky-clean, smiling faces feeling like a student who had just been caught cheating. "A whole week," I mused. "I wonder how bad this is going to be." I was attending a conference on the gospel called Sonship. Would I be bored? Hadn't I preached every single truth I was about to hear? As I sat there, I began to get in touch with what I was feeling. "Guilty" was the first word that leaped from my heart.

That seemed odd to me, a gospel preacher. We had started a church that quickly had a reputation for radically preaching the gospel of grace to any and every one. Week after week, I pleaded with people to believe the good news that, though their hearts condemned them, Jesus would not. He was safe with their secrets. He knew their sin way better than they did, and he loved them anyway. More than that, I told them Jesus' love was counter-conditional. It more than covered their indifference and sin. It showered them with crazy, adoring love even though they continued to run away from him; even though they played games with God; and even though they faked their love for him and others.

I proclaimed that the gospel was big enough for every sin and problem they could have. I championed that anyone could come—no matter who they were or what they had done. In Christ, they could be accepted, loved, and filled. I believed the gospel could conquer the prostitutes, the drug abusers, and even the wife beaters. Yet, the nagging guilt consumed me. Where was the disconnect? Why did those smiling Christian faces smother me? The gospel had yet to conquer the toughest nut to crack: the professional Christian, the pastor. Me.

So there I sat with my guilt, my failure, and my remorse. A guy stood up, looked at us with genuine compassion, and started talking about the reason the Sonship conference was started in the first place. Jack Miller created the course for pastors who knew all about theology yet lived in the absence of it penetrating their own hearts. They could preach the truths of Jesus, but their lives weren't characterized by joy, deep love, and a power that radically changed them. The good news was for everyone but them. "OK," I thought, "that's interesting. And it's perverted. And it's exactly where I am." And then this smiling-faced pastor to the perverted told us: "We know what it's like to do ministry. We know what it's like to fake it and to work hard helping others find God and yet find him quite elusive for our own souls. This is a place where you can let your guard down. Please believe me—this is a safe place for you."

That's how it started. And then, hour by hour, with each song, each story, each *Peculiar People* sketch, each teaching, this team of gospel-mongers proceeded to mount a full frontal assault on my soul. Jesus really was crazy about me and all he wanted was me—not my performance, or my efficiency in ministry plans, or my effective leadership. He just wanted me. They had the audacity to tell me that all that stuff I had been preaching to others—all that goodness and grace and glory—it was meant for me too. Within a short time, I found myself praying, "Father, break through. Just break through this cold, hard heart of mine and do your renewing work. I am so lost."

This is the good news. And it comes to those who aren't experiencing it, even if they are preaching it. It comes to those who have never wanted it, to those who have fought against it, to those who have lit the world on fire with their rebellion. It comes to those living in bondage, so afraid that sin is what keeps them from Christ. Amazingly enough, it comes even to those who have led communities of faith into an understanding of grace that they themselves, in their own hearts, have refused to believe. This good news of God is for them, too. This gospel is no respecter of persons. It comes quiet as a mouse and innocently enters into the hearts of the disbelieving, the disobeying, even those with mouths full of God-words, even those whose hearts are empty. Yes, it even comes to them. And when it comes in, it changes into a lion of love, a giant of grace, and does its work.

Throughout that week, I was encouraged to believe the good news of Jesus for me, not just for everyone else. During that week, I took a walk with my wife and I began telling her how I had been faking, how I had been hiding, how I had been preaching for others but not receiving it myself. As I came clean and told her my secret sins, she asked incredulously, "That's it? That's the deep secrets you are carrying?" I was shocked. "Well, yeah. That's what I've been wrestling with and hiding from you." With eyes full of compassion, she said, "John, I already knew that."

And it hit me. I had been faithful to proclaim the free and sovereign grace of Jesus Christ to others all the while succumbing to the lie of performance. My wife, my elders, my staff, my friends all saw it. They could see I was burdened down. I was exhausted—striving to earn my own righteousness by being right myself, and always feeling guilty of not being good enough. Somehow, I had believed, "If only I can be disciplined and hard working, and can lead with passion, courage, and wisdom; and only if I don't screw up, then Jesus will be pleased with me. And just maybe others will be, too. Jesus might delight in others just out of love, but I am a minister. I have to deliver."

Too long, I had believed the lie that the gospel was

true for everyone but me!

The week of disruptive grace ended in tears of joy as I took communion. At the table, I celebrated the beginning of a new freedom, a renewed gratitude, a new walking with my Redeemer King who was thrilled and delighted in me as I was, not because of my performance, not because of my theology, and surely not because I was a minister. He loved me. The verdict about me was in. There was nothing I could do to gain his acceptance or approval. I already had it. I was beginning to believe it.

I BELIEVE THE GOSPEL...DON'T I?
All of us think we fully and deeply believe the gospel—and most of us do. And yet, are there areas of our lives that remain untouched by the gospel? How often do its powerful implications get missed in our everyday lives?

The following questions can be indicators of places where we may not yet fully believe.

Do you feel bad about yourself if you haven't been productive?

Are you unable to take vacations or your days off?

Are you undone by failure?

Are you often afraid of not "looking good"?

Do you have activities in your life that you keep secret?

Do you regularly despair?

Do you feel as if you are not able to freely share with others?

Do you find yourself being self-conscious?

Okay. So, obviously, we don't believe perfectly. Is the point to shame us? No, our desire is to identify our deep and continuous need for the gospel for each and all of us, especially church people. The following tools and resources aim not to condemn our unbelief, but to woo us to see the implications of the gospel played out in our lives as love and freedom.

gospel

The Gospel Made Me Furious
by Shari Thomas

"WHAT THE HELL DOES THE GOSPEL have to do with moving?" Sitting on a box I had just packed for yet another move, I hurled these words across the room at my husband. The previous five years had been the first in our lives that we had lived in one house, in one location. The kids had good friends. I knew the neighbors well. I could feel the anger churning below the surface. The all-too-familiar misused Christian phrases came hurtling into my mind like boxcars on a speeding train I had no power to stop.

"Sacrifice requires giving up your desires for God."

"Ministry means doing what you don't want to do. What did you expect?"

"God has sacrificed his own Son for you. Don't you think you can at least pack up your house for him?"

I wished the phrases would shut up and leave me alone, that I could find a way out so I would not have to move. Or at least find some miraculous way to make this easier. I wanted to run to my resume of goodness to increase my chances of getting my way, but I couldn't. A few years prior to that day on the box, I had my first brush with the whole concept of the gospel being for *me* and not just for "the lost." Of the gospel promoting Christ's performance instead of mine.

This gospel was changing everything.

This gospel was unsettling.

This gospel left me without leverage.

This gospel made me furious.

Oh, don't get me wrong, I grew up as a missionary kid, so I knew the gospel. I had spent a lifetime of three decades sacrificing my life and myself for it. My resume of sacrifice was extensive and impressive. I had met my husband in seminary. Before spending several years on the mission field, I had sold our possessions (antiques included, all done in the Proverbs 31 style of good business). "It's the hardest country," we were told. "It's called the graveyard of missionaries." Well, it wouldn't be for us. We weren't quitters. When it was too hard for everyone else, it was just right for us! We were the disciplined! The diligent! The dependable! Of course the "weak" would call that driven. But I knew they secretly wished they could be as strong as I was. No one had been able to call into question my voracious appetite for language learning. To achieve language mastery, I had worked to erase all traces of an American accent. I was doing it all for the Lord, for serving him, for bringing in his kingdom. And it was possible because, "I could do all things through Christ who strengthens me."

From my Christian heritage and the tightly taught doctrine of the evangelical church, I knew exactly how to live. I knew what was expected of me as a woman. Theology had been transformed from mere doctrinal truths in my head to a deeply lived way of life. It had been preached to me as a child, lived out in Christian high school, later taught at Bible college, seminary, and now the mission field. I knew the only way to live a fulfilling life was to be firmly in God's will. I knew I would never want to refuse my husband and what he believed God had called him to do. I knew how to get the approval of our Christian world. I knew all the proper nods, the affirming words expected of me, the right phrases, verses, and all the answers. I knew there was no way to escape God, and giving in to Him, sooner rather than later, was a win-win.

Why fight? I didn't.

No one could ask more of me than what I was already doing. Frankly, I didn't know anyone who was doing more than me. What could even my husband say? I was the one up praying before dawn, fixing breakfast, feeding the family, caring for the poor and destitute, teaching the Bible. I was the perfect model missionary, mom, and ministry woman.

And I was miserable. The "good news"? This was no gospel at all. And yet I spent our several years in mission work living like this.

WHEN THE BOTTOM FELL OUT and we returned home from the mission field as failures, I was a raging volcano waiting to erupt. And erupt, I did. While there was human carnage in the wake of my eruption, the most venomous flames were aimed right where they should have been: at God. I felt betrayed, abandoned, and totally powerless before the hands of this maddening God whom I could never do enough to please. I'd given my life, my earthly possessions, and, as my grandmothers before me— my children. And I was furious! If there was really nothing required of me, then why all the hard work? Why all the sacrifice? Why all the incessant teaching and conferences and studies of never-ending ways to better ourselves? My Bible was the first thing to go—thrown out the window in a rage. Then I tossed all the wasted time on such things as prayer and quiet time. Next, I chucked any pretense— whenever I even dared attend church or church functions.

Still, my rage had not run its course.

For although I had thrown out the Bible, all the many verses I had "hidden in my heart" all those years came bobbing to the surface of my mind. They came unbidden, in the middle of the night; they came in the quiet of the day. In the absence of endless Bible studies to attend or lead, I finally had time to sit out in nature and listen. What came to me then were remnants of scripture, but not the ones of condemnation that I expected. Instead:

"Come unto me all you who are weary and heavy laden…"

"…I will give you rest."

They came in seemingly unrelated snippets:

"Blessed are they that mourn, for they shall be comforted…"

"All of your righteousness is as filthy rags."

"I will sing over you."

"I have not asked these things of you…"

"Where were you when I created the heavens?"

"Many will say Lord, Lord, have I not done all these things in your name?"

Surely my kids must have thought I was going mad. I began talking back to the 'voices.' "You're the one who required all this from me! You're the one who deceived me!" I would scream. "I have done all these things for YOU. I have given up everything for you. I did what you asked—what your law demands! You OWE me!!!"

LITTLE DID I KNOW THAT IN MY RAGE I was finally engaging with God. The real God. Not the one whom I had been taught to surrender to without a fight (oddly enough, the word surrender implies there *is* a fight), and not the God whom I had envisioned as so small. For so much of what I had been taught made women out to be strong, men weak, and God small. We were taught it was our fault if men stumbled. Our husbands could not do God's will if we didn't submit. The world would go to hell if we didn't go and tell others the good news. This real God I was beginning to engage was not the one whom Christian leaders had used to motivate me to serve by asking, "How will they hear if no one goes?"

Later I would learn that this engagement with the real God was what the Psalmist had the audacity to call worship.

I began to see that much of the doctrine and theology that had seeped so deep into my soul had not come from Jesus. But it was so confusing—which parts had and hadn't come from him? Everything I had been taught had come from very sincere Christians.

Yet my deepest doubt still loomed: How could God truly require nothing of me to earn his favor? If this was really true, if this was the crux of Christianity, then what

gospel

would keep all hell from breaking loose? What would stop any of us from living completely sinful lives? Yet, still, the good news of it all was irresistible. I had to test it out. What if there was truly no merit in succeeding in a church plant?

What if we could go out and fail and it would really be okay? Not just okay somewhere down the road in eternity, but right now! Did God really care if we got out of ministry altogether? Could I really enjoy life? It seemed to good to be true!

I made a list of things I had longed to do. Fun things I never took time for because ministry had kept me so busy. I signed up for salsa dancing classes. I began hiking. I tried things I had always been taught were edgy. You know, the slippery slope—the borderlands every Christian group marks out according to its own standard and culture. I found I loved icy beer on a hot summer day and smoking cloves on a cold winter night. I stopped hanging my clothes on the line to save on the laundry bill. I finally went out and purchased my first box of disposable diapers. Surely I would go to hell for not doing my part in saving God's good green earth, right? Yet I was beginning to taste the freedom of the gospel. It really was good news!

THEN CAME THE DECISION NOT TO RETURN to the mission field. I told my husband, "This sounds so strange. But it feels like I have two choices in front of me: going back to a belief system that is all about how I perform, or following the real God. For me, giving up missionary life is giving up my performance-based Christianity." I knew I was somewhere on the right track. Nothing scared me more than the thought of not being a missionary. All my worth, value, and importance had been wrapped up in this high calling.

Yet, little did I know that this was *still* not the bottom. We were not returning to the mission field, so I was no longer a missionary. I was not attending church regularly. I was not reading my Bible regularly (remember, I had thrown it out the window). I was no longer a woman others would point their daughters to as a godly example. My resume was shattered. What more had to go for me to see that it was not my righteousness but Christ's alone?

A lot.

One day I was working busily in the kitchen. Laundry was piled high. The house needed cleaning. Groceries were low. My toddler pulled on my legs wanting lunch. The baby was dragging Tupperware, pans, tins, you name it, from the cupboard. Our oldest was at school. John was out of state for a few weeks working on his Ph.D. My new-found freedom had given me courage to stay in a location where we had a strong support network even though I had been pressured with comments like "a woman's place is with her husband." Familiar feelings of being overwhelmed with mothering and housework loomed. The war in my soul continued to mount.

"Not motherhood too," I thought. "Surely the gospel doesn't apply to mothering." I was a great mom. I had a long list of my mothering accomplishments. "Come on, you can't take that from me too," I argued. "What's wrong with being a proficient homemaker and mom?"

Yet, deep inside I knew it wasn't about being a good mom or not. It was about the fact that here was one more area I was sucking life from. My worth came from mothering. One more filthy rag I was lifting up to Jesus saying, "Doesn't this count? Can't I add to what you did on the cross with a little of my own effort? Come on, my work is so very good. The whole world loves it. I'm the person they bring up on stage at churches to applaud my efforts and my work for your kingdom. Why can't You applaud?"

I was exhausted. I was tired. While I had given up some aspects of carrying the world on my shoulders, it was so deeply ingrained in me to make my mark on eternity, to work for Jesus, to be a good wife and mother, I just couldn't see that nothing I did was required. But how in the world does one keep house or mother with a view that nothing is required by God, I wondered. It just didn't make sense. Yet I knew if theology didn't apply to the everyday aspects of life, then it didn't apply to anything. I sunk to the floor and engulfed my toddler in my arms. New thoughts came into my head as I asked my son, "I bet you would like to fix your own sandwich, wouldn't you?" He nodded eagerly as he dragged a chair to the cupboard and climbed up to reach the ingredients. I watched him pull out the jar and sloppily wipe big slabs of sticky peanut butter on the bread, the shelf, the table, and the floor, grinning with his new accomplishment. This is going to be more cleanup than it's worth, I thought. But something propelled me into this new chaos of not knowing.

I can't remember how many days, weeks, and months I lived in this limbo land. But slowly I began to see that not having a clue about what to do was the first step of walking with Jesus. Being out of control was really resting in *his* control. Some days we would spend all morning swinging in the back yard. Other evenings we would eat cold cereal for dinner. (A sure sin for the perfect mother and cook). I put the clean laundry in piles on the floor in the living room and each child could pick what he or she needed from the piles. Some days we went to bed dressed in our clothes for the next day so we didn't have to get up quite as early. We would read favorite books long into the night, everyone falling asleep in our bed. One day my daughter asked me how she could know if a person was a Christian. I found a Bible and took her to the passage on the fruit of the spirit and we talked about what the Holy Spirit does in our hearts. "The fruit can't be helped," I explained. "It just comes." "Oh," she said. "so you must have just become a Christian."

SO WHAT?

Wouldn't it be nice if the story ended there? But it hasn't. Jesus continues to invite me to see that his righteousness applies to everything—meaning it's about figuratively holding my hands open to him, trusting him for what he does on my behalf. Trusting him to rescue me every day rather than trusting myself or my plans to save the day.

ON THE DAY WE STARTED PACKING TO MOVE and I hurled the words at my husband, "What the hell does the gospel have to do with moving?" his response was perfect.

"I have no idea, Shari. But think about this: What will it look like for you to rest in this move? What is it you really want to do?" Still angry, I retorted, "Well, for starters, how about if I just sit here?" Like in the past, I reverted to thinking if I didn't work hard to make this move happen, then there would be no way we could move. Yet when I

thought about why we were moving, I knew it was what I really wanted, too, and not because I thought it was my duty to follow my husband or God. As I slumped down to the floor, I knew there was another way apart from forcing myself forward. I just didn't know what it was yet, and so I sat, once again not knowing what to do.

I have come to love that I can't formulate a three-step plan for how the gospel will invade each situation I face. If I knew, then I wouldn't really need Jesus. But I do know to keep coming back to this question, "Jesus, what does it look like today to rest in *your* work accomplished for me on the cross?" Every day and in each situation, trusting Jesus continues to look different. Sometimes it is working hard. Other times it's not. Sometimes it's being effective and efficient, other times it involves disorder and chaos. I certainly don't have the answers I used to. I wish I could tell you that every day I love Jesus and I love the gospel. Some days, I do; some days, I don't. But even when I don't, I know God's love for me is not dependent on my love for him. Honestly, it was easier living a life where I had all the answers. Exhausting and miserable, yes, but certainly more predictable and much tidier.

Yet I wouldn't go back.

Life is like a tornado watch. You can hunker down in the basement or get up on the roof, let the wind give you rock-star hair and yell, "I knew you were coming! That's why I didn't rake the leaves!"
—Unknown

gospel

TOOLS on GOSPEL

What Is the Gospel?
by Scott Sauls

Why Use This Tool?
- To clearly define an often-used term
- To awaken the senses to the beauty, centrality, and enormity of the Gospel
- To consider our current views of the Gospel

The Gospel is more than the first step in a staircase of truths. It is better likened to the hub of a wheel, the central reality around which all of life is arranged. It is not a "basic truth" from which we "move on" to deeper truths, but is the central truth from which all other truth flows. Whether you are just beginning to investigate Christianity or are a life-long follower of Christ, the Gospel is the one, single thing you must grasp if your life is to be all God designed it to be. Without the Gospel, life becomes distorted in many, many ways. With the Gospel, life is set to a path toward beauty and wholeness.

Basic definition of the Gospel: The bad news is that the universe and everything in it is wearing down all the time, and people are more sinful and wounded than they even realize. The good news is that God, through the person and work of Jesus, intends to restore both the universe and his people to their original beauty and glory. This article focuses on recognizing three primary "big truths" of the Gospel—truths that are foundational for all other teaching about faith and life.

#1 God Will Restore All Things That Are Broken

The Gospel, at its essence, is the good news that through Jesus, the love and power of God have entered history to make all things new. This renewal certainly includes the hearts of people, but also much more. It is God's intent to renew (that is, to make beautiful as it was originally intended) the entire universe. The Bible teaches that things as they are now, particularly the broken things in our lives and in creation, are not the way they are supposed to be, and as a result both people and all God's creation groan in anticipation of all things being made new again—restored to their original beauty before sin entered the world (Romans 8:18-25; Revelation 21:1-5).

Setting Things Right. Life in the world as it currently exists can certainly be characterized by moments and seasons of joy and splendor (a good marriage, a new car, straight A's, an athletic victory, a delicious steak, beautiful music...). But all would agree that there is also much that is broken (frustration in work, pain in relationships, financial strain, sickness, death). In spite of the fact that all things eventually break down, believers in the Gospel, even in dire circumstances, can live with hope (2 Corinthians 4:7-18, 12:7-10). Though things aren't perfect now, it will all be made right when God renews all things.

Redemptive Discontent. Think of the last project you were excited about (remodeling a home, waxing your car, weeding your lawn, getting a haircut...). Both the frustration you felt before the work was done (this isn't how it's supposed to be... it could and should be so much better!), and the sense of satisfaction you felt when the project was completed, are a glimpse into the image of God in you—a God who eagerly desires, as the rock band U2 sings, to "make beauty from ugly things."

#2 God Will Rescue a People for Himself by Grace and Through Faith

The central teaching or crux of the Gospel surrounds not a list of ideas, rules or propositions, but a Person. That Person is Jesus Christ, who, being in his very nature God (Philippians 2:6; 1 John 5:20), took on human flesh to mediate the enormous gap between the holiness of God and the sinfulness of humanity (Isaiah 6:1-7). Whereas

gospel

religion focuses on behavior ("you can't be acceptable unless you perform and keep rules"), and irreligion focuses on personal freedom ("you can be happy apart from God's rule in your life"), the Gospel focuses on personal trust in God's heroic rescue. The average person believes that a Christian is someone who follows Christ's teaching. The Bible says this is impossible. You don't rescue people unless they are in a perishing condition and are unable to recover themselves (how many times have you seen a corpse do CPR on itself?). Jesus, knowing the helplessness of the human condition (Genesis 6:5; Ephesians 2:1-10), therefore gave himself as a sacrifice for those who would place their faith (or trust) in his gracious gift (unmerited and unearned by us) of himself. Jesus came, lived a perfect life, and died a sacrificial death, not to buy us a second chance but rather to be our substitute. Everything we needed to do to satisfy God, Jesus did for us. He died the death we should have died so that we would never be condemned (Romans 3:23-26), and he lived the life we should have lived so that God would regard us as blameless in his own sight (2 Corinthians 5:21). Because of what Jesus did as substitute, those who trust in and receive his free gift can truly say, "As far as God is concerned, everything that's true about Jesus is true about me. God regards me as blameless and beautiful. He loves me as much as he loves Jesus. He gives me credit for all the good that Jesus did, and he puts all the blame on Jesus for all the wrongs I have done and will do."

A "who," not just a "what." Christianity is not something that we do as much as it is a Person we trust—the doing merely flows out of the trust. Jesus lived the life we should have lived, and Jesus died the death we should have died. It is on this basis alone (John 14:6) that anyone can stand blameless and fully accepted in the sight of God.

Caterpillars. Martin Luther likened all people to a caterpillar caught in the middle of a ring of fire. For us, just as is the case for the caterpillar, the only hope for deliverance is rescue "from above."

#3 God Will Make His People Beautiful, Every Last One of Them

Returning back to the first point above: it is not only God's plan to rescue his people, but to start them on a life-long journey of becoming restored to their original beauty, to reflect his image in all of its radiance, perfection, and glory. Believers in Jesus and the Gospel will one day actually be like God in their character, way of life, and desires (1 Corinthians 13:8-12; Ephesians 4:24).

A Healing Journey. The Gospel leads us to a beautiful destination—it is, in essence, a journey we take with others who also believe and embrace it—and we help each other along toward the destination of knowing and becoming like Jesus. In this life, God's ultimate purpose for us is to shape us, to renew us, to re-make us into Christ-like people. This is therefore to become our goal and vision for our own lives, and it enables us to see everything that happens to us, even suffering, as a tool in the hands of God to artistically mold us into the beautiful workmanship he intends for us to be and to become (Ephesians 2:10).

QUESTIONS:
* In what ways has this teaching changed or sharpened your understanding? Encouraged you? Bothered you?
* Read Romans 8:18-25. If you could see one broken thing in your life, your world, or in the world in general renovated or made new, what would it be and why?
* Read Ephesians 2:8-10. "Christianity is not something that we do as much as it is a Person we trust—the doing merely flows out of the trust." Is this statement consistent with what you have been taught or have believed about Christianity?
* How does this view of the Gospel compare with the portrayal of Christianity in today's culture? In your church?
* Read James 1:2-4. What is your initial response to the notion that God is artistically molding you into his workmanship (Eph 2:10)—but in a way that sometimes takes us through pain? (See also Hebrews 5:7-9)

By Scott Sauls. Used by permission of the author.

Martin Luther's Preface to the Galatians
Paraphrase by Timothy Keller

Why Use This Tool?
- To learn practical implications of the doctrine of justification by faith
- To explore differences between active and passive righteousness
- To learn how to use arguments of the gospel against the law

1. The most important thing in the world

a. The one doctrine which I have supremely at heart, is that of faith in Christ, from whom, through whom, and unto whom all my theological thinking flows back and forth day and night. This rock... which we call the doctrine of justification... was shaken by Satan in paradise, when he persuaded our first parents that they might, by their own wisdom and power, become like God.... Thereafter the whole world acted like a madman against this faith, inventing innumerable idols and religions with which everyone went his own way, hoping to placate a god or goddess, by his own works; that is, hoping without the aid of Christ and by his own works to redeem himself from evils and sins. All this is sufficiently seen in the practices and records of every culture and nation....

b. The devil our adversary, who continually rages about seeking to devour us, is not dead. Likewise our flesh and old man is yet alive. Besides this, all kinds of temptations vex and oppress us on every side, so that this doctrine can never be taught, urged, and repeated enough. If this doctrine is lost, then is also the whole knowledge of truth, life, and salvation lost; if this doctrine flourish, then all good things flourish...

2. Kinds of righteousness

a. Paul expounds the Biblical doctrine with the goal of demonstrating beyond doubt the difference between Christian righteousness and all other kinds of righteousness, for there are many kinds. First, there is political or civil righteousness—the nation's public laws—which magistrates and lawyers may defend and teach. Second, there is cultural righteousness—the standards of our family and social grouping or class—which parents and schools may teach. Third, there is ethical righteousness—the Ten Commandments and law of God—which the church may teach (but only in light of Christian-righteousness). [Now it is right to be a good citizen, to be loved and respected by your social group, and to be a morally upright person. So all these may be received without danger], if we attribute to them no power to satisfy for sin, to please God, or to deserve grace.... These kinds of righteousness are gifts of God, like all good things we enjoy....

b. Yet there is another, far above the others, which Paul calls "the righteousness of faith"—Christian righteousness.... God imputes it to us apart from our works—in other words, it is passive righteousness, as the others are active. For we do nothing for it, and we give nothing for it—we only receive and allow another to work—that is, God.

3. The need for Christian righteousness

a. This "passive" righteousness is a mystery that the world cannot understand. Indeed, Christians never completely understand it themselves, and thus do not take advantage of it when they are troubled and tempted. So we have to constantly teach it, repeat it, and work it out in practice. For anyone who does not understand this righteousness or cherish it in the heart and conscience, will continually be buffeted by fears and depression. Nothing gives peace like this passive righteousness.

b. For human beings by nature, when they get near either danger or death itself, will of necessity view their own worthiness. We defend ourselves before all threats by recounting our good deeds and moral efforts. But then the

gospel

remembrance of sins and flaws inevitably comes to mind, and this tears us apart, and we think: "How many errors and sins and wrongs I have done! Please God, let me live so I can fix and amend things." We become obsessed with our active righteousness and are terrified by its imperfections. But the real evil is that we trust our own power to be righteous and will not lift up our eyes to see what Christ has done for us.... So the troubled conscience has no cure for its desperation and feeling of unworthiness unless it takes hold of the forgiveness of sins by grace, offered free of charge in Jesus Christ, which is this passive or Christian righteousness... If I tried to fulfill the law myself, I could not trust in what I had accomplished, neither could it stand up to the judgment of God. So... I rest only upon the righteousness of Christ... which I do not produce but receive; God the Father freely giving it to us through Jesus Christ.

4. Law and grace

a. It is an absolute and unique teaching in all the world, to teach people, through Christ, to live as if there were no Law or Wrath or Punishment. In a sense, they do not exist anymore for the Christian, but only total grace and mercy for Christ's sake. Once you are in Christ, the law is the greatest guide for your life, but until you have Christian righteousness, all the law can do is to show you how sinful and condemned you are. In fact, to those outside of Christian righteousness, the law needs to be expounded in all its force. Why? So that people who think they have power to be righteous before God will be humbled.

b. Therefore the communicator of the Word of God must be careful when dispensing the knowledge of both law and grace. We must keep the law within his bounds! If you teach that we can be accepted by God through obedience, then Christian righteousness becomes mixed up with earned/moral righteousness in the people's minds. Such a teacher is an ill logician—failing to "rightly divide." On the other hand, if you teach to persons outside of Christ about God's acceptance and love, with no mention of repentance and the cross of Christ, you also confuse and fail to "rightly divide." Rather, he that applies the law and works to the flesh or the old man [the unconverted], and who applies forgiveness of sins and God's mercy to the spirit or the new man [the awakened by the Spirit] does well.

c. For example, when I see a man that is bruised, oppressed with the law, terrified with sin, and thirsting for comfort, it is time to remove out of his sight the law and active righteousness, and that I should set before him by the Gospel the Christian and passive righteousness. Then the man is raised up and realizes the hope of being under grace, not under the law (Rom. 6:14).... But upon the man without Christ there must be laid the obligation of works and the law—we do have to fulfill the law. This burden must press him down until he put on the new man, by faith in Christ—then he may enjoy the freedom of the spirit of grace. (Nevertheless, no one fully does this in this life!)

d. Therefore, no one should think we reject the importance of good works or of obeying the Law. When we receive the Christian righteousness, we consequently can live a good life, naturally, out of gratitude. If we try to earn our righteousness by doing many good deeds, we actually do nothing. We neither please God through our works-righteousness nor do we honor the purpose for which the law was given. But if we first receive Christian righteousness, then we can use the law, not for our salvation, but for his honor and glory, and to lovingly show our gratitude.

e. So, have we nothing to do to obtain this righteousness? No, nothing at all! For this righteousness comes by doing nothing, hearing nothing, knowing nothing, but rather in knowing and believing this only—that Christ has gone to the right hand of the Father, not to become our judge, but to become for us, our wisdom, our righteousness, our holiness, our salvation! Now God sees no sin in us, for in this heavenly righteousness sin has no place. So now we may certainly think: "Although I still sin, I don't despair, because Christ lives, who is both my righteousness and my eternal life." In that righteousness I have no sin, no fear, no guilty conscience, no fear of death. I am indeed a sinner in this life of mine and in my own righteousness, but I have another life, another righteousness above this life, which is in Christ, the Son of God, who knows no sin or death, but is eternal righteousness and eternal life.

5. Living the gospel

a. Now both these things continue while we live here. We are accused, exercised with temptations, oppressed with heaviness and sorrow, and bruised by the law with its demands of active righteousness. These attacks fall upon our "flesh" —the part of our heart that still seeks to earn our salvation... Because of this, Paul sets out in this letter of Galatians to teach us, to comfort us, and to keep us constantly aware of this Christian righteousness. For if the truth of being justified by Christ alone (not by our works) is lost, then all Christian truths are lost. For there is no middle ground between Christian righteousness and works-righteousness. There is no other alternative to Christian righteousness but works-righteousness; if you do not build your confidence on the work of Christ you must build your confidence on your own work. On this truth and only on this truth the church is built and has its being....

b. This distinction is easy to utter in words, but in use and experience it is very hard. So you who would be teachers and counselors of others I admonish to exercise yourselves continually in these matters through study, reading, meditation on the Word and prayer—that in the time of trial you will be able to both inform and comfort both your consciences and others, to bring them from law to grace, from active/works-righteousness to passive/Christ's righteousness. For in times of struggle, the devil will seek to terrify us by using against us our past record, the wrath, and law of God. So if we cannot see the differences between the two kinds of righteousness, and if we do not take hold of Christ by faith, sitting at the right hand of God (Hebrews 7:25) who pleads our case, sinners that we are, to the Father, then we are under the Law, not under grace, and Christ is no Savior, but a Lawgiver, and is no longer our salvation, but an eternal despair.

c. So learn to speak to one's heart and to the Law. When the law creeps into your conscience, learn to be a cunning logician—learn to use arguments of the gospel against it. Say:

"O law! You would climb up into the kingdom of my conscience, and there reign and condemn me for sin, and would take from me the joy of my heart which I have by faith in Christ, and drive me to desperation, that I might be without hope. You have overstepped your bounds. Know your place! You are a guide for my behavior, but you are not Savior and Lord of my heart. For I am baptized, and through the Gospel am called to receive righteousness and eternal life.... So trouble me not! For I will not allow you, so intolerable a tyrant and tormentor, to reign in my heart and conscience—for they are the seat and temple of Christ the Son of God, who is the king of righteousness and peace, and my most sweet savior and mediator. He shall keep my conscience joyful and quiet in the sound and pure doctrine of the Gospel through the knowledge of this passive and heavenly righteousness."

d. When I have this Christian righteousness reigning in my heart, I descend from heaven as the rain making fruitful the earth. That is to say... I do good works, how and whenever the occasion is offered.... Whoever he be that is assuredly persuaded that Christ is his righteousness, does not only cheerfully and gladly work well in his vocation... but submits to all manner of burdens and dangers in his present life, because he knows that this is the will of God, and that this obedience pleases him.

e. This then is the argument of this Epistle, which Paul expounds against the false teachers who had darkened the Galatians' understanding of this righteousness by faith.

Paraphrase by Timothy Keller. Used by Permission.

How Free Is Free?

Why Use This Tool?
• To recognize common fears Christians hold regarding freedom
• To demonstrate the scandalous nature of the gospel in relation to our freedom
• To stimulate discussions on legalism, license, and the gospel—feathers will be ruffled

The QUIZ Please Answer True or False

TRUE   FALSE   1. Free means exempt or liberated from the control of some other person or some arbitrary power.

TRUE   FALSE   2. We must be careful of this freedom thing. People will take advantage of it.

TRUE   FALSE   3. What repeatedly hurts our witness is pretense, not freedom.

TRUE   FALSE   4. We are really and truly completely free.

TRUE   FALSE   5. Being free means that if I don't do what God says, he will still love me.

TRUE   FALSE   6. Being free means that God is pleased with whatever I do, no matter what it is.

TRUE   FALSE   7. Being free means that when Christians are upset with me, God isn't.

TRUE   FALSE   8. Being free means that God's love and grace are without condition, totally.

TRUE   FALSE   9. If I do something bad, God will still bless me and answer my prayers.

TRUE   FALSE   10. We have all played the freedom-robber role.

TRUE   FALSE   11. Freedom threatens religious people because it takes away their leverage and makes it more difficult to maintain control.

TRUE   FALSE   12. Freedom scares religious folks to death because a lot of ego goes into being right and "righteous."

TRUE   FALSE   13. Freedom scares us because we do not trust ourselves.

The ANSWERS

1. TRUE. The term Jesus used for "free" meant "liberated from bondage."

2. FALSE. What are you talking about, 'take advantage of freedom' by being free? Are you crazy? That's not freedom, that is a new kind of bondage. We inadvertently teach new Christians that they are free, but may God have mercy on them if they utilize what we taught them.

3. TRUE. It would be so refreshing to say to our unbelieving friends, "I really mess up sometimes, but let me tell you something really good: God is still quite fond of me. Wouldn't it be great if you belonged to a God like that?"

4. TRUE. There is no kicker. There is no if, and, or but. You are free. You can do it right or wrong. You can obey or disobey. You can run from Christ or run to Christ. You can choose to be a faithful Christian or an unfaithful Christian. You can cry, cuss, and spit, or laugh, sing, and dance. You can read a novel or the Bible. You can watch TV or pray. You're free… really free.

5. TRUE. That is exactly what it means. You might get hurt and regret what you have done, but you can do it and he won't stop loving you. You won't lose your salvation. You won't get kicked out of the kingdom.

6. FALSE. Of course not. God feels pleased when we do what he has asked of us; but, because of the imputed righteousness of Christ, he won't be angry with you nor will he ever condemn you.

7. TRUE.

8. TRUE. That's exactly what it means.

9. TRUE. What God does and doesn't do in your life rarely has anything to do with how good you are. Teachers act like that, not God. In fact, I preached some of my best sermons when I was doing some bad stuff. God demonstrated that his fondness for me depended on his love and the cross of Christ, not on my earning it.

10. TRUE. Therefore none of us can judge. In fact, I believe that we show our depravity less by the bad stuff we do than by our reversion to Pharisaism. It isn't our sin that is so bad (Christ fixed that on the cross), but our stiffness. There is something about religion that can make us cold, critical, and mean. It's a tendency we have to fight all the time.

11. TRUE. Some believe that the only thing that will make a Christian "go" is a bit of fear and guilt.

12. TRUE. It amazes me how irritated those of us who are right and righteous become around those who think they are right and righteous…. Self righteousness is one of the most addicting things in the world.

13. TRUE. We find it comforting to have others decide for us. If we are free, we could be wrong, and we don't want to be wrong. That's the essence of perfectionism: If I haven't done it wrong, I am still perfect; and even if I do it wrong when someone else told me to do it wrong, that takes away from their perfectionism, not mine.

Adapted by Tami Resch from A SCANDALOUS FREEDOM by Steve Brown. Copyright © 2004 by Steve Brown. Printed by permission of Howard, a Division of Simon & Schuster, Inc.

LEFT TURN   RIGHT TURN

FIRELIGHTING

But now, all you who light fires and provide yourselves with flaming torches, go, walk in the light of your fires and of the torches you have set ablaze. This is what you shall receive from my hand: You will lie down in torment.
—Isaiah 50:11

Waiting on your bed
Hosea 7:14

WAITING IN DARKNESS

I will give you the treasures of darkness and the hoards in secret places, that you may know that it is I, the LORD, the God of Israel, who call you by your name.
—Isaiah 45:3 (ESV)

Crying out to God from your heart
Hosea 7:14

TORMENT

SELF SAVING

FALSE Repentance & NO Repentance

TRUE Repentance

the OBJECT of our *desire*

epithumia

THE BLOCK

We begin here.

Created with the desire:
• to be loved
• to have worth
• to be safe and secure

delight in God

hope

LEFT TURN

FIRELIGHTING

But now, all you who light fires and provide yourselves with flaming torches, go, walk in the light of your fires and of the torches you have set ablaze. This is what you shall receive from my hand: You will lie down in torment.
—Isaiah 50:11

Fleeing *"I'm out of here."*
- escapes physically/emotionally
- cuts off relationships
- numbs feelings; is unaware of feelings
- unwilling to enter chaos, confrontation
- unwilling to cooperate with the sovereignty of God in that time and place

Despairing *"Nothing will ever change."*
- cynicism, dillusionment, self-pity, depression.
- expresses itself in substance abuse and addictive behaviors
- over indulges in food, sex, work, technology, spending money, etc.
- expresses anger in self-contempt

Fixing *"I will figure out a solution to get out of this mess."*
- shrinks desires
- attempts to use God and prayer to get my way
- relies on experts (books, wise counsel, seminars, etc) to solve problems
- employs strategies of: gossip, overwork, people pleasing, etc.
FIXING leads to self-righteousness (critical, judgmental, angry, manipulative, shaming).

We begin here.

FALSE Repentance or NO Repentance

False Repentance:
does not expose legitimate shame, our true fears, or the truth about ourselves.

In False Repentance:
- we fail to take sin seriously
- we set the will against superficial behaviors
- we are motivated by fear and not love
- we are sorrowful only about the consequences we suffer, not the pain we cause

We feel only TORMENT

Wailing on your bed.
Hosea 7:14

gospel

RIGHT TURN

WAITING IN DARKNESS

I will give you the treasures of darkness and the hoards in secret places, that you may know that it is I, the LORD, the God of Israel, who call you by your name.
—Isaiah 45:3 (ESV)

Crying out to God from your heart
Hosea 7:14

TRUE Repentance

- moves beyond repenting of our actions to repenting of our patterns that lead to our actions
- is a process
- turns from dead works: self-sufficiency, self-confidence, self-righteousness
- brings life
- moves beyond consequence-regret to true sorrow over our sin and the ways we cause harm
- leads to "clean" grief that brings life rather than inordinate shame that brings death
- loosens sin at the motivational level
- leads to BELIEF: that we are accepted and loved; that Christ is reliable and our idols are not

Fruit of True Repentance

- we become willing to wait
- we anticipate rescue with delight
- we rest
- we become willing to engage others
- we lose our defensiveness, impatience, ridigidy, irritability
- we become willing to hear how we harm others and we enter the path of reconciliation
- we become grateful and free of self-condemnation
- we trust God more
- we yearn for and...

THE BLOCK

We begin here.

delight in God

Left Turn/Right Turn Chart Explanation
by Shari Thomas

Why Use This Tool?
- To understand that our longings are created by God
- To identify our patterns for getting our longings met
- To grow in recognition of true and false repentance

THE HUMAN SOUL

We will not fully explore the vast profundity of being created in the image of God here, but one implication we want to discuss is that God has set eternity in our hearts. In other words, what God will one day fulfill in eternity has already been imprinted as a desire in our hearts. Our deep longings and desires were created by God, and these desires have hard-wired us, so to speak, to receive as well as to give.

OUR LONGINGS

All people desire:

Love

If a human being is not loved, she dies, or wants to. Studies conducted on children in certain orphanages have shown that if a child is not held, she dies. A child needs to know that he is loved, if not by his parents, then by someone. A child needs to be loved not just until she's 21, but until glory.

Worth

We need to feel that we matter, and that our lives count. The object of our longing could be someone who thinks I'm contributing at home or at work and tells me so. While it may not be a conscious thought, everyone has a reason for living, and anyone who loses his or her sense of worth eventually wants to die. For most people, the hardest part of aging is feeling that they no longer have value. Some people would rather be wanted for murder than not wanted at all.

Security/Safety

We need to feel we are secure and safe. A child not only needs to *be* protected, she needs to *feel* that she is protected. As with our objects of longing related to love and worth, the object of longing in regard to security will vary from person to person. The object may be money or it may be freedom from fear or it may be a person who will provide for me.

While we may not be able to place every longing into one of these three categories, it is important to recognize that all humans have legitimate longings and these longings have objects. Human behavior stems from the desire to satisfy our basic needs, and we are motivated when these needs are touched. Some people go through life with very little experience or sense of being loved, protected, or feeling their value and worth. The need to have these basic longings met is not wrong. We are created in the image of a God who is love, who has designed our lives with a purpose, and who is all-powerful; we are safe in that love. God, who is the embodiment of these attributes, does not need as we do. But our needs reflect the image of the God who created us.

gospel

THE OBJECT OF OUR LONGINGS

Love

We want someone who will love us and show it. No person can be satisfied apart from relationships with other people. Whether single or married, each person needs to be loved and know she is loved.

Worth

We ache for something to invest our lives in that gives us worth and purpose.

Security

This is the desire to live and live well, to not be annihilated either literally or figuratively. This incentive motivates us to search for others with whom we can feel safe and secure. It also draws us to situations, positions, places, and circumstances that make us feel secure.

THE DRIVE OF THE HUMAN SOUL

These legitimate needs drive the human soul. Just as our heart constantly pumps, think of the drive of the human soul as persistently pursuing. When our soul senses *need* (and it always does) it moves toward and goes after whatever promises to meet these needs. We move toward the objects of our desires and needs. Remember: our need to be loved, to have a sense of worth, and to feel safe is God-given. However, *the ways we seek to fill those needs* will not necessarily be God's way of having those needs met.

THE BLOCK

As we go after these needs, eventually we come to a place where we are blocked from getting what we want. The legitimate love needed from a mother may be withheld. The protection needed from parents may be compromised by neglect or poverty. Children growing up in a loving home may still experience the terror of living in a war-torn country, or the loss that death brings. A child may feel keenly a lack of ability in academics, sports, beauty, or some other area and decide he or she has no worth or value. All of us will experience the aching loss of life in a broken world.

Since we are all worshipers by nature, we will turn the objects of our desire into something we must have at all costs. Worshiping what we desire is dangerous because eventually we will destroy one another to get what we crave. Worshiping the living God is not some ego trip for God; it's our only hope of not destroying ourselves and the rest of humanity.

In Genesis 3, we see the first block to human desires: God not only allowed the Curse, but put it into effect. Even in the Curse, however, God does not leave humanity alone. Instead, God points to a way out, to a redemption that will come. So in the Curse, we see the first signs of blessing for the human race. We need the Curse—the thorns, thistles, relational pain and even death—to drive us to the living God, the only place our souls can find true rest and satisfaction.

Types of blocks we often experience:
* The failings or wrongdoings of the person who is the object of desire
* Circumstances
* Our own weaknesses
* When another person gets what I want
* Rules, customs, laws

NEGATIVE EMOTIONS

Another function of the soul is to feel emotion. When our drive is blocked we typically feel negative emotions: hurt, sorrow, shame, humiliation, anxiety, fear, and loneliness, to name a few. When we feel out of control, we frequently cap or cover these emotions with anger. Anger is often a sign of many other emotions the person cannot identify. It is much easier to be angry than to feel the pain of not being loved. Anger can be manifested as either other-centered or self-centered contempt. In other-centered contempt, we hate the object of our desire. In self-contempt, we hate ourselves for even having the desire. Though anger is destructive, we go to it because it helps us feel powerful when everything is out of control.

Signs of other-centered contempt include eye-rolling, sighing, sarcasm, deprecating humor, or making a person look small. Use of pornography (which reduces people to objects) demonstrates contempt. We can show contempt for others in our tone of voice, body language, or by verbal or physical violence. Even if we don't do these things on the outside, we can still play mind movies and do these actions in our heads.

Signs of self-contempt include self-deprecating humor, not allowing others to focus on us, beating ourselves up in our head, or not accepting compliments. Self-mutilation (cutting) and binge eating or drinking also indicate self-loathing. We can also shift attention off of ourselves in a way that might indicate self-contempt: "Well, just give God all the glory. He did it, not me."

Yet God knows that the negative feelings arising from our blocked goals may be our only salvation. Because God loves us, he also brings us into the darkness, into that sense of chaos and confusion. We can either trust in the unseen God, or we can trust in something we can do (self-salvation) for rescue. Isaiah describes this as encircling ourselves with lights or firelighting. Here, we either take a left turn (firelighting) or a right turn (waiting in darkness).

FIRELIGHTING: LEFT TURN

Even with a desire to please God, we don't know what to do with negative emotions. We find ourselves confused and want to get out of the dark as quickly as possible. Our tendency is to make a left turn. Listen to how Isaiah describes this.

"Who among you fears the LORD and obeys the word of his servant? Let those who walk in the dark, who have no light, trust in the name of the LORD and rely on their God. But now, all you who light fires and provide yourselves with flaming torches, go, walk in the light of your fires and of the torches you have set ablaze. This is what you shall receive from my hand: You will lie down in torment." Isaiah 50:10-11 (TNIV)

Firelighting can be described as our natural tendency and response when our goals are blocked. Firelighting is an attempt to see—to get out of the dark—brought about by our own efforts. Firelighting is movement that is motivated by a desperation for clarity: "I will get out of this confusion." So we light torches and get ourselves out of the mess. We commit ourselves to solving our own problems and to using all available resources (including God) to get the job done. But this commitment keeps us preoccupied with something other than discovering God.

"They do not cry out to me from the heart, but they wail upon their beds; for grain and wine they gash themselves; they rebel against me." Hosea 7:14 (ESV)

We appear to be calling out to God, but we really aren't. We wail to God because everything we have tried is not working, but we aren't crying out to God from our hearts. There is a big difference. One is true repentance (we cry out to God; take a Right Turn) and the other is false repentance (we wail on our beds; take a Left Turn).

There are as many ways to get around blocked desires as there are people, but we'll only focus on a few of the more common ones.

Fleeing: *"I'm out of here."*
This most often involves escaping physically or emotionally. What could it look like to flee our church plant? We might emotionally withdraw—present in body, but absent in our hearts. We might disengage from relationships, ministry, or knowledge of what is happening. We might stop going to church altogether, or only be involved in areas where we feel secure and where our contribution is valued. We might escape by attempting to convince ourselves and others that we really don't care. "After all, this is my spouse's calling. It's not really mine." This form of firelighting does not lead to repentance as we refuse to stay engaged.

Despairing: *"Nothing will ever change."*
Cynicism, disillusionment, and self-pity are signs of despair. Hopelessness can show itself in substance abuse or an overindulgence in technology, food, sex, addictions, reading, or fantasy. It can express itself in depression or pornography. The most likely form of anger expressed by a person in despair will be self-contempt. This form of firelighting usually leads to false repentance.

Fixing: *"I will figure out a solution to get out of this mess."*
This form of firelighting is often hard to detect as it can be disguised as spiritual. We often experience fixing as trying harder, and usually this has as its object self-control. When we identify the struggle within ourselves we often see that we are just trying to gain more self-control. (This can be seen in the example used later of my anger towards John.) But self-control is the fruit of the Spirit, not my fruit. Why is the scripture reference to *fruit of the spirit* singular? The term *the fruit of the Spirit* is one thing, the Spirit's fruit. We either have it or we don't. It is something we get from the Holy Spirit, not from our efforts. And it is not something we can attain by working at it. This is the argument presented in Galatians: "Oh, you foolish Galatians, did you think you could sanctify yourselves through your own efforts?" So many of us run to self-effort in order to fix our lives.

> *Shrinking Our Desire:* *"I should never have desired/wanted this to begin with."*
We do this when we walk around the house saying under our breath, "I really should not have expected him home for dinner. He is a busy man. This is what it means to be in church planting. I just need to get a grip and not expect him to care for my needs too." Shrinking our desire is just another form of self-contempt. It gives us some measure of control, even if it's just an explanation of why life isn't working. This is the function of a poor self-image.

Using God or Prayer
We think we need to change or do something to get God to do what we ask. It can look like more Bible study, memory work, or prayer, but the underlying desire is to escape our pain and compel God to fix our lives. This is not to say we shouldn't pray or read the Bible, but when we say, "Prayer isn't working," it may be a sign that we only pray in order to manipulate God rather than to know God.

Using/Over-relying on Experts
We often rely on experts as a substitution for relying on God. This can be done through books, seminars, discovering the newest ministry growth technique, or seeking more knowledge. We get into the frantic search for the next best thing on the market. Ministry couples are more likely to use this form of firelighting in order to ensure the success of their churches. But they are less likely to seek out experts to help their marriages, even when seeking marital help would be true repentance.

gospel   68

Gossip

Gossip is often a way to get a taste of intimacy even though it is false intimacy. We speak about the situation that's troubling us and something feels relieved (for a while, that is) but we go on as before until we complain to someone else.

Overwork or Legalism

We believe that if we just work harder, come up with the right program, or do what everyone wants us to do, that somehow we can solve the problem.

People-Pleasing

We are driven for people to like us because we don't want to have to feel or endure their disappointment or anger. This is a manipulative strategy that produces an exhausted and overworked person, and one who is unable to sit in the pain of disappointing others. People pleasers are nice but they are not kind. Their motivation to be nice is self-protection.

Fix-it solutions often lead to self-righteousness. When we pour enormous amounts of time and energy into solutions, it's quite easy to give ourselves permission to be judgmental, critical, and angry with others who do not share the same work habits or solutions. We may even manipulate others by shaming them or cutting off relationships. If our fix-it solution seemed to work for us, we believe others need only to do what we did in order to solve their problems. A sign that we have succumbed to self-righteousness is that our solutions leave us without compassion for others. Lack of repentance is revealed when we think we have done all we need to do, when we've done it all right, when we think we deserve better outcomes than we are getting.

FALSE REPENTANCE

"They do not cry out to me from their hearts but wail on their beds. They slash themselves, appealing to their gods for grain and new wine, but they turn away from me."
Hosea 7:14

In Hosea's culture, grain and new wine equaled security. One could literally live or die without grain and wine. We find ourselves in similar situations today. What do you believe you must have right now or you will not make it? What pushes you to the exhaustion of your mind and body?

In false repentance we often recognize the outward signs of what is wrong. We may even feel remorseful. We more than likely wail to God because we just want God to give us what we think we need.

IN MY STORY: During one of our church plants, I begged God to let our church fail and fail quickly because I didn't believe it was going to survive. I wanted to get out of my pain, and to do so quickly. I saw what was going wrong, or so I thought, and my way out was to flee. I wanted to use God to escape my pain. God would have none of it.

We may think we are turning to God, but rather than crying out from our hearts we are turning *away* from God. We are falsely repenting.

- *False repentance does not expose our legitimate shame and Christ's outrageous provision and love.* As in the Garden, we prefer to hide and make coverings. When legitimate shame is too much to bear, we quickly move into illegitimate shame. We say, "No one can really love me for me. I must bring something to the relationship besides just myself. I will bring my coverings, my masks, the things I think are good." I don't let my REAL

 gospel

sin show, not even to myself. This takes away from Christ's work on the cross because we think Christ is not enough (pride). The truth is we really are much worse than we know (legitimate shame), but someone does love us in spite of our substandard resume (unbelief).

 False repentance does not expose our true fear. Our true fear is that God and others can't handle us and maybe we are just too much for them. We are afraid God will abandon us and won't really forgive us. We are afraid we won't really be freed. This takes away from Christ's work on the cross because we do not believe Christ has rescued or will rescue us again (unbelief). We think others can't handle us (pride).

 In false repentance, the truth about ourselves is not exposed. We are scared to death of what we will find if we should happen to see our true selves. And that feels just a bit too risky. When we aren't facing the pain about who we really are, we aren't believing that we are as bad off as God says (unbelief). We think surely God could not love us unless we fix ourselves up (pride).

- *In false repentance, we fail to take sin seriously.* We continue to make excuses. We avoid, reject, or attack others. We attempt quick fixes. We gossip. We don't allow ourselves proper grieving time over real losses. We become impatient and resort to legalism to control behavior. We don't expect God to work. We take credit for what God has done. Or we fail to give credit for what God enabled us to do, refusing to recognize our dignity and how God used us.

- *False repentance tries to fix problems with rules, legalism, or superficial behavior.* Without an orientation to the gospel, our attempts at repentance tend to set the will against superficial behavior. We say to ourselves, "I should not be worrying! It's a sin! Christians shouldn't worry! I must stop it!"

IN MY STORY: When our children were young, it was difficult to get time away to focus on ministries outside the home. I blamed my husband for not honoring his promise to be home when he said he would be and I felt justified in my outbursts of anger toward him. A superficial analysis would say that I just needed to repent of the sin of uncontrolled anger. But the root issue was that I inordinately placed my value on being a successful missionary. "My life is worthwhile because I have given all to follow Christ as generations in our family have done before me." My husband's lack of participation in childcare threatened my idol system. The success of my contribution to the missionary enterprise gave me my sense of satisfaction, value, and worth. My entire way of thinking was off. A complete overhaul was needed. Only when God denied me the very things I was fervently asking him for did he expose and chip away the root of my anger and volcanic eruptions. My anger eventually shifted away from my spouse to God, where it needed to be, because my battle was really with God. "Why won't you give me what I want?" "Why are you so vindictive?" "I'm doing this all for you!" Eventually the truth began to dawn. "Really? I'm doing this for God? Or is it to suck worth from what I'm doing?"

If my actions can give me a sense of worth then I can keep God at a safe distance. I won't have to face the real God or the real me.

- *In false repentance we feel regret over consequences we or even others may suffer, but we fail to address what drives us.* Repentance because of fear is really sorrow for the consequences we will experience. It is sorrow over the *danger* of wrongdoing. False repentance bends the will away from sin, but the heart still clings to it.

When we are blocked from getting a legitimate need met, an added drive rises up. It's an energy that the scripture calls an over-desire, or in Greek, *epithumia.* Our craving for a legitimate need is blocked so we attempt to go around the block in our own way. When these strong desires are not met, we create something that will fill us. We refer to these as gods or idols. These are the systems we have set up to make our lives work for us. "But I say, walk by the Spirit and you will not carry out the *epithumia* of the flesh." Gal. 5:16 (NASB)

- *False repentance can be characterized as scrambling about for relief.* It leaves us frustrated, agitated, and distressed. It is indeed torment. But God is a God of compassion whose heart is set upon us. God allows the darkness, knowing that pain can bring us into the only life that will set us free. ✗

WAITING IN DARKNESS: RIGHT TURN

"I will give you the treasures of darkness and the hoards in secret places, that you may know that it is I, the LORD, the God of Israel, who call you by your name." Isaiah 45:3 (ESV)

"For thus says the high and exalted One who lives forever, whose name is Holy: I dwell on a high and holy place, and also with the contrite and lowly of heart, in order to revive the spirit of the lowly and to revive the heart of the contrite." Isaiah 57:15 (NASB)

This passage is saying something profound! In the darkness we discover God. We discover the God who knows our name and calls us by that name. In other words, we find the God who knows us.

There is one person, however, who experienced darkness in a profoundly different way from the rest of us: Christ. He knew the treasures of living in constant community with God, yet he chose to enter a darkness where there would be no treasure, and where he would lose access to God. He not only chose momentary darkness but the final darkness of death as well. He who did not have to know darkness voluntarily chose to lie down in torment so we would not have to. This is good news! We do not have to experience the ultimate torment that results from firelighting. Christ, who didn't light his own torch, experienced the ultimate torment of darkness. As we enter darkness without lighting our own way, without seeking our tried and true ways out, we will meet God. Listen, it's not just that we can meet God, but that *we will* meet God. We will be given the treasure of knowing the God of Israel, who calls us by name. The One who calls us by name, and knows us! We are not alone in the dark as Christ once was completely alone. This truly is good news—the gospel. When we firelight, we won't meet this God, not because God is vindictive but because the fires we light draw us to false sources of light.

We often experience feelings of threat whether they are real or not. Our stomachs clench up. Our chests constrict. Our backs go straight. Our throats tighten. We go numb. We can't speak or we speak too much. At this point, we often panic. We believe if we do not respond as we have grown accustomed to responding, all will be lost. All we hold most dear is threatened, or so we believe. However, this is where we have a wonderful opportunity. We can *choose* to wait in the darkness and invite Christ to lead us to true repentance.

TRUE REPENTANCE

"They do not cry to me from the heart, but wail upon their beds; for grain and wine they gash themselves; they rebel against me." Hosea 7:14 (ESV)

Although this verse is stated in the negative, it is actually an invitation to cry to God from our hearts.

In true repentance, we move beyond repenting of our *actions* to repenting of the *patterns* that led to those actions. We grapple with the depth of our sin and experience true healing. It is a process in which we continually turn from our dead works to Christ. We repent of telling God what must be done for us and how he is to do it. We repent of not believing that Christ has really rescued us and will continue to rescue us. We begin to uncover our many alternative salvations and are set free from the power of idols.

- *True repentance leads to real sorrow over real sin and the hurt and pain it causes.* This type of repentance melts our heart so that we long to turn away from sin. It makes the sin itself disgusting to us, and it loses its attractive power over us. We say, "This disgusting thing is an affront to the one who experienced ultimate darkness on my behalf."

- *True repentance is a process.* When I first began repenting of an idol system which said my worth came from serving God, it led us not only to leave the country in which we were serving, but to leave professional ministry altogether. My patterns were so ingrained that I had to breathe different air, so to speak, until I began to recognize idolatrous patterns around which my life was built. Ministry was my god. Radical repentance meant I had to forsake a lifestyle from which I derived my worth. This didn't mean that I stayed away from good works altogether, but I left a type of ministry for a season.

- *True repentance is a turning away from dead works.* (Hebrews 9:14) This involves repenting from self-sufficiency, self-confidence, self-righteousness, and from the fears, hardness of heart, and irritability that result. These come as the result of a proud refusal to accept that the Father's love is free through Christ, and that Christ's work is all we need to be deeply loved, accepted, and valued.

  IN MY STORY: I slowly grew away from putting my hope in my accomplishments. Growth could be seen as I let go of an inordinately clean house, yard, and organized life. My husband's repentance led him to good works born out of repenting from despair and a false idol of success. We saw this as he began taking care of the kids, cooking meals, and picking up around the house.

- *True repentance brings life.* True repentance looks at the objects of our false pride and our false securities and says to them, "You are not my peace! You are not my life or salvation! You may be good, but you are not a savior! Only Christ is that to me!"

- *True repentance cleanses and does not crush.* It creates the only kind of grief over sin which is 'clean' and brings healing. It says: "Look at Jesus dying for you! He won't leave you or abandon you—how then can you respond as you are doing? He suffered so you wouldn't have to experience the suffering of ultimate darkness like he did! You are not living as though you are loved! As his child! Christ is not asking us to be holy out of fear that he might abandon us, but because this is One who, at inestimable cost to himself, has said he won't ever abandon us!" See how the GRACE of God argues? It is the only argument that cannot be answered. This creates the only motivation that leads us to hate the sin without hating ourselves. It is the only motivation that will make sin lose its power over us.

- *True repentance loosens sin at the motivational level.* Because true repentance causes us to rejoice in the acceptance we have in Christ, it destroys the motivations for sin at the root. Idolatrous desires for power, approval, self-control, pleasure and comfort are roots of the flesh that can control our lives—even as Christians—unless we continually dwell in the gospel. Though we may refrain from external sinful activities, pride and envy and fear can still shape our lives, and especially our religious activities.

  In order to live in freedom from the power of idols, we have to remind ourselves of who we are in Christ and live in accordance with it. We ask ourselves, "What does it mean to live as if we are completely accepted and loved by grace?" We spend time thinking about what it means that he has justified us, that he has adopted us, that he has accepted us.

- *True repentance is a lifestyle.* Relying on Christ rather than on idols and works-based slavery is a matter of day-to-day living. As P.T. Forsyth says, "It is an item of faith that we are children of God; there is plenty of experience in us against it." This belief—larger than all the evidence—invites us to warm ourselves at the fire of God's love instead of stealing self-acceptance from other sources. This belief is the *root* of holiness.

As you move through your everyday activities, you may notice the motives of the flesh, e.g., "Father, I see how much I do out of a hungry desire to gain worth from the applause of others and to look good in their eyes. This trivializes your unwavering love for me in Christ. Forgive and cleanse me from these motives, which rise from the habits of my old life."

Then, articulate the motives of a child of God, as you proceed through the activity, e.g., "Father, I do this for you, not for the success it might bring me. I don't need that, nor am I worried that much about failure, because your recognition is all I need. Oh, let my heart fully experience what I just said to you!"

What does repentance and faith look like for you? As you recognize some of your patterns of firelighting, consider writing what a right hand turn looks like for you.

Fruit of True Repentance
- We experience an increased trust in God. We become willing to wait for him to revive us. Increasingly, we don't look to other measures.
- We begin to anticipate rescue with delight. There is an excitement as we wonder what Christ is going to do and how he is going to show up!
- We rest. We increasingly cease from fretting, from having to fix the problem.
- If previously we disengaged, we become willing to engage.
- We begin to lose our defensiveness with others, our impatience, our rigidity, and our irritability.
- If our sin is against others, we sincerely ask them, "Can you tell me how I harmed you?" We are willing to listen. We are willing to walk the path of reconciliation.
- Our lives begin to be characterized by gratefulness. We lose the attitude of entitlement or thinking that things are owed us.
- True repentance gives increasing freedom from self-condemnation.
- We yearn for God.

Notice that the fruit of repentance is not something we can produce. It does not come immediately and it grows in us much like fruit grows on a tree.

For Further Reflection:
- Can you name some of your current objects of desire?
- How are these goals being met or blocked? What negative emotions are you experiencing?
- Can you identify your firelighting techniques when you make left-hand turns? In other words, do you tend to flee, fix it, or move into despair? Or have you created a unique pattern all your own?
- Describe a recent time when you made a left hand turn.
- Can you identify idols that you were protecting?
- What might true repentance look like in this situation?
- If you are able, write a prayer of repentance for this situation. Include your particular firelighting skills and the motivation for lighting these fires. Include statements of your unbelief. Include how this is filled with pride. Write what you believe Christ has done and is doing in this particular situation.

The contents of this tool reflect contributions from James M. Hatch, Jim Peterson, Larry Crabb, and Kathy Bearce.

Honey Out of the Rock, Psalm 81:16

by Thomas Wilcox (1621-1687)

Pastor of a Particular Baptist Church in London

Why Use This Tool?

- To consider how we look to obedience and duties for acceptance
- To bring our focus back to Jesus

Believing is the most wonderful thing in the world. Put anything of your own to it, and you will spoil it. It is the hardest thing in the world to take Christ alone for righteousness: that is, to acknowledge Him as "Christ." Join anything to Him of your own and you un-Christ Him.

Whatever comes in when you go to God for acceptance, besides Christ, call it anti-Christ; bid it be gone; make only Christ's righteousness triumphant. When Satan charges sin upon your conscience, then for the soul to charge it upon Christ, that is gospel-like; that is to make Him, "Christ." When the soul, in all duties and distress, can say, "Nothing but Christ, Christ alone, for righteousness, justification, sanctification, redemption" (I Cor. 1:30)…that soul has got above the reach of the billows.

Make Christ your peace; "for he is our peace" (Eph. 2:14); not your duties and your tears, Christ your righteousness, not your graces (changes). You may destroy Christ by duties (your obedience), as well as by sins.

He that fears to see sin's utmost vileness, the utmost hell of his own heart, he doubts the merits of Christ. If you will do anything yourself, as to paying for your sin, you renounce Christ the righteous, who was made sin for you (II Cor. 5:21).

Don't you know? In all the Scripture there is not an ill word against a poor sinner stripped of self-righteousness.

You complain much of yourself. Does your sin make you look more at Christ, and less at yourself? To be looking at duties (obedience), graces (spiritual power), enlargements (spiritual changes), when you should be looking at Christ, that is pitiful. Looking at them will make you proud; looking at Christ's grace will only make you humble.

Look not a moment off Christ. Look not upon sin, but look upon Christ first. When you mourn for sin, if you see Christ, then, away with it (Zech. 12:10). Let sin break your heart, but not your hope in the gospel.

When we come to God, we must bring nothing but Christ with us. Any ingredients, or any previous qualifications of our own, will poison and corrupt faith. He that builds upon duties, graces, etc., knows not the merits of Christ.

Despairing sinner! You look on your right hand and on your left, saying, "Who will show us any good?" You are tumbling over all your duties and professions to patch up a righteousness to save you. Look anywhere else and you are undone. God will look at nothing but Christ and you must look at nothing else.

You say you cannot believe, you cannot repent. You would be fitter for Christ if you have nothing but sin and misery. Go to Christ with all your impenitence and unbelief, to get faith and repentance from him; that is glorious. Tell Christ, "Lord, I have brought no righteousness, no grace to be accepted in, or justified by; I have come for Yours, and must have it." We would be bringing our gifts of righteousness to Christ, and that must not be.

This will be sound religion: To rest upon the everlasting mountains of God's love and grace in Christ, to live continually in the sight of Christ's infinite righteousness and merits, they are sanctifying. Without them the heart is carnal; and in those sights, to see the full vileness, yet littleness of sin (in comparison to Christ's righteousness). And to see all pardoned: in those sights to pray, hear and so forth.

Looking at the natural sun weakens the eye. The more you look at Christ, the Sun of Righteousness, the stronger and clearer will the eye of faith be. Look but at Christ, you will love Him and live on Him. Think on Him continually. If you will see sin's sinfulness, to loathe it and mourn, do not stand looking upon sin, but look upon Christ first, as suffering and satisfying God's justice for your sin. If you would see your graces, your sanctification, do not stand gazing upon them; but look at Christ's righteousness in the first place.

A Christian never lacks comfort, except by breaking the order and method of the gospel: looking on his own, and looking off Christ's perfect righteousness, which is to choose rather to live by candlelight, than by the light of the sun. The honey that you suck from your own righteousness will turn into perfect gall, and the light that you take from it to walk in, will turn into black night upon the soul.

Again, if you would pray, and cannot, and so are discouraged, see Christ praying for you; using His interest with the Father for you; what can you lack (John 14:16)? If you are troubled, see Christ as your peace (Eph. 2:14), leaving you peace when He went up to heaven, charging you not to be troubled, as to obstruct your comfort or your believing (John 14:1-27). He is now upon the throne, having spoiled upon His cross in the lowest state of humiliation everything that can hurt or annoy you. He has borne all your sins, sorrows, troubles, temptations, and is gone to prepare mansions for you.

Do Christ this one favor for all His love to you—love all His poor saints and churches, the most despised, the smallest, the weakest, notwithstanding any difference of judgment, they are engraved on His heart. Let them be so on yours.

Thomas Willcox (1621-1687) was a Particular Baptist pastor in Southwark, London. Written before the Great Fire of London, this tract was originally entitled: *A Choice Drop of Honey from the Rock Christ*, or, *A Short Word of Advice to all Saints and Sinners*. It is based on Psalm 81:16. In the 19th century, this tract was used by the Holy Spirit to ignite a revival in Finland.

gospel

Gospel Resources

Children of the Living God, Sinclair Ferguson
Commentary on Galatians, Martin Luther, Modern English Translation
Counterfeit Gods: The Empty Promises of Money, Sex, and Power, and the Only Hope that Matters, Tim Keller
The Discipline of Grace, Jerry Bridges
The Divine Conspiracy, Dallas Willard
The Doctrine of Repentance, Thomas Watson
The Dynamics of Spiritual Life, Richard Lovelace
From Fear to Freedom, Rose Marie Miller
The Glory of the Christ, John Owen, abridged version by R.J.K. Law
The Gospel for Real Life, Jerry Bridges
Gospel in Life Study Guide: Grace Changes Everything, Timothy J. Keller
Gospel Transformation, small group curriculum, World Harvest Mission
Heart of a Servant Leader, John C. (Jack) Miller
Holiness by Grace, Bryan Chapell
How People Change, Paul Tripp
Instruments in the Redeemer's Hands, Paul Tripp
Jake's Story, Wayne Jacobson and Dave Coleman
The King's Cross, Tim Keller
Outgrowing the Ingrown Church, John C. (Jack) Miller
The Reason for God, Tim Keller
Renewal as a Way of Life, Richard Lovelace
Repentance: The First Word of the Gospel, Richard Owen Roberts
Repentance and 20th Century Man, John C. (Jack) Miller
The Return of the Prodigal, Henri Nouwen
A Scandalous Freedom, Steve Brown
Sonship conference and discipleship materials, World Harvest Mission
Transforming Grace, Jerry Bridges
Valley of Vision: A Collection of Puritan Prayers and Devotions, Arthur Bennett
When Being Good Isn't Good Enough, Steve Brown
What is the Gospel?, Tim Keller

SERMONS

How The Gospel Transforms The Most Vile Sinner—The Pastor, Ray Cortese; www.firstpresaugusta.org
How The Gospel Transforms The Church, Ray Cortese; www.firstpresaugusta.org
Free Sermons by Timothy Keller; www. sermons.redeemer.com
Free Podcasts available on iTunes by Timothy Keller

HELPFUL WEBSITES

World Harvest Mission; www.whm.org
Peculiar People: Theatrical Theology; www.peculiarpeople.com

IDOLATRY

WHAT ARE IDOLS ?

HOW ARE THEY DISMANTLED ?

Sometimes I wake, and, lo! I forgot / And drifted out upon an ebbing sea! / My soul that was at rest now resteth not, / For I am with myself and not with thee.   GEORGE MACDONALD

The Myths of Idolatry
by Tami Resch

"Idols are little statues on a shelf."

"Idols are material in form."

"Idols represent evil things."

"I am a believer in Jesus Christ, not an idol worshiper."

"Churches do not serve idols."

"The only way to preclude over-desires is to not desire."

At a concert I recently attended, a musician who had been raised Hindu told of the 330,000,000 gods he worshiped as a child.

"330,000,000 was a little too abstract, so in our house, we picked five. Five blue gods. And we worshiped them. But when our family needed additional help, we worshiped the other 329,999,995. "

Not so very long ago, I would have scoffed at the seemingly ridiculous idea of worshiping little blue gods or looking to a myriad of gods when I needed help. But as the musician spoke, I did not sneer. I saw. I saw my Hindu-like heart that readily worships and serves created things rather than the Creator, that readily worships and serves ideologies rather than the Creator, that, in fact, readily worships and serves just about anything rather than the Creator. We can make idols out of anything.

John Calvin poignantly stated, "Our hearts are little idol factories." I can imagine red brick smokestacks jutting from the factory of my heart and emitting their toxic fumes as idols roll off the assembly lines within. This picture would make a clever illustration, but there's nothing funny about how vividly it portrays my overworking heart choking on its own fumes.

So why talk about idols in a toolkit for the hearts of ministry leaders? Men and women in vocational ministry are notoriously adept at identifying idolatry (spiritual adultery) in the lives of others. But to what degree are we accomplished at recognizing *who we are sleeping with?* Who and what are the other gods we serve when we break the first commandment? And why is it so hard to see idolatry in our own lives?

Idolatry is insidious and evil. In his Ephesians 6 sermon "Spiritual Warfare," Tim Keller speaks of the complexity of evil.

From the beginning, the Bible says

evil never comes pure. Evil never comes openly. Evil never comes at you obviously. Evil is... always intertwined with good. It is always hidden. It's always multilayered. It's always complicated.... When you finally figure out that evil is upon you, you'll be wrestling— it will be that close. When you finally wake up to evil, the hands are always around your throat. As a general rule you never see evil

> We are not machines that can be repaired through a series of steps—we are relational beings who are transformed by the mystery of relationship. We are radically disposed to idolatry, illusion-making, and attempts to secure our lives without bowing to God. Our core problem is not a lack of information—it is flight and rebellion.
>
> —Dan Allender, The Cry of the Soul

coming. You put on the armor but you end up wrestling. You never have a shoot-out with evil—you wrestle with evil! Because you're not smart enough to have a shoot-out with evil. Not REAL evil!

Idolatry is REAL evil. Idols are rarely little blue statues. In fact, only some idols are material in nature. So if they aren't statues on a shelf, what are they? The Scriptures call them *epithumia*— over-desires or lusts. Idolatry is taking an object or desire, whether good or evil, and making it ultimate. The idolatrous heart says, "I must have [blank] to be happy" or "I need [blank] to be a person of worth and value." We come to believe that something of ultimate value is being withheld from us, and we don't like it! But we rarely see the subtle movement from good to ultimate. In fact, our first inkling that evil is upon us often comes in the quietly nagging or raucously unsettling emotions of fear, anger, or despair.

We handpick our idols based on our stories. There's something specific we want from each of them. They make us promises and they often deliver. Don't be mistaken, there is a reason we turn to idols—*they work*. At least for a season. But ultimately, they never satisfy. Over and over we trade in our faulty and worn-out idols for newer and more promising ones. Yet they never bring us the satisfaction we long for in our lives or our ministries.

In this section, we invite you again to see how your story intersects with God's redemptive story. In the "now and not yet" world we live in, we continue to create false, counterfeit gods while the one, true, and living God shouts, whispers, and woos us to return to Him. Therefore, it is the norm of life, even for ministry leaders, to expect the ongoing construction and dismantling of idols, personally and corporately.

To avoid *epithumia*, and in an attempt to thwart sin altogether, it is not uncommon for ministry leaders to attempt to detach themselves from desire, to embrace the many postures of under-desire—a Buddhist-like absence

of longing to preclude the tension of holding desires loosely. "If it's God's will that our attendance stays flat, I just need to accept that," we might shrug. Perhaps ministry leaders are not so over-desiring when it comes to sports cars, homes, and large 401Ks (at least, not out loud), but who among us has not wrestled, and perhaps been choked, by other good, yet elevated desires: be-

> *If we keep clamoring for things we want from God, we may often find ourselves disappointed. In a very real sense, God has nothing to give at all except Himself.*
> —*Simon Tugwell*, Prayer

ing used by God, being a great parent, or being respected in our communities.

Where have you, your spouse, your launch team, or your ministry team taken good desires (open palms) and formed them into ultimate desires (grasping palms)? In your worship of these desires, what promises have the idols held out to you? What sense of pleasure and righteousness do you receive from them? Sometimes, the ways we most like to describe ourselves reveal idolatrous places in our hearts and in our churches. "We are reformed, and right!" "We are not like our mother church!" "We are small and relational!" "We are urban." Remember, we can make an idol out of anything: our core values, our hip location, our not-so-

hip location, our methodologies, our language, our denomination, our gifts/talents, even the fact that we are gospel centered.

As you enter this section, listen to your story. Can you identify at least five personal idols (functional trusts, little "s" saviors that provide your sense of rightness?) Can you identity at least five corporate idols? Do you have a community of friends to whom you've revealed your idols? Do you have a coach or mentor who knows your ministry idols?

In the following pages, we will look at our stories and also dig beneath the surface of our words and actions to begin naming the enslaving inordinate desires that reside in our hearts. However, just as naming our cancer does not remove the tumor, simply identifying our idols is not repentance. We will look at true repentance. And we will be reminded that our idols do not define us—even though they are things to repent of, surely. We will be challenged to arm ourselves for the spiritual battle and to ask others to join us in our fight against the gravitational pull of idolatry. We will not denounce God's design for us as creatures full of desire and who long to worship; rather we will learn to hold fast to the one true and living God, Father, Son, and Holy Spirit!

> *What does it cost the soul to lie?*
> —*Paullina Simons*,
> The Bronze Horsemen

Idolatry: Beneath the Slamming Surface
by Tami Resch

What happens when we learn to look at the deeper motivations of our hearts? For me it has meant discovering some of the contours of my heart and my deepest motivations. I tell the following story in a more simplified, rather than real-time version, so be aware that these types of discoveries often take a long time.

I slam my hands against my daughter's closet door screaming, "Why do you have to make messes all over the house? When will you stop making more work for Mommy?" I run sobbing into my room slamming the door behind me. Thoughts swirl in my head. I have just scared my three-year-old daughter. I am out of control over something as minor as a messy room! I want to justify my yelling with righteous indignation towards her for not following my instructions. But I can't. Between my gasps come clear, nagging insights that treating her in this demeaning way is sinful. I hear her crying alone. I feel horrible for scaring her. My fury against her and her mess changes into contempt toward myself that I am the kind of mother whose love of order regularly triggers outbursts of rage. I wait—for God, for the intermittent gasps to subside, for the ability to talk without the choking lump in my throat. I wait—for the desire to go to her, and the desire to have someone come to me. I wait—for the desire to hold her, and the desire to have someone hold me. I wait—for the desire to comfort her, and the desire to have someone comfort me. I wait—for the desire to forgive her, and for the desire to have Someone forgive me. I wait. God comes, holds me, comforts me, forgives me.

Awash with his love, I now have the courage to ex-

amine my heart. I know it is foolish to examine my heart alone, without the presence of the Holy Spirit. Otherwise I am just like the girl in a bad horror flick who hears a noise in the dark basement and wanders down to check it out. We all know she's headed to her doom. And I, too, am headed for my doom if I wander into the darkness of my heart alone. So, with the Holy Spirit's presence and comfort, I examine my heart. I see that much resides below the slamming/screaming surface. I see sin's taproots of pride and unbelief. I pride myself in being organized, in control, and in gaining the approval of others. This is often expressed in wanting people to think that I can keep both my home and my children under control. I fail to believe that Christ's righteousness is sufficient for me. My compulsion to supplement Christ's goodness with my good housekeeping is a breakdown of my faith. My belief that another's good opinion of me defines my worth or value functions as a source of trust in something other than Christ. In my room, I confess to Christ that he has not been enough for me. His approval has not been sufficient. I want the approval of others more than his.

Eventually, I leave my room. Asking my daughter to forgive me for yelling would only be a starting point. In my earlier years of parenting, that was all I knew to do. But over the past few years, I have been ambushed by the gospel. I have been ambushed with the truth that my sin runs deeper than what is visible and audible. Likewise, I have been ambushed with the truth that God's forgiving grace runs correspondingly deep. I have discovered a correlation between my angry outbursts and my inability to control my surroundings—and my children for that matter. I love order! Open a drawer and I'll straighten it. I love

idolatry

control! Let *me* be the doorkeeper of change, risk, and even the status quo in my life. Oh, how I have longed for my children to assist me in feeding these idolatrous needs instead of fighting me on them. This day, my daughter had interfered with my intent to have a neat, orderly home, first, for our morning Bible study and, second, for an overnight guest. My daughter kept me from what I wanted most and bore the wrath that often accompanies unattained idols.

The messy room was not my primary issue. The primary issue was dealing with my heart's desire for control, for order, and for looking good in front of others. Awash with the powerlessness of these things (my idols) to give me real joy and life, my perspective changed. Oh, change was not immediate. And most times in my life it has been slow and brutal—the prying open of reluctant fingers. Occasionally repentance washes over me quickly and my hands open with ease. But any time idolatries are identified, named, and released, I find the Spirit of God entering and working in ways that are astounding. In this particular incident, I was filled with thankfulness for Christ's forgiveness, and so my internal dialogue was not an unending bitter diatribe against my daughter and my woes. Astounding! Blame-shifting to my daughter ended. Astounding! I had no desire to shame her or deny my sin or hers. Astounding! She was no longer the only sinner in the situation. Astounding! My heart became tender toward her as I took my eyes off of myself and rested them on Christ. Yes, astounding.

My heart cried out to God. *Father, thank you that my worth is not dependent on a clean house or an ordered life. Intellectually, I know that Christ is my righteousness but sometimes that doesn't filter down into my everyday life. Help me believe! Help me put to death again and again these inordinate desires for order, control, and approval. May I hold fast to the truth that you love sinners such as my daughter and me! May your Spirit bear his fruit of love and patience in me. May your love overshadow my many fears—of what others think, of being out of control, of never outgrowing this sinful pattern, of driving people away and being alone.*

There was much crying that day. My daughter had

cried in fear of Mommy; I had cried in my rage, and over the ugliness of my anger, and I cried still more with the dread of letting go of my obsessive need to be in control (like prying fingers off a life-giving rope). Lastly, there were tears of faith and hope that Christ—not order—could and would give me life. I could face the mess and my daughter.

I began by telling my daughter in three-year-old lingo that I was wrong for yelling. I told her I was angry about the room because I wanted other people to like me and think that I'm the kind of mommy who works hard. I expressed my sorrow for not loving her and leaving her unprotected against my anger. In each other's arms we cried tears of love's relief.

Later, while caring for and enjoying the guests in my home, waves of accusation sneered at my heart. Was I nothing more than a mommy version of Jekyll and Hyde? I battled by plunging myself into the beautiful truth of God's love for me. My heart is desperate for this truth, because I am so often tempted to "condemnation instant replay." Too often I believe the lies that I am the sum of my repeated patterns of sin, that I am a "bad mommy." God's love for me was my sword and shield against the lies.

There was much loving that day. Repentance, rather than "bad mommy guilt," moved me to love, which, that particular day, was expressed by cleaning my daughter's room alongside her without grumbling or complaining. There was a new peace and patience in my heart toward her, evidenced in my actions, words, and tone. At other times, the outworking of the Spirit regarding my desire to control has become evident in letting the house stay messy or in having people over without cleaning up.

The exciting part of this journey is that while love is the outflow of letting go of idols, it will have a different look tomorrow and next year. My goal is not one of striving for or conjuring up the 'look' of love, but rather, my goal is to let go of idols, while holding fast to Christ as my worth and fulfillment. Then I wait to see how that will express itself in love. I can't even control love's appearance and outcome! Ouch! A painful truth for control worshipers. Oh, but what life and freedom itself for those of us putting away idols!

TOOLS on IDOLATRY

idolatry

Idol Identification: From Fruit to Root & Root to Fruit

by Tami and Steve Resch

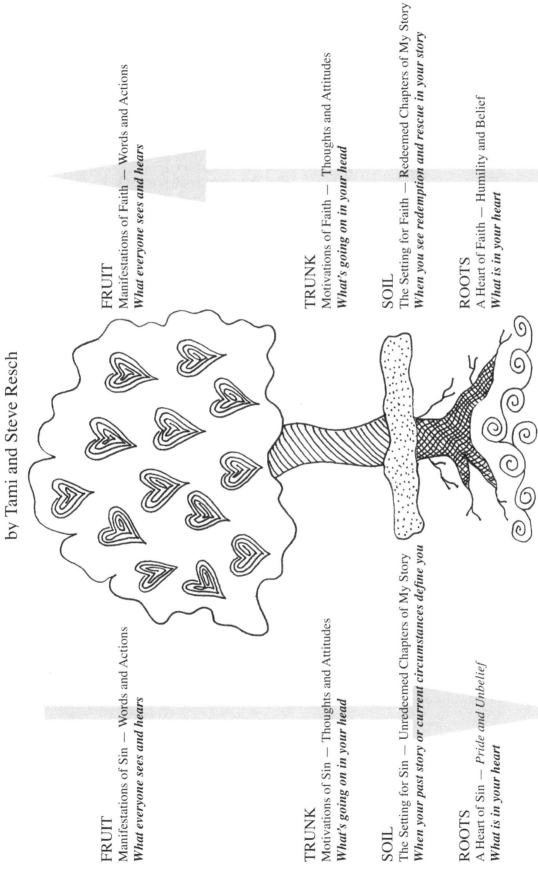

FRUIT
Manifestations of Faith — Words and Actions
What everyone sees and hears

TRUNK
Motivations of Faith — Thoughts and Attitudes
What's going on in your head

SOIL
The Setting for Faith — Redeemed Chapters of My Story
When you see redemption and rescue in your story

ROOTS
A Heart of Faith — Humility and Belief
What is in your heart

STREAMS OF LIVING WATER
Turning Away from Lesser Gods — Nourishment of Faith
When we soak our hearts in Jesus

FRUIT
Manifestations of Sin — Words and Actions
What everyone sees and hears

TRUNK
Motivations of Sin — Thoughts and Attitudes
What's going on in your head

SOIL
The Setting for Sin — Unredeemed Chapters of My Story
When your past story or current circumstances define you

ROOTS
A Heart of Sin — *Pride and Unbelief*
What is in your heart

DRY STREAMS
Turning To Lesser Gods — Nourishment of Sin
When we are unwilling to wait for Jesus' comfort and nourishment

idolatry

FROM **FRUIT** TO **ROOT**: *Digging Deeper Into Your Heart*

If you want to know the truth about your heart and what is ruling and filling it, look at the heart's fruit: your thoughts, words, and actions. These reveal the state of your heart.

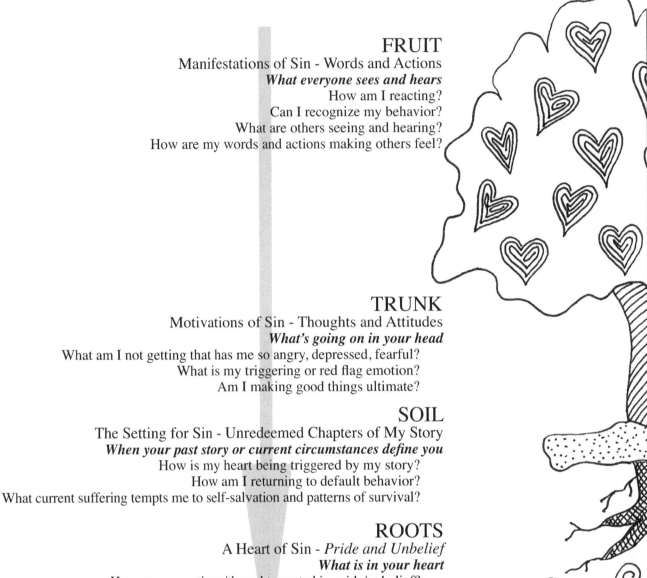

FRUIT
Manifestations of Sin - Words and Actions
What everyone sees and hears
How am I reacting?
Can I recognize my behavior?
What are others seeing and hearing?
How are my words and actions making others feel?

TRUNK
Motivations of Sin - Thoughts and Attitudes
What's going on in your head
What am I not getting that has me so angry, depressed, fearful?
What is my triggering or red flag emotion?
Am I making good things ultimate?

SOIL
The Setting for Sin - Unredeemed Chapters of My Story
When your past story or current circumstances define you
How is my heart being triggered by my story?
How am I returning to default behavior?
What current suffering tempts me to self-salvation and patterns of survival?

ROOTS
A Heart of Sin - *Pride and Unbelief*
What is in your heart
How are my actions/thoughts rooted in pride/unbelief?
How is my self-pity or anger revealing pride?
What draws me to solution-seeking rather than to Jesus?

DRY STREAMS
Turning To Lesser Gods - Nourishment of Sin
When we are unwilling to wait for Jesus' comfort and nourishment
How am I seeking temporary relief that will further dehydrate my soul?
What lies am I living on?

Prayer of Repentance
"I confess... [what I did], ... [how I did it], and ... [why I felt motivated to do it]."

FROM **ROOT** TO FRUIT: *The Outworking of Faith*

Since transformation is a work of the Holy Spirit, change and good fruit is inevitable, but not predictable. We can know that the Spirit's fruit will become evident, but we can not dictate how or when. Avoid artificially adding "good" fruit to your life; rather, allow the changed roots and trunk of your heart to bear the new fruit.

FRUIT
Manifestations of Faith - Words and Actions
What everyone sees and hears
>How am I reacting?
>Is the Spirit's fruit visible?
>Can I recognize joyful gratitude in my behavior?
>Are my new actions revealing God's power instead of my power?
>What are others seeing and hearing?
>How are my words and actions making others feel?

TRUNK
Motivations of Faith - Thoughts and Attitudes
What's going on in your head
>How are my thoughts changing about God, others, myself, my circumstances?
>How is my inner dialogue matching what God says about me?
>Am I asking the Spirit to transform me and fill me with joy?

SOIL
The Setting for Faith - Redeemed Chapters of My Story
When you see redemption and rescue in your story then and now
>How am I seeing redemption in my story?
>In what ways is God inviting me to hope?

ROOTS
A Heart of Faith - Humility and Belief
What is in your heart
>What does a heart of repentance look like?
>How am I brought back to humility?
>How can I accept responsibility for my sin?
>Do I believe God sees me clothed in righteousness?

STREAMS OF LIVING WATER
Turning Away from Lesser Gods - Nourishment of Faith
When we soak our hearts in Jesus
>How am I seeking the comfort of Jesus?
>Am I finding my soul stilled in the truth of the gospel?

Prayer of Belief
"I believe you have taken away all my sin, that you call me your beloved, and that you have clothed me in Christ's righteousness. I believe that the very power that raised Christ from the dead is the same power that is in me right now. I believe; help my unbelief."

idolatry

Explanation of Fruit To Root
By Tami Resch

Why Use This Tool?
- To answer the question, What makes me act this way?
- To help identify some of our sin tendencies
- To encourage a more honest and thorough repentance
- To help us see the log in our eye when we are obsessing about the specks in the eyes of others

How to use From **FRUIT** to **ROOT**

Draw a tree with heart-shaped fruit, a trunk, soil, and some roots. Draw a stream at its base.

The Fruit: Begin with the fruit. Think of a specific event or season of your life (i.e., a recent conflict, or your church plant fundraising season) and label the hearts with specific words and actions that came out of you during this time. Not all the fruit will look terrible, so include some that looks good. Self-righteous fruit is less obvious than unrighteous fruit but indicates something equally awry below the surface. Don't be shy or soft. Ask the Spirit to help you see clearly the words and behaviors with which you responded during the struggle, situation, or season. Example: Verbal, angry insistence that my children and my husband act according to my ways while visiting a donor church. Difficulty sleeping. Relentlessly checking our teenagers' Facebook pages (to ensure they don't make us look bad—again). A growing stinginess.

The Trunk: List the thoughts, attitudes, and motivations that nurture and sustain this fruit. Example: Worry and fear of the kids' bad behavior reflecting poorly on us in front of potential donors or church members. Our thoughts give us clues to our idols. Remember, you can make an idol out of anything. For example, "being a responsible steward of money" is a good desire, but if it becomes an ultimate, consuming desire—it is an idol in your life. Visible or obvious idols often have deeper, hidden idols attached to them such as comfort, approval, control, security, power, etc. If you are unsure which idols are impacting this situation or season, ask yourself, "What is/was being withheld from me that prompts my anger, despair, or anxiety?" (See "Hidden Idolatries," page 94.) Label the trunk with one or more identified idols. Example: I must have the approval of our donors or members; control over my family's behavior; and the security of a full paycheck.

The Soil: Spend some time reflecting on your story and your circumstances leading up to this precipitous event or season. Don't forget to consider your childhood and adolescence. What parts of your past are influencing the trunk and fruit? What aspects of your current story feed and fuel the trunk and fruit? Label the soil with a few realities of your story that, while not excusing your ugly fruit, provide a fertile habitat for the fruit's growth. Example: I was raised in poverty and the only way we escaped was by hard work. Our current debt load is burdensome and accompanied by a nagging guilt that I could have prevented it if "I had just worked harder at fundraising."

The Root: Out of the overflow of the heart, the mouth speaks. Our fruit and its idolatrous trunk are nourished by deep taproots most commonly in the form of pride and unbelief. Label the roots demonstrating how the fruit and trunk of your tree show pride and unbelief. Example: Pride: Fundraising is only about how hard I work. Unbelief: God will not provide unless I do my part and my kids do their part (behave). Unbelief: I cannot be generous until I feel financially secure.

Caution: Be alert to the temptation to blame, explain, justify, and excuse away your sin. Even if the other parties involved have sinned more grossly, you are still responsible for your own fruit (behavior). Ask the Spirit of God to help you own 100% of your sin even if only 5% of the situation is yours.

Repentance involves turning away from one thing and turning towards something or someone else. Ask God to give you a willingness to turn away from the things (idols) you habitually use to gain life on your own. Ask God for a willingness to rest in Jesus to give you life. Use words when you go to God and others and own up to not only the fruit of your actions and the idolatrous trunk, but also the deep taproots of pride and unbelief (see "A Lifestyle of Repentance," page 110). Do not despair. Martin Luther declared in the first of his ninety-five theses that the life of the believer would be one of continual repentance.

Believe what you sometimes doubt to be true: you are completely unable to change your heart apart from a work of the Holy Spirit. As you rest in this truth, allow time for change and growth to take place. Repentance makes room in your heart for a growing belief in Jesus and his promises. Ask the Father to make real to you what Christ has accomplished for you: a completed atonement with no penance required. Take Martin Luther's advice, "For every one look at your sin, take ten looks to the cross!" Marvel and revel in Christ's work on your behalf which paid the penalty for all your sin, past, present, and future, and which clothed you in his righteousness "for if righteousness could be gained through the law, Christ died for nothing." (Galatians 2:2b)

Pause and celebrate what the Holy Spirit is doing in your life. Even though it feels awful to be face to face with our depravity, the degree to which we see our baseness will be the degree to which we delight and bask in the generous forgiveness of Christ and his righteousness credited to us.

The Streams of Living Water: Seeing the raw depth of your sin can parch your soul, bring shame, or intensify a thirst for significance, approval, value, etc. Identifying our sin patterns does not automatically draw us closer to the Father. "My people have committed two sins. They have forsaken me, the spring of living water, and have dug their own cisterns, broken cisterns that cannot hold water." (Jeremiah 2:13)

Drink deeply therefore, from the streams of living water: Jesus, his Word, his promises. Drink as the Psalmist describes, "But his delight is in the law of the Lord, and on his law he meditates day and night. He is like a tree planted by streams of water, which yields its fruit in season and whose leaf does not wither." (Psalm 1:2-3)

What aspects of God's character as seen through the scriptures or the person of Jesus compel you to thirst after him? Even if going to God's Word is difficult at this time, ask him to quench your thirst with the beauty and truth of Jesus and to surprise you with a thousand ways he can satisfy you. Wait with him. Wait on him. Do not fret about bearing good fruit. Allow Jesus to be the Hero of your story rather than trying to rescue yourself. In Isaiah 50:2, God asks, "Was my arm too short to ransom you? Do I lack the strength to rescue you?"

How to use From ROOT to FRUIT

Be on the lookout for surprising changes!

The Root: As the root of your soul is nourished by the Stream of Living Water, change begins to take place. Movement from pride to humility and unbelief to belief begins to happen. Prayer becomes a reflex — a sincere leaning into God, as you wait for rescue from God rather than turning to your cisterns of habit. Label the roots with the truths your heart is holding fast to at this time. Example: I do not have to overwork to the exhaustion of my body and soul, because like the lilies of the field who are here today and gone tomorrow, God will take care of me and of my family.

The Soil: This side of heaven, we may see parts of our story redeemed. But full redemption is something we look forward to when Christ makes all things new once and for all. When you see glimpses of God's restorative work in your story, you may want to jot them down. Keep your eyes open and fight the temptation to tell God what your redeemed story must look like, as your demand will cloud your ability to see God's hand at work. Example: Amazingly, in revisiting my childhood story, I've begun to see where God provided others who helped in my deliverance from poverty. Previously, I didn't recognize this was God. I am now on the lookout to see how God will help our family.

The Trunk: How are your thoughts and attitudes different even if the circumstances have not changed? Label the trunk with sound bites of your new inner dialogue and new perspective. Also, label the trunk with continued longings that have changed from over-desires (idols) to desires. Example: I'm not demanding that God provide for us with one big chunk of money. I find myself almost expectant of what God may do. I still want financial security, but I don't need it in order to sleep at night.

The Fruit: As you notice new actions or heart changes, identify these. Do not be shy or dismissive with your change, but celebrate! The Spirit of God is at work, bearing fruit and showing forth glory! Example: When I check my teens' Facebook pages now, it is to dialog and connect with them, not to reassure myself that I look good for donors and church members. I am growing in my ability to be generous.

Fruit to Root and Root to Fruit is an ongoing process with a promise.
"And we, who with unveiled faces all reflect the Lord's glory, are being transformed into his likeness with ever-increasing glory, which comes from the Lord, who is the Spirit!" (2 Corinthians 3:18)

Fruit to Root and Root to Fruit can be dangerous.
Be careful of using a growing knowledge of idolatry and its roots as a weapon against others. You could easily look at the fruit of someone's life and declare/judge what you believe to be their idols. Remember we do not know another's heart nor all of his or her story. He or she could have the same fruit as you but be motivated by vastly different idols.

Also, extend kindness to your spouse, children, and extended family. You know well the soil of your family's stories, thus you can more quickly delude yourself into believing your judgments are correct. Remember, From Fruit to Root is an exercise to help us remove the logs in our own eyes. (Matthew 7:5) Only after you see the log in your own eye and are reminded that any good fruit in your life is a work of the Spirit, will you be able to regard the sawdust in another's eye.

An Example of Using From Fruit to Root

Gabriella is perpetually worried about many things. Her vague feelings of unease are growing more intense daily. The calendar shows only one month until August, the bleak month when their church start-up funds run out. She wakens in the night, grabs the journal by her bedside and asks God to help her see what is going on in her heart....

Fruit:
- Ongoing short fuse with the kids when they don't help me

- Exhausted trying to serve others in our church and neighborhood
- Inability to shut off my brain at bedtime and occasional eye twitch
- Verbally scolded launch team members last night when they failed to bring friends
- Worried about money
- Replaying the conversation with Mrs. X over and over in my mind
- Demanding husband spend time with Family X so they won't leave and possibly take Family Y with them

Trunk:
- *Idol of Control* (Although I wouldn't say it out loud, I am motivated to do whatever it takes to keep people from leaving and to make the church grow so we can get paid.)
- *Idol of Security* (My happiness and meaning are tied to the success of the church plant and the subsequent ability to stay in the house and city we currently live in.)
- *Idol of Approval* (I need Mrs. X's approval of my husband in order to feel good about him, my family, and myself.)

Soil:
- After my parents divorced, we had little money and had to move often. I hated it! I vowed I would never do that to my children.
- Always felt like I had to be the "glue" in the family. I worked hard to bring harmony into our shattered family dynamics.
- Mrs. X recently told me she does not like my husband's preaching style.

Root:
- *Pride*: I think I know exactly what my husband should do to grow our church. I did not see my arrogance when I shamed our launch team.
- *Unbelief*: I am not sure if I really believe that God will grow his church—especially if I don't serve everyone to the exhaustion of my own body and soul. I don't believe we can keep Family X and Family Y unless I make it happen (or unless my husband preaches better).

Streams of Living Water:
- Father, make me lie down in green pastures and restore my soul…starting with sleep tonight. This burden does not feel easy or light. I truly cannot imagine bearing up under the weight of it another day. Help me tomorrow to trust you, see you, and hear you singing over me. Help me see my husband through your eyes instead of through my fear.

Several weeks later, Gabriella picks up her journal to reflect on the changes going on in her heart and in her behavior.

Root:
- *Humility*: I cannot hold my family together, my church plant together, or my world together. I am not in control. I am not God. This is good news but soooo hard.
- *Belief*: Lord, I am a mess when I don't trust your promises—please continue to help me believe you are for me, regardless of whether the church plant survives!

Soil:
- This past Sunday at the launch team meeting, I felt no compulsion to spend extra time with Mrs. X. But I still wished my husband would do more to woo them.

idolatry

- Still waiting to see how God will change my inclination to be "the glue" of this church plant.

Trunk:
- I still very much want to have the church plant continue and to have a paycheck.
- I am using my arsenal by reminding myself, "God will build his church" and even singing a children's song to calm me, "When I am afraid, I will trust in you…"
- I can see my need for others' approval becoming less powerful the more I remind myself of God's love and approval. This idol feels the hardest to let go.

Fruit:
- I'm sleeping better and am able to return to sleep more quickly when wakened by anxious thoughts.
- I notice a growing patience with the kids.
- I have growing peace about money and what we will do in August if we close the church even before we officially start services. I feel sad about this but I am crying out to God about it instead of frantically trying to make it all work.
- I was able to tell the launch team the depth of my fears, my lack of trust in God, and my pride in thinking I know how my life ought to play out and how this church plant needs to grow. It was a beautiful time of honesty and forgiveness… not sure I expected that… but it grew my desire to pray for God to rescue us somehow in August. Now our whole launch team is praying for God's rescue. While we continue to labor planting the church, we are looking for God to do what we surely can't! No eye twitch this week!

Idol Identification Chart

Why Use This Tool?
- To explore the costs of idolatry
- To employ scripture in the dismantling of idols

Problem Emotion — What am I feeling? How am I reacting?	Seen Idol (More concrete, specific, recognized)	Hidden Idol — Are further from the surface of things and may be hidden.	What price am I willing to pay?	What is my greatest nightmare?	What do others often feel?	REPENT 1) Name 2) Unmask 3) Confess	REPLACE 1) Repent 2) Rejoice 3) Rest
		Identify Idols		**Cost of Idols**		**Dismantle Idols**	
Cowardice		**Approval** Affirmation, love, relationships. I need to be loved and respected by _____. I need permission or consent from others. I need people to tell me I'm ok.	Less Independence	Rejection	Smothered	Joshua 1:9; Ps 27:10 Zeph 3:14-17; Rom 8:1 Phil 4:19; Col 1:22	Ps 17:8; 56:8; 78:39; 91:11 103:14; 139:2; 139:13; Mt 6:30; 10:30 Eph 2:10; Col 1:22 Heb 13:5b, 6b; Rev. 21:4; I Jn. 3:1
Boredom		**Comfort** A pleasure experience, a consolation, a particular quality of life, privacy, lack of stress, freedom.	Reduced Productivity	Stress, Demands	Hurt	Ps. 16:11; 81: 10 Ps 107:9; Pr. 4:18 Is 66:13; Phil 4:13 Matt 5:6	Mal 3:10 Numbers 6:24 Ps. 104:33; 42:8
Anger		**Power** Success, winning, I want power and influence over others. I want significance. I am worthy of respect. I should be respected.	Burdened; Responsible	Humiliation	Used	Deut 32:4 Ps. 37:6; 145:8 Matt 18:21-35 II Cor 3:5; Eph 4:32	Eph 6:10-18 James 5:15
Worry		**Control** Self-discipline, certainty, standards. I will be in charge so it gets done right. The more I control, the less I have to trust; the less I will be disappointed or let down.	Loneliness; Lack of Spontaneity	Uncertainty	Condemned	Ps. 37:5; 56:3; 138:8 Pr. 3:5-6; 19:21 Ecc 3:14 Jer. 29:11 Rom 8:28 I Cor 28:20 Phil. 4:6	Ps 9:9; 45:11; 143:8; SS 2:3-4 Is 40:11; 41; 49; 54:5 Is 62:5; 62:12 Eph 5:25-27 Col 2:10
Stress		**Security** Safe place, protection; freedom from danger, fear or anxiety. I won't risk loss.	Co-dependent; Driven	Hurt, Vulnerable	Controlled	II Sam. 22:31; Ps 37:25; 57:10; 68:6 Is.41:13; 43:25; 58:11 Matt 10:30-31 James 1:5	Ps 46:10 Ps 62:1-2; Ps 91:1, 4 Ps. 146:6; Is 30:15 Is 43:1-3 Matt 11:28

Adapted by Jenny Dorsey from materials by Tim Keller.

idolatry

Obvious and Hidden Idols Chart
by Jenny Dorsey

Why Use This Tool?
- To deepen our understanding of how idols present themselves
- To uncover our less obvious and hidden idols

Problem Emotion	Idols that are Obvious (More concrete, specific)		Idols Hidden (Farther below the surface of things)
What is my "problem emotion?" What am I feeling? Why am I so upset? How am I reacting?	An idol is anything (and often a GOOD thing) that has become inflated to function as a substitute for God. Idols come from our desires: an obviously sinful desire or a good desire that has become a sinful demand. James 4:1-2	**Obvious idols** are concrete and specific. They are on the surface and easily seen.	**Hidden Idols** live deep down. Like roots, they are hidden underground. They are the hidden motivations that drive you. They are what you really want!
Fear of others, Fear of rejection Sense of Worthlessness, Despondent, Hating Yourself Guilt, Cowardice Fearful, Worried	A physical object A property A person An activity A role An institution A hope An idea An image A pleasure A hero	Work Family Being Well Liked Money Sex Helping Status Addictions Pornography Alcohol Drugs Being well-liked Helping Workaholic Family Relationships	**Approval** Affirmation, love, relationships. I need to be loved and respected by…. I need permission or consent from others. I need people to tell me I'm ok.
Temptation, Lust, Craving Boredom, Laziness, Emptiness Despair, Disappointment, Disillusionment, Cynicism Envy, Coveting, Greed: you want more and are not happy with what you have.		Food Ministry Workaholic Relationships Shopping: buying things Food Shopping TV Sex Money Knowledge	**Comfort** An experience of pleasure, a consolation, a particular quality of life, privacy, lack of stress, freedom.
Anger, Bitterness, Hard Hearted, Irritable Pride: you think you are better than others. You don't like to be wrong.		House Car Furniture Government Workaholic Money Knowledge House Car	**Power** Success, winning, wanting power and influence over others. I want significance. I am worthy of respect. I should be respected.
Worry, Anxiety, Fear		Ideology Business Hobby/interest Wisdom Clean House Easting Disorders Physical Health Ordered Life Ideals Knowledge	**Control** Self-discipline, certainty, particular standards. I will be in charge so it gets done right. The more I control, the less I have to trust; thus: the less I will be disappointed or let down.
Stress, Fear, Anxiety, Panic Vulnerable, Scared Low self-worth, Don't think you have what it takes to get the job done		Knowledge Music Physical health Ability to teach, communicate clearly Bank account Homeownership Relationships Career/Job	**Security** A safe place, protection; freedom from danger, fear, or anxiety. I won't risk loss.

Building An Arsenal of Truth and Beauty

by Tami Resch

Why Use This Tool?

• To arm ourselves for the battle for our hearts
• To discern if our inner dialogue is one of truth and beauty, or death and duty

What is an arsenal of truth and beauty? It is a personal collection of words, songs, scripture, film clips, poetry, pieces of art, objects, bits of nature, photographs, quotes — anything that points us to Christ, mends our heart, moves our soul, and propels us to love and faith. Your arsenal will be different from anyone else's because it will be unique to your story, your own recurring threads of faith, and the ways in which you are moved and comforted.

By literally and figuratively stocking your arsenal, you create a place to turn and specific weapons to use when you are weary in the battle, when you have lost your footing, when you are suffering, and when you want to step purposefully into God's presence and the reminders of his goodness toward you. Your arsenal will often take you into a larger story and offer a panoramic view. It can help you battle your strategies of self-salvation and it reminds us how to destroy sin's grip.

Scripture teaches that our world is not divided between the secular and the sacred, the holy and the mundane. James tells us that every good and perfect gift comes from our Heavenly Father. When we believe this to be true, we view our world and the pieces, objects, and images in it differently. A movie showcasing redemption can be a gift of hope. A poem recalling the weight of suffering can be a gift of comfort. A downpour of cleansing rain can be a gift of refreshment. A well-composed piece of music can be a gift of beauty in the world's chaos. Redemption and hope, suffering and comfort, cleansing and refreshment, chaos and beauty — all can point us to Christ.

It's important to remember that what is comforting or faith-building to one person isn't necessarily so to another. What might invite one person to deeper faith could repel another. Our stories, our personal experiences, and our particular inclinations impact the flavor of our arsenals. A verse of scripture might be refreshing to one person, yet feel heavy-handed to another. A certain movie might propel one person to faith and action, yet make another feel paralyzed. One person might be most reminded of Christ's love by hearing about it, yet another would need to speak aloud Christ's words of love in order to feel their truth. One person might need to view art, another might need to create it. We can never assume that what invites our heart to faith in Christ will necessarily invite another.

How To Build Your Personal Arsenal

It is important to remember that your dominant voice of influence is your own internal dialogue. This is why it is essential to build your personal arsenal of truth and beauty, so that apart from husband, coach, or friend you are equipped to take the hope of the gospel to your own heart by remembering and returning to the words and objects and avenues God's Spirit has used to call you and comfort you.

Listen to the way you speak to yourself, with others and in prayer. Is your arsenal one of truth and beauty or death and duty? Do you use scripture for repentance, hope, and life, or to motivate yourself by accusation, condemnation, and fear? Are you a tactile, visual, or auditory learner? Let your arsenal reflect you. What motivates you? What crushes your heart? If you hear scripture as condemning, are there other ways to hear God's voice as sweet and comforting? Watch what draws your heart to Jesus. Arm yourself in the battle for your heart!

This article is excerpted from the Parakaleo Leader Handbook.

Idols and Me

by Tami Resch

Why Use This Tool?
- To identify the idolatrous themes in our life story
- To be alert to red flag emotions, thoughts, speech, or actions
- To battle idolatry personally and communally

Idols are good things with disproportionate value—good things made ultimate. They are not just things we *enjoy* in life, but things we *live for* in life.

Idols are God substitutes. Idols take the place of God as our functional savior, and we attach our happiness and well-being to their presence.

Idols are personal. We choose them carefully and specifically according to our needs. Our decision to remain steadfast to an old idol or to abandon it for a newer and more promising one all depends on our needs.

Idols are attached to personal things. **My** reputation, **my** rights, **my** longings, **my** things, **my** family and friends, **my** roles, **my** values, **my** choices, and **my** needs.

Idols are liars and thieves. They promise us freedom, pleasure, control, comfort, and power (or whatever we happen to be looking for). They deliver for a season, but will leave us in slavery as we experience the disintegration of body and soul.

Idols are prolific; John Calvin said, "Our hearts are idol factories." As we demolish the foundation of one idol, others are already under construction.

What are my IDOLS?
List the decades of your life and two to three idols that corresponded to each decade or chapter of your life story.

Example: *Before I was 10, life only had meaning, or I only felt worth if...*

What are my PATTERNS of idolatry?
Identify repeating idols in your story.

What are my RED FLAGS of idolatry?
Certain feelings, thoughts, actions, words and ways of speech alert me to the controlling presence of idols.

When [idol] is being kept from me:
I feel...
I think...
I say...
I do...

My common RED FLAG EMOTIONS are:

My common RED FLAG THOUGHTS are:

My common RED FLAG WORDS/SPEECH are:

My common RED FLAG ACTIONS are:

Knowing my tendency for certain idols and the red flags that accompany them enables me to be more aware of when and how my heart is worshipping and serving something other than God. Yet sin by its very nature is deceitful. I usually do not see idolatry coming. I recognize my idols when I realize my outstretched hands have grasping fingers. What am I grasping so tightly to? What am I clawing after? About what am I saying, "I have to have [*this*]!"

What are MY WEAPONS?
My personal arsenal is chock-full of weapons with which I fight against the idolatry in my heart. The words, phrases, objects, pieces of art, song lyrics and such remind me that Jesus alone is ultimate, and the only satisfier of my body and soul. My weapons help me find my perspective and return my desires to their proper proportions. My weapons help loosen my grasp. With palms up and open I stop clawing and instead wait for Jesus to give me what he has for me and for him to take me by the hand and lead me.

My weapons are….

Who is MY COMMUNITY OF SUPPORT?
The people in my community of support know my idols, my red flags, and they also know some of the weapons and helps in my personal arsenal. I invite them to journey with me as I wrestle with the competing desires of my idolatrous heart.

My community of support is…

How the Gospel Changes Us
by Timothy Keller

Why Use This Tool?
- To unpack how the gospel defuses the idols of our heart
- To bring our thinking in line with the gospel
- To discern moralistic, relativistic, and gospel approaches to life

SUMMARY: The default mode of the human heart is to work moralistically on external behavior and outer appearances. If we truly grasp the difference between religion and the gospel, we will discover that the gospel not only saves us but transforms our hearts and defuses the idols at the root of our sin. This talk was given at a training conference at Redeemer Presbyterian Church in New York City.

Today we want to talk about how the gospel—this comprehensive thing that is so full of meaning—actually changes you. The gospel, just like the doctrine of the Trinity, is a little too hard to stick into a nutshell, but we should try. Nutshells tend to push you down into one aspect or another.

The basis for our understanding of how to do ministry at Redeemer Presbyterian Church is this: The gospel is "I'm accepted through Christ; therefore, I obey." But functionally, the human heart's default mode, both before and after conversion, is "I obey; therefore, I'm accepted." The default mode of the human heart, whether inside of religion or outside of religion or whatever, says, "I obey, and therefore I am accepted."

Martin Luther, especially in his famous commentary on Galatians, lays out the basic principle. The book of Galatians is this incredibly great, clear proclamation of the gospel of grace—but it is written to *Christians*. It's written to people who had started to lose their grasp on it, and the meaning and implications of it. Luther's fundamental insight is that even though we understand the gospel enough to get converted and we embrace the principle of it in joy, the actual way in which our heart works is not immediately changed, and that over the years, in every moment, you have to beat the old principle out of your heart and the gospel principle into it.

There's a famous place where Luther says in his commentary on Galatians, "The truth of the Gospel is the principal article of all Christian doctrine.... Most necessary is it that we know this article well, teach it to others, and beat it into their heads continually."[1] Basically, all deadness, divisiveness, fear, pride, and spiritual stagnation in the church and in your life are due to the fact that you still, at some level, in some sense, are failing to believe the gospel. You have to beat it in.

That doesn't mean there aren't times when you do things because they're in the Bible: "It's the way a Christian's supposed to be, and I'm going to do it. I don't want to do it; I don't like it; it's going to be hard, but I'm just going to do it." There are plenty of times when that happens—but that can't be the prevailing wellspring, the prevailing motivation, of your life. The gospel is not just the ABCs of the Christian faith, so that you enter with the gospel and then you try hard the rest of your life to live according to biblical principles. The gospel is the A to Z of the faith, which means the gospel not only saves you, but then every single part of your heart and mind has to be transformed, bit by bit by bit, by more deeply believing, reflecting on, rejoicing in, and applying the gospel. That's how anything ever happens in your Christian life.

To try to show you how that works, I'm going to take two aspects, you might say, of how the gospel renews you: your mind and your character.

How the gospel renews your mind. The gospel is like a set of basic beliefs that influence the way you look at absolutely everything.

Galatians 2:14 has had a very profound influence on me. In it, Paul lays down a powerful principle in the way he deals with Peter. The gospel had begun to bring Peter out of his own racial pride. Previously Peter had not eaten with Gentiles or dealt with Gentiles. The gospel brought him into fellowship with Gentiles who also believed in Christ, but he was starting to slip back into racial segregation and not eating with Gentiles, because they were "unclean."

In Galatians 2:14, Paul confronted Peter, but here's how he did it. He confronted his racial pride and cowardice by declaring that he was not living "in line with the truth of the gospel." Notice Paul did not say, "Peter, Christians are not supposed to be racist, and you're breaking the 'no racism' rule of Christianity." He could have said that, as it's true. There are rules, and that's one of them. But he didn't say that. He said, "You're not living in accordance, in line, with the gospel. You're not thinking out the implications of the gospel. You're not letting your mind and heart be influenced and shaped by the gospel." Because frankly, what are the reasons for obeying the rules? If your reasons for obeying the rules are fear and pride, it's temporary — you're not really changing your heart. You're only restraining your heart.

If you really want your heart to be changed, you've got to apply the gospel to it. We're going to get to the heart part in a minute, but obviously when Paul says this to Peter, he's saying that the Christian life is a process of renewing every single dimension of your lives — spiritual, psychological, corporate, social — by living out the ramifications of the gospel. Out of the gospel comes a line, and you say, "I've got to bring every single part of my life into line with the gospel."

Most people think, "The gospel's how you get saved. The gospel doesn't have anything to do with your inner attitude toward people of other races." Yes, it does. Paul says, "Absolutely! That's where the change comes from."

"Walking in line" gives us a metaphor. It's only a metaphor, but metaphors are important in the Bible. This metaphor implies that you can get off to one side or the other. When Paul speaks of being in line with the gospel, you can extend that metaphor and say that gospel renewal occurs when we keep from walking off-line to one side or the other. Left and right — that doesn't mean politically, at this point. What it means is that the key to understanding the implications of the gospel is to see the gospel as this third way between two mistaken opposites. This does not mean the gospel is a compromise or a mid-point between the two poles — it's not a half-way point between the two things. It's neither religion nor irreligion. It's something else.

Tertullian, the early church father, said it like this: "Just as Christ was crucified between two thieves, so this doctrine of justification is ever crucified between two opposite errors."[2] Isn't that interesting? The early church fathers were quite pictorial in the way they spoke. He says, "As Jesus was crucified between two thieves, this doctrine is always crucified between two opposite errors," and what he meant is that on the one hand, there's an error of legalism. In theological terms, moralism and relativism are both basically the danger of legalism, which is to say, "You've got to obey God, because that's how you're saved." On the other hand, there's the danger of "antinomianism." Antinomianism is the theological term for the view that says, "It really doesn't matter how you live, because you're fine. You're accepted, and therefore it doesn't matter how you live. You can do whatever you want." That's moralism/legalism on the one hand, and antinomianism/relativism on the other.

When the gospel is preached, to legalists it sounds like antinomianism. They say, "Oh, you're just a bunch of dirty antinomians." And when the gospel is preached to antinomians, you sound like "a dirty legalist." In New York, unless you're really, really careful, the average person hears any preaching of the gospel as moralistic, legalistic, and judgmental. In other words, if you're living in an antinomian culture, you're going to sound legalistic. If you're living in a legalistic culture, which parts of America are like, and you preach the gospel, they're going to think that you're a "wishy-washy liberal"—you know, all that talk about grace and accepting people and all that stuff. But it's not half-way. It's not half-way. It's something else.

Tertullian says these thieves can be called moralism or legalism, and hedonism or relativism. Another way to put it is "The gospel opposes both religion and irreligion."

On the one hand, moralism stresses truth without grace. It says we must obey the truth in order to be saved. On the other hand, relativism—irreligion—stresses grace without truth. For they say, "Oh, everyone is acceptable and everyone is a child of God, and we have to decide what is right or wrong for us." But truth without grace isn't really truth, is it? Because the gospel is part of it. Grace without truth is not really grace, because it's really a kind of sentimental syrupiness. Truth without grace is not really truth, because it's leaving out the essence of what Jesus has said.

But Jesus Christ was full of grace *and* truth (John 1:14). Full of grace and truth. Any philosophy of life that de-emphasizes or loses one or the other *falls into* one or the other. Either way, it's a thief, and that's what Tertullian is trying to say. If your understanding of the Christian faith is two clicks to this side of the gospel or two clicks to that side, to the degree that it's off to one side or the other, the thief on that side is robbing you of its power. It's robbing you. The gospel has power. And to the degree that we hit it—and by the way; nobody does; *I* don't—and we get the gospel right, to that degree it releases power in your life. To the degree your understanding of the gospel is several clicks to one side or the other side—into very legalistic churches or churches that kind of believe anything and "we just accept everybody and it really doesn't matter what you believe"—you can see where at the extremes you lose the power. But can you see that the further it gets to one side or the other, those are *thieves*? Those are spiritual thieves, says Tertullian, and you lose power.

Moralism steals joy and power. Let's go a little more deeply into this to help you think about the different areas of your life. First, how does moralism steal joy and power? Moralism is the view that you're acceptable to God, the world, others, and yourself through your attainments. Although they usually are religious, not all moralists are religious, by any means. Dr. Lloyd-Jones told a story about someone who once said to him, "If I ever become a Christian…." The man said his father was an Episcopalian, but he was also an alcoholic who was always falling off the wagon and always in trouble. Sometimes his father would take him to the Episcopal church, although he was an utterly inconsistent Christian in every way. His mother was, at one point, a Unitarian and then eventually decided she didn't believe in anything, but she was incredibly moral. She was incredibly strong and upright and absolutely a better person—a more moral person, a more disciplined and successful person, an incredibly "pulled together" person. And Dr. Lloyd-Jones said that this guy said to him, "My mother's character was the beauty of a snowflake: perfect, intricate—and freezing. And my father's character was a ruin, an absolute ruin. He didn't have any character. But if I ever, ever, ever, ever decide, I'd go to my father's religion if I ever decide I need something, because there was forgiveness there. There was something there."[3]

Moralism is not necessarily religious, but when moralists *are* religious, their religion is pretty conservative, filled with rules that focus on behavior. Often moralists view God as very holy and very just—which is true, right? This view will either lead to self-hatred, because they can't live up to their standards, or it will lead to self-inflation, because they think they have lived up to their standards. One or the other. Moralists either produce absolute atheists—who were raised in it and they try it and they can't keep up with it and they blow up completely and then they hate Christianity—or utter Pharisees. Always produces one or the other. It's ironic to realize that inferiority and superiority complexes have the same root: moralism. Whether the moralist ends up smug and superior or crushed and guilty just depends on how high the standards are and on the person's natural advantages, like family and intelligence, etc. Moralistic people can be deeply religious, but there's absolutely no transforming joy and power there. That's the reason why this person said to Dr. Lloyd Jones, "I'm not going to go in the direction of my mother, if I go in any direction at all."

Relativism steals joy and power. Secondly, how does relativism steal joy and power? Relativists are usually irreligious, or they prefer liberal religion, if any. On the surface, they're often more tolerant than moralistic and religious people. They believe everyone needs to determine what is right and wrong. Often they view God as a loving and personal force. They talk a lot about God's love.

Here's what's important about this. People in this category do not really believe there's anything bad about them, and they don't think of God as holy. They just think of God as loving. God's love is not transforming love. Over the years, and usually only when I'm in a little bit of a grumpy mood, if I'm talking to somebody who says, "Well, I just don't see why Jesus had to die. I think God just loves everyone," I'll say, "That's your understanding of God—he loves everyone. What did it cost the god you believe in to love us?" And the person always will say, "Well, nothing. He just loves everyone." And I say, "In that case, frankly, my God is more loving than yours. My holy, just God—who had to have Jesus die in order to accept us—is more loving, because he loved us enough that it cost him something."

If you ask, "Are you right with God?" the moralist says, "Yes, of course." And if you ask irreligious people, "Are you right with God?" if they believe in God, they'll say, "Well, of course. He loves everybody." It's just, "Of course." There's no joy. There's no power. There's no "It's incredible!" They're not electrified. So they're both thieves. You see? Both moralism and irreligion are thieves.

Bringing your thinking in line with the gospel. I want to give you some examples here, because to walk in line with the gospel is not to fall off into one thief or the other. How would you actually bring your thinking in line with the gospel? I'll give you three examples related to the moralistic approach to a subject, the relativistic approach to the subject, and the gospel approach.

Bringing your thinking in line with the gospel takes a lot of thinking. You have to think it out. You're trying to bring every area of your life in line with the gospel.

The first example is suffering. Without the gospel being the real heart of your life, when bad, bad, bad things happen to you—and in many cases, they have, right?—you either fall into an "I hate thee" or an "I hate me" mindset. In other words, you're temped very strongly to get into an "I hate thee! How dare you do this to me" mindset, or into an "I must be bad! I hate me" mindset, where you get down on yourself. You start to flagellate yourself. Why?

The person who says, "I hate thee," tends to be a relativist who really feels, "I'm a good person, and God is a loving person." When bad things happen, the relativist starts saying, "I can't believe that God would let something like this happen." The relativist believes that if there is a God, he certainly owes the person a good life. He should be stopping all the problems. There's no good reason why he should allow all these things to happen. The relativistic mindset has a light view of sin and a light view of God's justice, and when difficulties develop, relativists get mad.

Here's who else gets mad: Moralistic people who think they've been living a pretty good life. If you're a moralistic person and you've really tried very hard and you've lived a pretty good life but suffering comes, you get

 idolatry

incredibly mad, because you think God owes it to you to protect you. They, too, get into the "I hate thee" mindset. Who gets into the "I hate me" mindset? "I hate me" happens if you're in a moralistic framework but you haven't been living that good a life. Tons of people who are professing Christians are not living very consistent lives. Morally, they're not really living as they should. They're not really coming to church. They're not really praying. And suddenly, when bad things happen to them, they start to hate themselves. They say, "Oh, my gosh, I'm being punished." Moralists who are not living up to their standards go into an "I hate me" mindset, and relativists and moralists who feel they are living up to their standards go into an "I hate thee" mindset. But the gospel keeps you out of both of those.

The gospel approach to suffering is different. On the one hand, the gospel humbles us out of being mad at God. It *humbles* us out of being mad at God. Jesus, the very best person who ever lived, suffered terribly. People say, "I've lived a pretty good life," but Jesus lived a perfect life—and he died suffering, because of God's redemptive purposes. As soon as you realize that, it demolishes the idea that good people should have good lives and bad people should have bad lives. Jesus just completely destroys it. And it humbles you, because you realize, "If God *really* gave me what I deserve—." When people say, "I'm being punished for my sins," are you kidding me? You think God has such low standards? If you were being punished for your sins, you wouldn't even be here. You'd be gone. "He must be punishing me…" Think about it.

One of my teachers used to say to me, "Don't ask God for justice. If God gave the world justice at 12:00, there wouldn't be anybody here at 12:01." Jesus, the very best person who ever lived, suffered terribly, and this just demolishes the idea that good people should have good lives. If God himself, out of love, was willing to become involved in terrible suffering, and if he could not live a good life in this world without suffering, what in the world makes us think we'll be exempt?

By the way, if God loved us so much that he'd get involved in the world and suffer so horribly, then I don't know why God hasn't ended suffering. I don't know why God hasn't brought in the kingdom—but he must have a good reason. Whatever his reason is, it can't be indifference. It can't be remoteness. It can't be that he doesn't care.

On the other hand, the gospel affirms us out of feeling guilty or mad at ourselves. Jesus suffered and died for us, which means whatever problem you're experiencing right now, it can't be punishment for your sins. It might be a wake-up call. It might be smelling salts, yes. But it can't be retribution. Retribution fell onto the heart of Jesus. Your retribution fell onto the heart of Jesus. There may be a million reasons why you're going through the suffering you're going through right now, but one of them can't be "tit for tat." *Quid pro quo* punishment for our sin is something it can't be.

Jesus got the punishment. If we realize we're accepted in Christ, then and only then will suffering humble us and strengthen us rather than embitter us and weaken us. As others have said, Jesus suffered not that we might not suffer, but that when we suffer, we'll become like him. That's the gospel approach to suffering. It's very unique—not, "I hate me / I hate thee."

Of course, you'll find that since none of us is living right in line with the gospel, when suffering comes you'll probably find yourself pulled into one side or the other. Then you'll see where your heart really is. Your heart doesn't operate on the gospel paradigm. What it means to grow into Christlikeness is to spend all of your life getting it in line, and in times of suffering you start to see where your heart really functions. Very often you don't otherwise know, because you say, "Oh, I believe in Jesus. I believe the gospel." Well, you don't. You believe it and you don't believe it—totally. And sometimes you don't even realize to what degree your heart doesn't believe it. Suffering brings that out.

Let me give you a second example of how being in line with the gospel is neither falling off into this thief nor into that thief. This concerns the gospel approach to discouragement. I'm not talking about clinical or physiological depression, or the medical side of depression, however.

When a person is depressed, the moralist says, "If you're discouraged—really, really, really discouraged, and really despondent—you're breaking the rules somewhere. Repent." On the other hand, the relativist says, "You just need to love and accept yourself."

In other words, in answer to the self-esteem problem, moralists ordinarily say, "You're probably just not living right. You need to repent and do the right thing, and then you'll feel better about yourself." Relativists say, "You're not accepting yourself. You have to see that God loves you and people love you and everybody loves you."

But, assuming there's no physiological base for your depression, the gospel doesn't say either. The gospel leads us to examine ourselves and say, "If I'm really despondent, it's probably because something in my life has become more important than God to me. A pseudo-savior. A form of works-righteousness." The gospel leads us to repentance, not just setting our will against superficialities. Without the gospel, superficialities will be addressed instead of the heart. The moralist will work on behavior. The relativist will work on emotions. And the gospel will lead us to say, "What is your heart's functional trust?" Did you hear that?

"You're doing something wrong. Repent." "Oh, you just don't love yourself." Both of those approaches are superficial. But what if you're really despondent and you're a Christian? I'm going to give you an illustration about a woman I know. She's married, living in Virginia, and has two children. She's a strong Christian woman, but when she was in my church in Virginia as a fifteen-year-old, she was so skinny, and she had a sister who looked better. They were the same age, basically, because it was an adoptive family that had come together. I remember she sat in my office once, despondent, and I said, "You know, you're a Christian and you're going to heaven and you're adopted into the family." And she said, "But what good is that if nobody wants to date you?" At fifteen. "No guy will look at me, so what good is it?" And she was despondent. You don't want to be nasty to a fifteen-year-old, and you understand exactly why she felt that way. But the gospel is saying, "Something is more important to you than Jesus Christ, at that point. Something is more important to your self-image, or to your hope and happiness and meaning."

And what's interesting about the gospel is it's not a pat answer. It's more likely to make you go deep and look at how your heart really operates. It's not the kind of condemning, moralistic approach that says, "If you're feeling bad, just buck up. Do the right thing." It's not the psychology approach that basically says, "You have to just get people who love you and accept you and support you so you see how wonderful you are. Think good thoughts about yourself." It basically says, look underneath the surface.

There is a moralistic, a relativistic, and a gospel approach to everything. To everything. Think about evangelism. The literal, pragmatist approach is to deny the legitimacy of evangelism: "You shouldn't evangelize, because who's to say who's right?" The conservative, moralistic person does believe in evangelism, but because "We're right and they're wrong." The gospel, however, leads you to evangelism with these kinds of characteristics:

1.   You're compelled to share the gospel out of love, not guilt. You're not doing it because you feel, "I've got to do it, or else God's not going to let me into heaven."

2.   We're free from the fear of being ridiculed or hurt by others, because we have God's favor. In theory, if you

really believed the gospel, you wouldn't be afraid of looking a little weird.

3.   There's humility in our dealings with others, because we know we're saved by grace alone. There's not the slightest bit of a sense that you're superior to those that don't believe. You're not saved because of your right doctrine or because of your serenity; you're saved by grace, so you're no better than they are.

4.   We're hopeful about anyone, even the hard cases, because we know that it's a miracle that we're Christians—so why not anyone else?

5.   We're courteous and careful with people. We don't have to push or coerce them. It's only God's grace that opens hearts.

The gospel approach is a whole different approach. It's neither the moralistic approach nor the relativistic approach. Now, I'll get as intimate and as pragmatic as I can. What does it mean to say, "The only way you're actually going to change your heart is by applying the gospel"? Not just simply "sucking it up" and trying to conform your behavior to what you see in the Bible. Not just trying to conform your behavior to the model of Christ. (Of course you're trying to conform your behavior, but not directly and simply.) Rather, how do you actually apply the gospel?

Let's go to Martin Luther. His *Treatise on Good Works* was basically an exposition of the Ten Commandments. Here are two excerpts:

> All those who do not, in all their works or sufferings, life and death, trust in God's favor, grace, and good-will, but rather seek His favor in other things or in themselves, do not keep this First Commandment.[4]

What's the first commandment? He says if you don't believe you're saved by grace alone—if you don't believe in justification by faith alone, not works; if you don't look to God's grace but instead look to other things for his favor; if you're trying to earn your own salvation—you're breaking the first commandment.

If you don't believe the gospel, you're breaking the first commandment.

If you don't believe you're saved by sheer grace, you're breaking the first commandment.

Isn't that odd?

He says they're "breaking this first commandment and they practice *idolatry*"—which is the first commandment.

> ...even if they were to do the works of all the other Commandments, and in addition had all the prayers, fasting, obedience, patience, chastity, and innocence of all the saints combined.[5]

He says it's possible to obey all the other commandments and be breaking this first one. How could that be?

> If we doubt or do not believe that God is gracious and pleased with us, or if we presumptuously expect to please Him through our works, then all [our compliance with the law] is pure deception, outwardly honoring God but inwardly setting up self as a false savior. Note for yourself, then, how far apart these two are: keeping the First Commandment with outward works only, and keeping it with inward [justifying faith]. For this last makes true, living children of God, the other only makes worse idolatry and the most mischievous

idolatry   104

hypocrites on earth.[6]

That's Luther and the way he talks. Here's what he's saying. If you break Commandments Two to Ten, it's because you've already broken Commandment One. The sin underneath every other sin is that you're breaking the First Commandment, and breaking the First Commandment is not believing the gospel. Let me give you an illustration.

Kathy and I have been married for a number of years. Those of you who are married know about this and those of you who are not married don't know, but when I tell you about this, you won't be unhappy about not being married, anyway. It takes a period of time, but after a while, when you're married you start to just forget the other person is there. You actually start to act in ways that you never ever would let anybody else see. But you know, you can't keep that up—the person's there all the time, all the time, everywhere you go. You're eating with them. You're sleeping with them. They're everywhere, practically. And so, after a while, you just can't help it and you start to forget they're there and you start to act like you really are. You do things that even your parents don't see—nobody sees. Suddenly, your spouse starts to see them.

And Kathy and I noticed that one of the things you never let anyone else see is how you spin the truth—how you twist it, shade it—to suit yourself in certain situations. That's something nobody likes to have anybody see, but, you know, it started happening when you were on the phone and you heard your spouse say, "Well, no, I can't because I really won't be home on Thursday night." And, it could be me, it could be her, puts down the phone and the other spouse says, "That's not exactly the truth, is it?" And you say, "Oh, come on! You know." It's quite an insight, and when you actually begin to see those places where you kind of twist and shade and spin the truth, and each of you gets to hear the other one all the time, you start to realize something weird.

We're both sinners. "Thou shalt not bear false witness" is one of the Ten Commandments. And yet, we came to notice that we're tempted to lie in extremely different situations. It's not as simple as, "We're both sinners and we both tend to do that." We began to realize we're tempted to lie in very different situations.

I am tempted to do it when I think the other person will not be happy if they find out the truth. So, for example, the person comes up to me and says, "Did you get to that thing I asked you to do?" And I say, "Oh, yeah, it's almost done. In fact, I was going to give it to you tomorrow." As I walk away, I start to realize that I had utterly forgotten about the person's concern. I didn't want the person to feel snubbed. So, as I walk away, I say, "That's not really true. And you're a senior pastor. And you didn't tell the truth." I will shade the truth. I will be tempted to lie when I think the person will be unhappy with me. Kathy is only tempted to lie when she'll be unhappy if the other person finds out the truth, because she doesn't care what other people think about her at all. She's never, ever, ever tempted to shade the truth or lie just so that person won't be upset with her, because she doesn't care what people think. It does not bother her. She is tempted to lie in other situations, which I'm not going to tell you about because she's not here, and it's not fair, and I'm serious. So let me go into my own.

What we began to realize is this. If I say, "I want to start working on my heart. I see a certain lack of integrity. I see a tendency to kind of fudge the truth and to twist the truth and to spin it," what am I going to do? I say, "Well, I know the reason. The reason that I do it is because I'm a bad person. I'm a sinner. I have a wicked, sinful heart." And so what I start to say is, "You're a pastor. What if somebody finds out? What is God going to say?" And this is basically how you work on your heart: You go, "Bad Christian! *Bad* Christian! Tell the truth!" But what's going to happen is, if I'm almost caught, I'll probably be good for three months. Then my motivation wears off and back it will come. It doesn't really change the heart. But let's ask Martin Luther what's going on.

idolatry

Martin Luther is saying you would never break this, the lying commandment, unless you're already breaking the First Commandment and making something else your real salvation, your real hope, your real meaning; and, therefore, you are not really believing the gospel.

What would it be in my case? I'm only tempted to lie at times when Kathy is not, and that's what triggered us to have this discussion together. I'm only tempted to lie when I'm not getting the thing that I really, really, really seem to need—which Kathy doesn't, but I do—and that is human approval. If I utterly believe the gospel, then it doesn't matter what anybody else thinks. I'm okay because of what Jesus thinks. If I actually believed that, there'd be no incentive for me to ever lie again. And, therefore, if I'm ever tempted to lie, it's because there's a sin underneath the sin—and the sin underneath the sin is always, always, always unbelief in the gospel.

Now let me put it in the most positive possible way. You're only looking at superficialities if you're telling yourself, "I've got to change this" by saying, "Bad Christian! Don't do that." What you do is bully the heart into changing, out of fear alone, by saying, "This is going to happen and that's going to happen." And the heart says, "All right, all right, all right!" But, eventually, the consequences go away and it comes right on back in.

But what happens when you actually go underneath and say, "Why is the heart tempted to do this?" The heart is not tempted to do this just because I'm a sinner in general, even though I am, but because I'm failing to believe the gospel habitually in a particular way. And that means I'm failing to rejoice in Jesus. It's a failure of joy in him. It's a failure of love for him. It's a failure of belief. In other words, I believe the gospel intellectually, but I don't believe the gospel down deep, and I am only tempted to lie to the degree I am trusting in the approval of people—rather than Christ—to be my worth, to be my salvation, to be my hope, to be my meaning, my functional trust.

Let me give you just one more example, because if I only give you one example, you'll think, "Oh, the honesty thing, the integrity thing." Years ago, I was pastoring in my first church. There were two women in the church, both of whom were Christians, but they had non-Christian husbands who didn't come to church with them. Each of them had a teenage son, about the same age, who was starting to get into trouble, doing badly in school, and probably acting out, as it were, because their fathers were so completely emotionally remote and distant from the wife and the son. I remember pastoring, in a sense counseling, both women because they were mad at their husbands. They were really mad, because they said, "It's one thing to ignore me, but now, the way he acts is ruining my son's life, too." They were getting very bitter, and in both cases, being a young minister, I simply said, "Forgive them"—which, by the way, is what I'd say now, but I would take longer, or I'd listen longer. I'd be nicer, and I'd be more careful. But I'd say, "You have to forgive them. You're a Christian"—that's what they told me in seminary. I was twenty-five years old; what am I going to do?

These two women said, "How do I forgive?" And I gave both of them a little book on forgiveness, and they were good books on forgiveness. Here's what's interesting. The wife with the better husband of the two was unable to do it. She was a stronger Christian, from what I could tell. At least she was more active. Her husband was really a better person. And she could not do it. She stayed bitter. The other woman, who didn't seem to be as strong a Christian or as active a Christian, and who had a far worse husband, and who had, I felt, far more warrant for being mad, was able to do it. She took the book, really worked through it, and really broke through. And I was sitting around saying, "I don't get this. What's going on? Why was she able to do it and the other wasn't?"

Years later, I looked back on it and I realized that for the stronger Christian—the woman with the better husband—her son was her whole life. Even though she said, "Jesus is my salvation," deep in her heart, her heart was saying, "Here's how you know if your life has been worthwhile: if your son loves you, and if your son turns out to be a good person." In other words, her son essentially was the idol. Better yet, being a good mother was the main thing that she looked to as her pseudo-savior. It was the replacement. And because of that she couldn't possibly forgive her husband. She wasn't able to change her heart on the surface unless she went down underneath and began to realize there was a lack of joy in Jesus—that the smile of her son on her was vastly more valuable, emotionally, to her than the smile of Jesus. It didn't mean that she wasn't a Christian. It didn't mean she wasn't saved. It just meant that she believed the gospel at one level but she didn't believe it at a deeper level, and until she did, she was not going to be able to make any progress. See that?

So now somebody asks the question, "Wait a minute. What, then, is my motivation, really? If you're saying, 'You just have to believe Jesus loves you,' how do I really get motivation to make these deep changes in my life?"

Making the deep changes in life. Here's the first of three things: Only the gospel gives you the power to admit what's wrong with you.

If I'm a moralistic person, the very foundation of my self-image is that I'm an honest person. I tell the truth. I'm a good person. I obey the Ten Commandments. That's the very foundation of my self-image, so how could I possibly admit the problem I have with telling the truth? I'm going to look at my tendency to shade the truth and I'm not even going to call it a lie. I'm just going to say, "Oh, I shade the truth, and I'm just trying to be sensitive to what people think. They would be unhappy, and I'm just really thinking of their happiness." You see? I cannot bear to admit that I am a liar, because I don't know that I'm accepted. Only if I know that I am radically and unconditionally accepted—only when the very foundation of my self-image is that God loves me, not that I'm a better person than others because I'm pretty good; only if the foundation of my self-image is not that I'm an honest person, but that I'm a saved sinner—can I begin to admit what's wrong with me.

In fact, I'd say only Christians who really, really, really, really deeply believe the gospel are going to be able to look at themselves and admit what's there. Really admit it. It's silly to think that somehow, if I just believe that God loves me and accepts me completely, I'm going to go light on sin. Instead, I'm going to finally be able to admit my sins. So the first thing is the gospel gives you the power to admit what's wrong with you.

Secondly, as we've seen, the gospel gives you the power to understand what's wrong with you.

The moralistic approach just looks at behavior, and the relativistic approach just looks at emotions, but the gospel approach makes you look underneath, under the surface. What am I really after? What am I really trusting? What am I really hoping in? What's my functional salvation, even though I'm giving lip service to the idea that Jesus is my Savior? What's my real savior? So it helps you to *understand*.

But, most of all, the gospel gives you clean motivation to change. Not dirty—clean. What do I mean?

Jonathan Edwards wrote a book that is almost impossible to read (so don't say, "I'm going get it out of the library and read it." It's not a good use of your time yet—at least, there are about three thousand other books you need to read first). He wrote a book called *The Nature of True Virtue*, a remarkable book, and in it, he basically says there are two reasons why people are virtuous. One he calls "common virtue" and one is "true virtue." Common virtue is when you do the right thing out of fear and pride and, therefore, for yourself. True virtue is when you do the right thing just for God's sake.

For example, he says, "Common virtue is always out of fear and pride."[7] Let's go to lying again. Why should I tell the truth? Common virtue says, "Fear. Tell the truth, or you'll be caught." Or Harvard Business School says,

"Be ethical," because why? Why do they tell you in Harvard Business School to be ethical? Because it's good business—which is fear, by the way, and greed. There's also a secular version of that: "Tell the truth, or you'll be put in jail. Tell the truth, or people will find out." And then there's a conservative version, you might say a Christian version, that says, "Tell the truth, or God will get you."

Pride is another reason to be virtuous. Pride says, "You don't want to be like those awful liars." A conservative version says, "You don't want to be like people who are not virtuous," and a liberal version says, "You don't want to be like people who are greedy and who cheat and who are not concerned for the common good."

Fear and pride are the main reasons why most people don't lie. Jonathan Edwards says, "That's great. We're so glad that God is keeping the world from being the horrible place it really could be by having billions of people telling the truth millions and billions of times a day, making the world a livable place—but out of fear and pride."

There's something inherently unstable in that, isn't there, because why do you lie? The same reasons. And therefore, if you take fear and pride and you jury-rig the heart so that it's your fear and pride that make you into a virtuous person, you have restrained the heart but you haven't really changed the heart. You haven't gone to the fountain of the evil of the heart, and you've actually nurtured the roots of sin within your moral life. Isn't that wild? So what that means is that you have incentive to do well, to do the right thing moralistically, but it's dirty, because what will very often happen if this is the main thing running your engine of trying to live a good life, is that at some point, you'll finally find it's not profitable to your fear or to your pride to tell the truth. And you'll lie. And the next thing you know, you'll say, "I can't believe I did this. Why did I do this? Why did I embezzle? Why did I tell that lie? I wasn't raised that way." But it's because you have nurtured the roots of sin in the center of all your moral life. The only way to change your habit of lying is not just to try harder, but to apply the gospel.

Fear and pride can, in a sense, bend the heart in a kind of unnatural way, but it will spring back. It's like trying to bend a tree. You tie it down, but eventually the tree will spring back. To really be melted and shaped into a whole new person, you have to see what Jesus has done for you. You can only be melted by joy. Every sin is a lack of joy in him. Every sin is just a lack of joy. Isn't it great to know that the essential dynamic releasing real change in your life is gospel repentance?

What is gospel repentance? Gospel repentance is repenting for a lack of joy that the thing that most assures you that God will never reject you is because of what he has done at infinite cost. He has put you into a relationship with him so that he doesn't have to reject you. Gospel repentance means the thing that most assures you is the thing that most convicts you—the reason you're convicted of sin is not because, "I'd better do the right thing or God will cast me off" but "I'd better do the right thing, because how can I treat the one who will never cast me off, at infinite cost to himself, like this?"

If you are afraid that God's going to reject you and just throw you into hell if you sin, then the reason you so desperately want to do the right thing is not for God but for you. If you know what he has done—at infinite cost to himself he has put you in relationship so that you'll never be rejected by him—then your motivation when you sin is to go get him. You want fellowship with him. You want him, him, him. And you realize the ultimate thing is your lack of joy.

So, when the thing that most assures you is the thing that most convicts you, you'll be okay. When you're convicted of sin in a gospel way, it drives you toward God. It drives you toward prayer. But when you're convicted of sin in a moralistic framework, you have to beat yourself for three months until you feel good enough to drag yourself back to church. Can you see the difference?

Paul says in Romans 1, "I am not ashamed of the gospel, for it is the power of God unto salvation" (v. 16). Listen carefully. Does Paul say, "I am not ashamed of the gospel, because it *brings* the power of God?" Or that "If you believe in the gospel, it *results in* the power of God"? Or "It *causes* the power of God"? It's a pretty remarkable statement—he says, "I am not ashamed of the gospel, for it *is* the power." The gospel is God's power in verbal form. To the degree you get it, it releases the power of God in your life.

Or, go back to 1 Peter 1:12, that great spot where it says they "preached the gospel to you by the Holy Spirit sent from heaven, into which even angels long to look." If your understanding of the gospel is, "Oh, I believe the gospel. Jesus died for my sin. Now let's get on to something advanced," angels are a lot smarter than you. Their IQs are way beyond yours, and they've been looking at the gospel, probably from all eternity. Jesus Christ, we're told, and this boggles the mind, was slain before the foundation of the world. The sacrifice of Jesus came into history at a certain point, but there is some sense in which the self-donating, sacrificial love of God saved us outside of time. The angels have been looking at the gospel through all eternity, and they're not tired of it yet, because there's always something else in there.

For every one of your problems, there's an aspect of the gospel, an application of the gospel, a reflection of the gospel, with your problem's name on it. It's in there. You have to go find it. You have to go look for it.

Let me just close with prayer:

Our Father, we're grateful to you that the gospel is something that can change every area of our lives. We're so grateful that the gospel is something that we can use on our hearts in such a way that we can finally, because of it, see what's wrong with us, understand what's wrong with us, and finally have clean hatred of sin. Without the gospel, we hate ourselves instead of our sin. Without the gospel, we are motivated through awful fear and pride to change, and it doesn't really change our heart. It just restrains our heart.

O Lord, let the gospel have its way in our lives so that we can truly be changed by it, grow through it. And we pray that you make us a church that's characterized by an understanding of the full meaning of the gospel. We want to be a church marked by the upside-down values of the kingdom, a church filled with people who really have finally changed because of their spiritual awareness of how loved they are. We want to be a church filled with people to whom the Holy Spirit is saying, "You are my beloved child, with whom I am well pleased and in whom I delight." So we ask that you make us a church like this and people like this. We pray it in Jesus' name. Amen.

idolatry

A Lifestyle of Repentance
by Shari Thomas

Why Use This Tool?
- To pursue a lifestyle of repentance instead of a lifestyle of resolve
- To see ourselves as the chief sinner
- To understand the difference between worldly sorrow and godly sorrow

A lifestyle of repentance means we give up our need to be right and instead receive the righteousness of Christ. Most of us think we grow in our Christian life by discipline, but Paul, in Galatians 3, says growth comes the same way we received Christ in the first place—through repentance and belief.

Jesus began his public ministry with the word *repent* and he repeated it over and over—a never-ending call to repentance. (Mark 1:15: repent and believe the good news; Matt. 4:17: repent for the kingdom is near; Acts 2:38: repent and be baptized.)

As we grow in repentance, we see more of God's grace and experience his resurrection power in ways we never imagined. The more we are able to understand the evil of our own hearts, the more we are able to understand evil in larger contexts. A repentant faith—one in which we open ourselves up to Christ and simultaneously cast ourselves down before him—is quite different from attempts to just try harder to believe and behave.

Luke 17 tells us that when someone sins against us, the person to watch out for is not the one who sinned against us, but ourselves! Why? We instantly want to retaliate. We want revenge. We are dangerous when we are sinned against because our natural instinct is to retaliate and wound someone else.

In Matthew 26:31-35, Peter promised Jesus he would never fall away. Yet minutes later, he disowned his Lord three times. Peter's resolve did not give him the power to persevere. Like Peter, our resolutions have no power to change us. Yet so often, we are inclined to pursue a lifestyle of resolve, not repentance. We believe too much in the power of our active righteousness. What we need is a hunger for Christ's passive righteousness.

In Luke 15, we see that repentance leads to celebration, not condemnation. Even though the prodigal returned to his father with the attitude of a slave, he *made a move* toward his father. The father celebrated the son's return and the son was able to join in, or receive the celebration of the father. His self-condemnation turned to celebration. When we repent, we also move toward our Father. And like the prodigal son, we often return to our Father burdened with a slave mentality, but the point is that we come! Celebration will not be far off. The longer we live a lifestyle of repentance, the more we see how much we need Jesus. A gospel interpretation of every biblical passage reminds us how desperately we need Christ.

For example, Ephesians 6:4 says, "Parents, do not exasperate your children but bring them up in the fear and admonition of the Lord." If we think this verse merely means that we are to raise our children knowing Christ, then we get busy teaching them how to behave. Nevertheless, the real job description is *to not exasperate*. But do we have the power to stop exasperating our children? Guess what! We can't do it! A parallel passage, Colossians 3:21, says, "Parents, don't embitter your children or they will get discouraged." These passages are a call to us as parents to cry out to Jesus. How do you embitter and exasperate your children? How many times have you broken this one command per kid per year? This is just one of God's laws regarding parenting that we break, and yet we get so upset when our kids break our laws and don't obey us. Are we lovingly disciplining our children with

110

compassion (we know how difficult it is to obey) and hope (Jesus can change us and our kids!)? Or are we punishing them and making them pay because their inability to obey is so frustrating and insulting to us? We need to see ourselves as the bigger sinner. Interpreting scripture through the gospel enables us to have compassion on others and to live by repentance and faith, whether it's with our children or those in our churches.

When a relationship is broken and reconciliation is being sought, effective restitution requires two people to pay the cost of their reconciliation. The very word, *restitution*, means payment. We often force two parties to reconcile because the right words have been spoken. We need to look deeper, however. Has there been a currency of repentance? Words are not the currency of repentance, pain is, godly sorrow is. There is a cost involved. Both parties pay. Without payment, repentance is shallow and reconciliation virtually impossible. Remember, we can forgive people who sin against us regardless of their response, ability, or willingness to interact with us. But for restitution to occur, both parties must look at what has occurred and be willing to pay a currency of repentance.

It is not wise to trust people who are unrepentant. If a person has not come close to paying the cost of his or her repentance, they are most likely feeling and exhibiting only worldly sorrow. This is where we often misunderstand the concept of grace and assume it to mean that a person does not need to pay the cost of their repentance to another. This only encourages worldly sorrow, which eventually negates an experience of true grace.

A person exhibiting godly sorrow (i.e. Zaccheus, Luke 19) recognizes his sin and offers a currency of repentance. In the movie *Get Low*, the protagonist Felix Bush isolates himself for 40 years as self-inflicted payment for his sin. He experiences pain, but it is not the pain or currency of repentance we are talking about. It is not until old man Bush comes clean before his community and experiences the pain of openly owning the truth of his actions that there is even the possibility of reconciliation between him and the few remaining people who know him. Of course there is no payment Felix can offer—and neither is there one that we can offer—that actually covers our sin apart from what Jesus has already accomplished on the cross. Yet, there is a currency of repentance that passes between two people walking the path of reconciliation. If this currency is absent, be cautious to assume that true repentance is present.

Guidelines for Repentance

1. Ask God to teach you the difference between godly and ungodly sorrow.

In Hosea 7, the Israelites were wailing from their beds. They wanted to change their circumstances and fix what was wrong in their lives. Notice they used generalities in speaking of their sin, not specifics.

But in Hosea 14, they cry from their hearts. Repentance puts our sin on the table and names it. We see that the problem is the sin of our hearts, not the pain it causes us. In Hosea 6 and 7, the Israelites just want to get rid of the pain. But in Hosea 14, we see a deeper change. Verse 2 says, "Take words with you." In other words, be very articulate about your heart sins. Be specific about the specific sins. "Repent of particular sins particularly" says the Westminster Confession. God promises in this passage that he will fill our tongues, our hearts, and our lives, and his love will know no bounds. His desire is to heal us of our idolatry. To make us fruitful people.

Confession is a lot more comfortable than repentance. We can confess without the help of the Holy Spirit. But we can't repent without the Holy Spirit. Repentance will feel like death to our souls because it is costly and painful.

Worldly sorrow (WS) is how we typically say, "I am sorry." It does not cost us much pain. Godly sorrow (GS), on the other hand, is a dying to self that will cost us pain which we are willing to bear.

Here are some typical examples of how we often apologize. In worldly sorrow, we try to minimize the impact of our sin and defend ourselves. Godly sorrow allows us to own the impact of our sin and makes us willing to die to ourselves in humble repentance.

Worldly Sorrow: I am only sorry for what I DO.
Godly Sorrow: I am also sorry for what I AM.

Worldly Sorrow: I confess after I have sinned.
Godly Sorrow: I am continually repentant because of my sin.

Worldly Sorrow: I focus on my behavior and desire moral reformation.
Godly Sorrow: I focus on my disposition and desire spiritual transformation.

Worldly Sorrow: I want quick resolution so you will get off my back.
Godly Sorrow: I want deeper insight, so I need you to hang in there with me.

Worldly Sorrow: I can't believe I am like that. Let's not talk about it any more.
Godly Sorrow: I can believe I am like that. We need to talk about it more.

Worldly Sorrow: I have an explanation.
Godly Sorrow: I am sick of my explanations.

Worldly Sorrow: I repent by trying to do it right the next time.
Godly Sorrow: I repent that I don't have it right and I trust Christ to be my rightousness.

Worldly Sorrow: I am sorry because I got found out.
Godly Sorrow: I am thankful you brought this to my attention.

Worldly Sorrow: I am sorry that I offended you.
Godly Sorrow: I am sorrowful that my sinful heart is so offensive.

2. Ask the person you sinned against to tell you how your sin impacted them.
We typically cannot see how our sin impacts others. So after going to a person and naming specific sins, ask, "Is there anything from this that you want to tell me?" Since we don't feel the impact of our relational sins, ask others to speak into your life. How does your relational style affect them?

3. Repentance is ongoing.
After you have gone to the other person, maybe a month or even a year later, return to the topic of your sin. "I wonder if there is anything else you want to say to me about the incident that happened last month at the beach? Is there something you want to tell me that you haven't told me?" Just because you repented once does not mean the impact of your sin has stopped, or that the person just needs to forgive you and move on.

4. Repentance does not mean you necessarily say "Please forgive me."
Scripture tells us to ask God for forgiveness but doesn't mention anything about asking the other person for forgiveness. It's not that this isn't a good idea, it's just that we often use this as a cop out in order to get the focus off ourselves. Saying, "Please forgive me," can actually put more of a burden on the other person. Instead of just

asking for forgiveness, go back to step #2 and ask the other person to tell you how your sin impacted them.

5. Do not minimize your sin or make atonement for it.

Don't make any explanations for what compelled you to sin. "If you hadn't provoked me, I would not have…." That is not confession, but blame shifting. Don't short circuit the process by minimizing your sin and getting your guilt off your chest. It's more powerful to ask for insight. Listen to comments people make about you and ask them about it. Do this especially if you are in an authority position such as a parent or church leader. You will need to take the initiative for others or your children to tell you the impact of what you are like. Make it easy for people to talk to you about the impact of your sin on their lives. Be alert to how easily your apologies become apologetics. So often our apologies are just a defense of ourselves.

6. Pray for the Holy Spirit to open the eyes of your heart.

We see in Ephesians 1:18 that we can experience the power of the Holy Spirit to change us.

7. Realize your sin is against God.

Even though your sin is horrendous against the other person, ultimately you have sinned against God. David says, "Against you only have I sinned." The universe and all it contains belongs to God. When we sin against another person, we are marring God's creation which was blessed and called good. Racism, bigotry, misogyny are all sins against God because we are dishonoring and harming what God created and blessed.

8. Holiness requires relationship.

God uses people in our lives. Nathan had to go to David to tell him of his sin—a full year later! So for a full year David just covered up his sin. We do not repent automatically. We don't readily see our sin. We need each other.

9. Invite your close friends to speak into your life.

"Is there anything I can do to make it easier for you to forgive me?"

"If there is one thing about me you could change, what would it be?"

"If I'm getting irritated, impatient or critical with you, could you stop me right when I'm doing it, so I can see myself?"

Are you tired yet of your petty and sinful ways? Learn to hate your own sin more than the sin of others. Remember we are referring to hating sin, not yourself nor others.

Adapted with permission from Stu Batstone at World Harvest Mission.

Idolatry Resources

The Allure of Hope: God's Pursuit of a Woman's Heart, Jan Myers
Confessions, St. Augustine
Counterfeit Gods: The Empty Promises of Money, Sex, and Power, and the Only Hope that Matters, Tim Keller
The Enemy Within, Kris Lundgaard
Idols of the Heart, Elyse Fitzpatrick
The Inner Voice of Love, Henri Nouwen
The Prodigal God (book and workbook), Tim Keller

SERMONS:
The Healing of Peter by Tim Keller; www.redeemer.com
Mortification Through Joy, Tim Keller; www.redeemer.com
Splitness, Tim Keller; www.redeemer.com

CALLING +
IDENTITY

WHAT IS MY IDENTITY ?

HOW DOES IT AFFECT MY CALLING ?

Doesn't everything die at last, and too soon? /
Tell me, what is it you plan to do / With your
one wild and precious life?   MARY OLIVER

The Myths of Calling
by Shari Thomas

"Women are called by God to all sorts of ministries just as men are. Gender should not affect their calling nor how it is lived out."

"Since my identity is firmly rooted in being a child of Christ, calling doesn't really matter."

"Full-time ministry is a wonderful calling just like other callings. In our day and time it doesn't impact the spouse as expectations are not what they once were."

"Of course I have a calling from God, and since my spouse and I are two separate people, we have separate callings. Just because he has a call to ministry, doesn't mean I'm called to it by default."

"The term 'call from God' has everyone confused. We put the term 'calling' on anything we want to do as a means of getting God's stamp of approval and a way to raise money. Just relax and live the life you want. God is in all of it."

"I really don't need to think about calling in our marriage. God has given that job to my husband. If he messes it up, he is the one accountable to God, not me."

"I'm excited that my husband is going to be planting a church. But I really don't think it's going to be affecting my life that much. Maybe this is something that only impacts women who don't have their own career."

"If you are married and have children, you are called to care for your husband and children before anything else."

"If a woman has a profound mind it should be kept a profound secret."
—Becoming Jane

IF A MINISTER WANTS to be a church planter, what does that make the spouse? Is the spouse automatically assigned a certain role? Is that then her call? Men and women who love scripture and are life-long scholars are coming up with many different answers to these questions—and all with answers based in scripture.

But what is calling? Is it merely a feeling in my gut? A desire? A longing? The term has become quite clouded as we freely interchange words such as guidance, God's will, desire, and spiritual direction with the word call. Might the term calling be broader than how we tend to use it?

Humans share a universal desire for meaning. Whether verbalized or not, we all ask variations of: Why am I here? What is my purpose? Am I of value? Do I matter?

The Hebrew word for call used in the Old Testament is pretty much the same as the English word used today. We call each other by name. We ask an expectant couple what they are going to call their baby. Looking at Genesis 1-3, the amazing point about the word call is that it is God who calls us. God names us. God gives us purpose. God gives us meaning. Calling is the answer to our questions of meaning, identity, and purpose. Calling is powerful stuff!

I love what Os Guinness says, "When we rise to answer the call, that call names us. Only when we see the Caller will we get our name because we've become who God called us to be."

I can't tell you how much I long for you to enter this wide-open, spacious life. We didn't fence you in. The smallness you feel comes from within you. Your lives aren't small, but you're living them in a small way. I'm speaking as plainly as I can and with great affection. Open up your lives. Live openly and expansively!

—the Apostle Paul, II Corinthians 6:11-13 (The Message)

calling + identity

This understanding of call goes far beyond accepting a specific position in ministry, making a decision about a job, or assuming certain roles.

Understanding our calling and our identity is so powerful that ignoring them can have devastating effects in our lives. Because the two are so intricately linked, we felt we couldn't separate them. If we don't understand

> *Don't ask what the world needs. Ask what makes you come alive, and go do it. Because what the world needs is people who have come alive.*
> —*Howard Thurman, American theologian*

our true identity, we quickly turn to our performance and other qualifiers to define who we are. Without a growing understanding of our calling, we too easily attach it to a role, a ministry, or what we do. Misunderstanding either will quickly sink us. Understanding both identity and calling leads to a buoyant freedom—one that propels us to look at the larger story of what God may be doing in and through us.

Our purpose in this section is to present the main struggles ministry couples report when dealing with the topic of identity and calling, as well as the areas we feel are crucial for a couple to address when accepting a ministry position. While we will share our beliefs on call and hopefully

debunk a few myths, it is not our intention to write an exegetical article on this topic. Check our resource section for that.

COUPLES ENTERING MINISTRY often report conflicting internal struggles as to what to do when one partner senses a call to a particular ministry and the other one does not. While many couples have entered ministry without both of them becoming convinced of a mutual call, these decisions often produce deep tension and struggles for the marriage. Many women have followed their husbands into ministry even when they did not share the same desire. And more and more men are following their wives into ministries when they do not sense as strong a passion as their wives do. Others who believe God has called their spouse—but not them—into ministry still face the impact of ministry on their personal lives.

Your beliefs and views will impact your understanding of calling and how it is lived out. Regardless of theological differences, our desire is that each of us humbly submit to Christ with a willingness to take an honest look at our marriages and at scripture, as well as a daring look at who God might be calling us to be.

> *The place God calls you to is the place where your deep gladness and the world's deep hunger meet.*
> —*Frederick Buechner,* Wishful Thinking: A Seeker's ABC

Shari's Story On Calling
by Shari Thomas

My earliest recollections conjure up sights of strutting roosters and mangy dogs running in and out of church services; smells of garlic, olive oil, plantains, black beans; and feelings of security within an ever-growing community of "aunts" and "uncles." I grew up as a missionary kid. But, it wasn't until later in life that I learned that the name given to our unique atmosphere was church planting. We had a team that, while fraught with the typical struggles that plague teams today, was made up of men and women from all nationalities dedicated to bringing God's Kingdom to our Latin American country. I was surrounded by women who served alongside local pastors. Among my early heroes were women who went to remote villages and planted churches when there was no one else to go. Our home was one where my parents valued the equal contribution men and women brought to any given topic or task. As he has always done with young leaders, my dad opened doors for me to use my verbal and leadership gifts. Naively, I figured everyone raised in a Christian home was also given these opportunities.

My extended missionary family brought before us the needs of the world, the mandate to make disciples of all nations, and the challenge of how we might participate in the great commission. There was never a question in my mind that I, too, would have my part to play on the stage of life.

When we married, my husband and I saw our marriage as an opportunity in which we could not only face the challenges of life together, but could serve the church and mankind together. We were drawn to each other for many reasons, but one was seeing how our lives could blend to give more fully to others.

And then we had children.

For the first time in my life I began to face the confusion many women in ministry have faced all along. Everyone, including my family, husband, and myself assumed my primary responsibility would be to care for our children. I *loved* being a mother, yet something felt oddly out of place. I was torn between my desires to serve outside the home and my family. I became frustrated with the expectation that my husband would be out and I would be home. While I loved my family, I also loved ministry outside the home. For years I struggled with guilt and shame that I did not feel content at home. Why was caring solely for my family not enough? Had I somehow missed my calling? Was I supposed to have remained single? How could I raise a family, care for my children well, and still have these passions? Even when I taught school before we had children, I always spent the majority of my time in new and developing ministries, in leadership, teaching, and speaking.

But now we were serving as missionaries in another country, and added to caring for my children was the intensity of city life and living in another language and culture. There just was no time left for anything but survival. At times the struggle was so intense I could hardly bear to go to church and hear a sermon. I couldn't help but exegete the passage, draw up an outline, and fill in stories and examples. But how could I use these and other

calling + identity

abilities while my children were still young? And where was a place for a woman with these types of passions in a conservative setting?

I was confused about my role as wife, mother, and missionary, and I didn't understand if my role was my calling or if calling was something else. Much later I came to see that these *roles* gave me great responsibility and tremendous opportunity to use my *calling*, but they were my *roles*, not my *calling*. In a progressive culture, many women struggle with the idolatry of work and a need to find fulfillment in what they do. But likewise, family is often a dominant idol for women in a conservative culture. I struggled with both. I was often tempted to place such a high value on mothering and our children, that when our family needed to sacrifice for the good of others, I did not want my children to suffer, so I chose comfort and safety out of fear. Other times I have wrestled with misplacing my identity in ministry and have demanded from my husband that I get 'equal opportunity' to follow my passions.

I did not realize that even though these abilities were God-given, it did not mean that I had to have a career or position to fulfill this calling. My calling could, and can, be used in many ways and in different measures, especially depending on my season of life. I also didn't realize that these deep desires and passions were a part of God's purpose for me, and that as I followed them I would one day come to know my naming and my calling. They were not to be ignored or squelched. Often, I would envy other women's gifts, like hospitality—which seemed so naturally used in the home when children were young. I would try hard to force myself to be gifted in this way. The evenings usually ended with my total exhaustion, tension between John and me, piles of dishes, and me still running to my computer to write.

But even as I, and others, began to recognize my calling, it still reflected dignity and depravity. In other words, just because my calling was from God didn't mean it was filled only with dignity. Depravity was also reflected in how I used this calling. Even when great good was accomplished and I saw dignity, just as readily I could see depravity.

Depravity: Insisting how or when my calling would

be used. Accepting opportunities that came my way even if I had to manipulate to do it.

Depravity: Comparing the measure of my gift to others. Comparison is a game where no one wins. There will always be someone better than me, and always someone worse. Comparing kept me from rejoicing with others, cheering them on, and rooting for them to be the best they could be. It also kept me from recognizing when God was using me, especially if it was not how I envisioned it.

Depravity: Complaining, whining, and losing hope when I was exhausted with raising children, and my husband didn't see my need for his help.

Dignity: Taking joy in God using my calling however he wants.

Dignity: Letting it be used when I don't get the credit.

Dignity: Receiving praise and acknowledging a job well done.

I also had to come to grips with the depravity and dignity in my husband and how these were demonstrated in his calling. It seems that mixed with the tremendous gifting church planters have, there is a proclivity towards narcissism. It is a beautiful gift when one can paint a picture for others, helping them see what will one day be, what God is doing, and how they might join kingdom endeavors. But this gift's dark side brings a misplaced fervor that unless all hands are on deck helping, it will fail. When compared with a child's birthday party or cleaning up the kitchen, the demands of church planting tend to win out. It takes great personal humility and much honesty from others for a person with this type of gifting to recognize his/her depravity.

While John and I have wrestled with this area of calling and its implications, we have come to see that God has called us together for a reason and that both of our passions and giftings need to be explored so we can come to a place of opportunity that uniquely fits our marriage. Even so, there have definitely been periods in our lives when we have placed, and rightly so, opportunities for one of us above the other. We are learning how we can honor each other better and how our callings are not separate. When I have intense deadlines, he often takes over grocery shopping or laundry. When he has people he wants me to work

calling + identity　　120

with, I adapt my schedule to be part of his plans. We are loosening our expectations of each other. He is letting go of the priority of exquisite meals and often cooks himself. And I am letting go of the priority of yard work and order for the home. Thus, we are both allowing each other to fully be who we are created to be. And we are both working toward a common goal.

While it has taken a lifetime to wrestle through how this practically plays out in our marriage, we have both grown in respecting each other's voice and abilities, all the while discerning how God wants to bring us together—not apart—for his purposes.

When you engage in a work that taps your talent and fuels your passion—that rises out of a great need in the world that you feel drawn by conscience to meet—therein lies your voice, your calling, your soul's code.

—*Stephen Covey,* The Seven Habits of Highly Effective People

121

calling + identity

The Myths of Identity

by Tami Resch

"The search for identity is just psychological mumbo jumbo."

"My identity is found in my roles."

"My identity is tied to my performance."

"I am what I do; I am what I say; I am what I eat."

"Our search for identity is firmly settled as Christians. We really shouldn't have to revisit this."

"Focusing on discovering your identity is the problem with the world today. It just takes your eyes off Jesus."

Our longing to be identified, described, and assigned a place in this world isn't just a modern day issue. Augustine was the first to reflect on and write about our need for doctrine and theology to break into our personal world. He wrote a psychological self-portrait in his book, *Confessions*. Go back farther still to the first family, to creation. In Genesis, God identified and described Adam and Eve as creatures made in his own image. He blessed them and gave them meaningful work, his presence and provision. They received a benediction. All was good. Very good.

But all too soon we come upon malediction. Because of the fall, Adam and Eve's earth, their work, and their relationships would be fraught with decay, toil, and pain. Little did Adam and Eve know that even as they were escorted out of their home, they wore on their backs a hint of their true identity. God had spilled blood to provide garments to cover their sin

> *Who am I? They mock me, these lonely questions of mine.*
> *Whoever I am, thou knowest, O God, I am thine.*
> —Dietrich Bonhoeffer, from his poem, Who Am I?

and shame. One day, much later in the story, God would spill the blood of his Son to provide garments of righteousness, restoring Adam's race to its truest identity—image bearers in Christ!

Ephesians 1 tells us that our status as adopted image bearers is not a post-Edenic afterthought; "We were chosen in Christ before the creation of the world to be holy and blameless in his sight. In love, we were predestined to be adopted…" All who wear Christ's garment of righteousness are identified and described as holy and blameless sons and daughters.

Are you saying my truest identity is in Christ? That I'm holy and blameless? Me? Yes, I know. It sounds outrageous! I've yet to hear anyone introduce me by saying, "This is Tami, who is in Christ. She is holy and blameless in God's sight." Rather, introductions sound like resumes of what I do, what I say, my accomplishments, my roles, and my latest performance in those roles.

The spouse of a church leader experiences extra layers of this description-by-performance-and-roles phenomenon. "This is Tami, the wife of our pastor. She's generous, a great hostess, and everyone feels welcome when they are around her. She helped found an organization that coaches women in ministry." These are the kinds of introductions we are used to hearing and often where we go to find our identity—to other people and our roles and performance and what they say about us. However, in this section we are inviting you to take a risk—a challenge. Will you dare to leave your resumes behind and live out of your truest identity?

Our one firm place to stand in the presence of God and in the presence of humankind is *in Christ*—not in our roles or qualifiers. The most fundamental and beautiful thing about me is that I am *in Christ*, one with the Father, Son, and Holy Spirit because of the work of Christ on my behalf.

When I let the qualifiers *about* me

> *It is the normal state of the human heart to try to build its identity around something besides God. Spiritual pride is the illusion that you are competent to run your own life, achieve your own sense of self-worth and find a purpose big enough to give you meaning in life without God.*
> —*Soren Kierkegaard,*
> Sickness Unto Death

define me. My contempt and my idolatries do not define me. My gifts and talents do not define me. My culture and my context do not define me. What I do, say, and eat are things that go in me and come out of me—but they do not define me. God has reserved the right to place the only defining mark upon me, the seal that speaks louder than all descriptors: *You are mine in Christ.*

Now it is God who makes both us and you stand firm IN CHRIST. He anointed us, set his seal of ownership on us, and put his Spirit in our hearts as a deposit, guaranteeing what is to come.
—*II Corinthians 1:21-22*

Jesus received God's blessing before he completed his work, *"This is my beloved son, with whom I am well-pleased."* He went on to live a perfect life and die our death so we could receive God's blessing based not on our performance, but upon Christ's performance. Christianity is the only religion where you get the blessing before the performance. Phew!

Oh, if only this were the end of our struggle! How difficult it is to believe and live out of our truest identity. But to the degree that, like Jesus, we believe God's spoken word over us, we can stand firm.

This section focuses on taking our unchangeable identity and fleshing out how it can be lived in our calling. If we could get one understanding embedded deep into our hearts—yours and ours—it would be this one!

> *Define yourself radically as one Beloved by God. This is the True Self. Every other identity is illusion.*
> —*Brennan Manning,* Abba's Child: The Cry of the Heart for Intimate Belonging

become the most fundamental thing defining me, I move toward taking these good things and making them my firm place to stand, and letting them be a measure of my worth and righteousness: *I am hospitable, kind, and generous.* Or I move toward taking the ugly things about me and making them the thick mire into which I sink: I am a poor listener, self-absorbed, and self-reliant. When I look to qualifiers—whether positive or negative—to support me, I will become unstable either in the false footing of good works or the sinking sand of my self-contempt and shame.

Qualifiers and descriptors can display glory or shame. They can be true, partially true, or utterly false. Even the qualifiers that are true of me do not ultimately define me. My successes do not define me. My failures do not

> *Tear man out of his outward circumstances; and what he then is, that only is he.*
> —*Johann Gottfried Seume, 18th century German theologian*

calling + identity

Tami's Story on Identity:
Trusting the Gospel, Living in Ambiguity
by Tami Resch

Black and White

I love color. Paint palettes at Lowe's and Home Depot captivate me. I love bold colors. I love subdued colors. I love black and white.

But gray—gray is different. Looking around my house, I don't find a speck of gray. Gray is not in my home.

But gray is in my heart. By the work of the Spirit, gray is seeping in and adding beautiful shading and depth to the colors of my faith.

Before the gray, and in the second year of our church plant, I lived soothed by the clarity of a black and white life:

- We were Christians. They weren't. (Maybe some of those in other denominations weren't either!)
- We were right. They weren't.
- We were growing kids God's way. They had kids who did not obey the first time.
- We were a small, relational church. They were big, program-driven machines.
- We had God. They needed God.

Black and white living allowed me to feel good about myself as I checked off my daily Christian chore list. Black and white living allowed me to put people in boxes. Boxes make highly efficient storage systems, and I like highly efficient, and I imagined God liked it, too. Black and white living allowed me to stay clean, to avoid getting messy with people whose lives were murky and muddied with sin.

I was clean. Black and white kept me that way.

The Graying

I did not want to go gray.

But it began when I witnessed a fellow black and white friend experience crippling waves of anxiety. My efficient paradigm cracked. She was a Christian. She was "right." She was growing kids God's way. She attended our church! She had God. What was happening here? I was truly frightened.

That week, black and white blurred before my eyes. I began to experience dramatic GI symptoms and feared cancer (a common occurrence with nurses who know too much.) For four days, I lay on the couch unable to be the church planter's wife—the Proverbs 31 woman—who freed up my husband, served my neighbors, homeschooled our kids, and managed an efficient household all with a smile on my Mary Kay® made-up face. I spiraled into depression. It literally felt like a vortex of swirling fears and condemnations I could not escape. *Who was I if not the woman described above?* With no firm place to stand, I panicked and shut down. I desperately wanted my life safely back in that organized and efficient box labeled: *Effective, Efficient Woman Who Serves People*. Not "is served *by* people."

But I couldn't go back to a box that no longer fit anything I was experiencing. Instead, the Spirit of God came and graciously held up a mirror that revealed:

- I did not love people.
- I wanted to be right and found it easy to judge others as wrong.
- I thought my kids should make me look good, building up my reputation.

- I thought a church methodology would make us "the right kind of church."
- I thought being a Christian meant the gospel was no longer necessary for me. I was beyond the gospel and now needed the deeper truths.

The mirror of the Holy Spirit doesn't lie. I became even more undone. I knew how to *do* Christianity. I didn't know how to *be* a Christian whose "rightness" was already won for her by Christ. I couldn't grasp that my truest identity was *in Christ*—not my roles or performance. I became acquainted with a different black and white—the clarity of the gospel: I was more sinful than I could ever conceive… yet more wildly loved than I could imagine! I had lived for years believing that in the gospel, I was 100% forgiven. What I had not believed was that I was 100% righteous by grace through faith. On the cross, an eternal white robe was secured for me because Jesus had become the substitute for my sin. I was clothed. All of my nakedness and shame were covered. I had known this theologically—in my head—yet somehow it had never invaded and changed my heart. My skewed thinking and living made that clear!

This gospel began changing my world and my worldview. Instead of drawing legalistic lines where I could earn points for good behavior, I stopped counting my merits and began resting *in Christ* alone, and began experiencing the gospel freedom of living by grace. Instead of checking off boxes in my head, I began to listen more intently to this God who chose to live in our hearts. Instead of being secure in my orderly lists, I plunged into the ambiguity of risk-taking—otherwise known as living by faith. Instead of seeing the black and white delineations in every decision-making dilemma, I began to see gray. Not the muted, watered down gray of "anything goes," this was an entirely other gray. I can only describe it as a rich shading that gave depth and substance to my flat black and white world. It was everywhere! Had God really intended for me to need him so much in my everyday living and decision-making? Suddenly I had more freedom than a black and white woman was comfortable having. And, again, I was scared!

Ambiguity is Gray

It is easier to go to a consistent extreme than to stay at the center of biblical tension.
—*Robertson McQuilkin*

Black and white is easy: good guys and bad guys; good choices and bad choices; good churches and bad churches.

Gray is, well, gray.

Gray shatters our seeming sense of order and alludes to chaos. Who wants chaos?

Ambiguity is a fun word to say; it is not so fun to have in our lives. It feels a lot like chaos. Kathy Bearce says, "Tolerance for ambiguity is tolerance for the state of things not being clear, a tolerance for things being indefinite, a tolerance for seeming inconsistencies and outright contradictions, a tolerance for mystery." Who wants that?

"Ambiguity is endemic to ministry," says Shari Thomas. If I had known this before seminary, I might have steered my husband into a life of sports broadcasting. But there we were, our second year into a church plant, being transformed by the power of the gospel. Being stripped of our moral self-righteousness attire, feeling naked and exposed as sinners who did not have their act together. Our world didn't just seem gray, it seemed upside-down.

Of course this new gray seeped into ministry. Before, I had always known there was a "right way" to be a church planter's wife and I was striving very hard to do it. My personal construct was that church planters' wives (and therefore I) should:
- Be nice
- Smile
- Always say "yes" to serving others (even if it means saying "no" to family)
- Store, take care of, and transfer any and all gear needed for the church
- Always welcome interruptions (I used a quote to help me with this one: "Ministry is the interruptions!")
- Don't make boundaries—they are selfish ways of keeping people out of your life
- Shop for and provide all decorations for the church
- Oversee hospitality and any women's ministry
- Keep the house clean—always.

- Don't share anything with anyone that makes self or family look bad
- Don't miss any gathering, unless you are really sick or out of town
- Etc. Etc. Etc.

Black and White

My old construct had kept me clear of the gray zones. And it rarely forced me to wrestle with decisions or to have to wait on hearing from the Spirit for direction. Of course this was directly related to identity, because if I followed Christ in freedom, in a way that was contrary to the identity/reputation I had been painstakingly building for so long, I would be undercutting my own worth and value. People might think less of me. I might think less of me.

Gospel gray freedom unraveled my old construct and revealed a world, not only of ambiguity, but also of paradox and mystery.

Did we have to host every newcomer in our home? Could we go out to eat on Sundays? Could someone else do the church laundry and buy the bagels and cream cheese for Sunday morning? I wanted to say, "No, that is my role, I will do it." But was it my role? Did it have to be? Was God nudging me to these tasks, or was it my need to look like the kind, hospitable, and competent pastor's wife that was driving me on? As my belief in my truest identity in Christ grew, I could begin to wrestle with these and many, many other questions. I have found delightful freedom! I have the freedom to say, "Yes." I have the freedom to say, "No." And neither of these answers defines who I am.

Three Types of Ambiguity

Years later, I participated in a groundbreaking research project by Shari Thomas which endeavored to uncover the primary sources of stress and satisfaction among church planting wives. Like many who have read her findings, I was relieved to learn that I was not a head case! Most women experienced the same identity confusion I faced. Many also struggled with the ambiguity of ministry, wanting to organize those gray areas into black and white.

In her research, Shari identified three major forms of

ambiguity endemic to church planting spouses: role ambiguity, emotional ambiguity, and physical ambiguity.

The gray, the fuzzy, and the unclear permeates and creates stress in the church planting journey. But if neither height nor depth can separate us from the love of God in Christ Jesus, what is a little fuzziness?

Roland Wise stated, "Ambiguity is the perfume of God." In my mind, this conjures a picture of sitting in a gray fog calmed by the scent of the presence of my Father who has declared that he will never leave me nor forsake me. *Even in the fog, I am not alone.*

Role Ambiguity

What role(s) will I have in this church plant? Do I choose those roles based on the expectations of others? Of my husband? Based on my gifts? Is the need the call? Is the gift the call? Is the squeaky wheel the call? Is relieving my husband's burdens the call? How and when can these roles change? Will attending to the unanticipated needs of people keep me from expressing my gifts in the manner in which I had always dreamed? Are those dreams one more thing to die to? How will my choices affect church health and growth? *Even in the fog, I am not alone.*

Emotional Ambiguity

How much should I know? Should I help bear my husband's load even if I am not responsible? How do I support him when he is depressed and/or questioning his call? How do I deal with resentment toward those who have hurt me, my husband, my kids, or others in our church? How do I deal with the awkwardness when friends leave our church? Or when they come back? *Even in the fog, I am not alone.*

Physical Ambiguity

Does my home have to be the office, nursery, worship center, and boarding house? Do I have to store and tote church gear? When can I say, "STOP!"? Can I say, "Stop!"? Do my kids have to share all their toys with the children who visit our home? Do my teenagers have to babysit kids during our small group time? Can we leave the cell phone outside our bedroom? *Even in the fog, I am not alone.*

Today, a decade after my world turned upside down (or should I say, right-side up?), I sometimes still long for the good ol' black and white! Gospel gray freedom in Christ can make decision making a time-consuming exercise in which I must examine the motives of my heart (a complicated matter of pride/humility and belief/unbelief.) Gospel gray freedom in Christ challenges me to hold loosely the reputations I strove for years to build. Black and white seemed so much easier when I just thought of myself as right and put everyone else in boxes. May it never be! May God continue to invite each of us into the fog with him! He has given us a firm place to stand. May we hear his voice, smell his perfume, and move out in love where he leads.

IN CHRIST, even in the context of ministry life, *we can go gray* enjoying God's presence, his freedom, and a most colorful life!

calling + identity

TOOLS on CALLING +IDENTITY

calling + identity

Calling: Do I Have One, and What Is It?
by Shari Thomas

Why Use This Tool?
*To encourage discussion between husband and wife on what is often a difficult topic
*To encourage husbands and wives to look at how they can better honor each other's calling
*To consider God's calling for your marriage

When I was conducting research on the effects of church planting on spouses, the question "Do you sense a call from God to partner with your spouse in planting a church?" received such intense, polarizing responses that I realized I had hit on a deep and confusing topic.

Several women responded with variations on this theme: "My calling is to be a wife and mother. It doesn't matter what he does—if he's a computer technician or a church planter, I know what I'm called to."

There were others who had different leanings: "I'm drawn to church planting. I sensed a call to this ministry before we married. We see this as a joint effort although we aren't sure how it will look in our marriage."

Others had callings seemingly unrelated to their spouse: "I'm called to bring physical healing to people. I work in medicine. I'm a physician's assistant and I love what I do. I know my husband is called to pastoral ministry and I will support him just as he supports me as a PA. But church planting is not my calling."

Confusion about calling seems to be a common experience for women inside and outside the church. Some wonder, do they put their dreams on hold when they marry? As Christian women it is a constant challenge to hear conflicting teachings on the same passages of Scripture. We must sift through our own cultural and personal biases, as well as wrestle with conflicting views held within our denomination.

Basic Assumptions We Wish To Name

Christian Marriage: Christian marriage is meant to mirror the relationship of the Trinity (unity and diversity). As couples we want to ask: What do we want to be about in this world? How do we, as a couple, want to shape order out of chaos? Yes, we are two unique individuals joining together to become one. But how is our one-fleshedness going to serve a purpose greater than just ourselves?

Our marriage commitment clearly takes precedence over any dedication to vocation or personal happiness. In other words, marriage will impact how we live out our calling. If one spouse is convinced of his or her calling and the other is unsure as to how to fit into that calling, this does not give the confident spouse permission to override the other when life decisions are being made. Nor does it give the uncertain spouse permission to avoid the conversation.

Vocation: Biblical Christianity does not distinguish between the secular and sacred. Whatever we do, if we do it by faith and to the glory of God, it carries equal value and importance in God's eyes and should in our eyes as well. Abraham Kuyper said, "There is not one square inch of the entire creation about which Jesus Christ does not cry out, 'This is mine! This belongs to me!'" All callings are sacred. We should not honor one calling above another. In marriage, when the callings of both spouses are not recognized as equally important, often one person's job becomes more valued and important than the other's. Which partner thinks he or she deserves more sleep?

calling + identity

Has a right to less household chores? Is entitled to more training in their field? This sense of rights not only has devastating effects on the partner's identity but also destroys relationship in the marriage and family.

Before my husband and I married, we were both aware of what we thought was a calling. When we came to the decision that church planting in other countries was the best way to join our "callings" we thought we were off to a good start. We verbally stated that we believed there was no division between the sacred and secular, yet we quickly saw that the way we lived belied a different commitment—the one we truly believed. We highly prized our study, preparation, and teaching time, and each of us competed for who would get the most. We each longed for the other to take over the chores of survival so we could do what was really important. Along with a multitude of underlying issues, we were placing a higher value on the perceived *sacred* vocation.

It has taken us years to understand the components of calling as they relate to our identity, purpose, meaning, and naming. And we still wrestle with what it means in our marriage. Yet, as we continue to live in the reality of our identity in Christ, we have come closer to discovering our true meaning and purpose. When we look back on the early years of our marriage and the specific call to church planting, we see that we allowed that call to supersede God's calling us to himself. We were so fixated—as so many are in intense ministries—on the specific call that we became blinded to the overarching call. So of course this affected us, especially in our roles in the home. While we both verbally affirmed the other in what we saw as a specific calling, we were not living as one, with a joint purpose, a joint call.

The question we needed to wrestle with was, how and where could we best live out our joint calling? And how would we join together to make this happen, especially in the practical areas of life?

For us it has meant laying down certain dreams and aspirations—mine at some stages of our life, and John's at others. For both of us it has meant trusting God for our dreams in his time frame, and not ours. It has meant taking big risks. It has involved giving up opportunities when prospects seemed like a fit for one, but not the other. It has also meant taking opportunities that we believed fit with God's call when we didn't see the exact match for both of us. What we have come to firmly agree upon, however, is that God doesn't call just one of us and a call to 'the ministry' is not somehow higher than other callings.

General Calling: Our Identity and Meaning

Each person is formed by the Creator to know him and to be known deeply by him whether they recognize him or not. This is the longing of every human soul, giving us our identity and our meaning. Being known by our Creator will be an exclusive knowing because each of us is a unique individual. God calling me to himself is an intimate, holy knowing. Not only does he know me as no one else does, I know him as no one else does. This is not a proud statement, but one of the reasons why community is so important—together we see God in ways we cannot see him when we are alone.

The more I come to know him, the more I come to know my purpose for existing. I will want to live for his glory. I will want to join Christ in seeing redemption come to my arena of influence. And I will see aspects of being made in the image of God and where, as a female, my voice is uniquely needed.

While knowing our specific calling is important, we can still live for God's glory even when we are confused about what this calling may be. All of us have experienced those fear-filled nights when we roll over in bed and exclaim, "Did we just make the biggest mistake of our life?" "Is God really in this? Did he lead us here?" Yet, our choices are not what define us! Sure, they affect us, but our choices are not our identity. Being in relationship with the living Trinity is where life exists, not in our decision-making ability. Of course how we live will flow out of being known by him and thus profoundly affect our life choices. Yet, we can live by faith, and to his glory, putting our hope in the One who will one day redeem all things—even our choices.

Because of the Fall, we will struggle to flesh out our calling as a couple. Sadly, more often than not, only one person in the marriage is encouraged to explore their calling—especially if that person senses a call to ministry. Something beautiful is lost, though, if a couple doesn't explore what their joint call may look like; or what a call to ministry will look like for both of them; or what each gives and gives up in order to live out their joint calling. Frankly, it's much easier to refuse to wrestle with the issue at all. But don't we want to live out our marriages as God intended?

Psychologist and author Diane Langberg describes marriage as a duet. At times one or the other voice carries the melody. Or one voice may be silent for a time and we hear a solo within the duet. Yet in a duet, both voices are needed. The same applies to calling in our marriages. If one voice overpowers the other, or if one person's calling is seen as the more important one, something very needed and intended by God is lost.

When we try to overpower the other's voice, we are giving into the Fall. We are fighting to rule and subdue one another, each building our own kingdom rather than building God's kingdom together through our one-fleshed marriage. When we are yielding to Christ, he gives us the ability and power to recognize and name our own self-focused kingdom-building tendency. That same power then draws our lives together without fear of losing our individual voices, and helps us to participate fully in the new duet that God calls us to sing.

Among other things, being created in the image of God means that we are created to be interdependent. Why? Because God is a "we" and not an "I." Marriage is modeled after the Trinity. If in marriage only one person's goals are being accomplished, doesn't that marriage model an "I" and not a "we?" Abuse of power becomes a danger. This can lead us to forget that the essence of being a "helper" (Gen. 2:18) is to bring components to the marriage, to the church, and to our work that would not be there without us. Recognizing that the image of God is reflected in both sexes means we need the input of both. We greatly hamstring our lives and our work when we do the easy thing and let one sex make all the decisions, whether it's in the home, workplace, or the church. As male and female, we are in desperate need of one another in all aspects of our lives.

Women have confided to me that years before a ministry failed, they recognized that their calling as a couple would best be used in a context other than church planting or the pastorate. But under the guise of submission they never said anything to their husbands. After church planting assessments, I have seen wives cry tears of joy when they receive recommendations to pursue ministry other than church planting. Fear had kept them from speaking truthfully with their spouse about what they believed would be a good fit. In the name of submission some wives may be willing to go anywhere to do anything. However, by not bringing their unique perspective and voice, are they neglecting their God-given responsibility?

When we follow our calling, risk will almost always be involved. Likewise, submission and surrender involve risk and they model Jesus' way of servanthood. By the very nature of the word, surrender implies that there is first a struggle. If there is no struggle or conflict in our marriage, or in our relationship with God and others, it is questionable if we have ever engaged in a real relationship in the first place. True submission comes only after wrestling.

In the context of calling, some Christian circles believe marriage and motherhood to be the only legitimate calling for a woman. However, this view diminishes the meaning of the word *calling* as it implies that calling is small enough to fit into one role rather than to transcend many roles. This view has been devastating for women who are not married, can't have children, or know their callings are larger than one role. Likewise, the church and the advancement of the kingdom is crippled. Just as men and women are needed to mirror the Godhead when raising a family, so both are needed in the church and the broader community. This is not to say that there aren't occasions when we work only with women or men. But if we are never influenced by the other gender, we need to make changes. The other gender shows us aspects of God's image we don't see in ourselves or in our gender as a whole.

Ephesians 5 paints a beautiful picture of mutual sacrifice and submission. If the husband is truly giving up his life for his wife (that is, he is loving her), then he is submitting his needs for her best. If the wife is submitting to her husband, then she is sacrificing herself for him. Without this posture for both, there isn't hope for marriage to mirror the Godhead. Both should be sacrificing for the other with the will of God in mind. When one or the other fails to follow this model, things get ugly. And frankly, this is where most of us live our daily lives. Rather than giving ourselves for the other (whether in sacrifice or submission), we would rather point out how our spouse is failing at their part of the duet. Ephesians 5 truly calls both partners to radical repentance, to sacrifice, and to submission for God's purposes—not our own—so that the unique melodies, harmonies, and tempos of our marriage can be performed before a world that desperately needs to see how refreshingly different, healthy, and beautiful a Christian marriage can be. If this is true, are we listening to one another to see how both voices blend to form a mutual call?

When we first had family devotions with our young children, John led them. It was disastrous. Does this mean we shouldn't have them? No. But because of our unique giftings, I was able to love my husband and kids well by creating devotions that were kid friendly. When our kids became older, I couldn't hold a candle to my husband's ability to discuss deep philosophical issues with them and their friends. So, of course, I yielded to him.

Understanding how our general calling influences our roles in marriage is no easy task. Yet, as we continue to imagine how it could be and how it is meant to be—knowing that God delights to rescue us—true biblical hope will surface, showing us how God wants us to live, and giving us glimpses of redemption, not just for the future, but for our marriages now!

With a deeper understanding of Christ's love for us, we can live boldly even when we are confused and uncertain about the particulars. Okay, maybe that doesn't sound all that reassuring! But if we are really known and loved by God, then we can have the freedom to stay in a difficult marriage. We can have the freedom to risk and make really big mistakes! Yes, we can even risk planting a church. Or we can risk telling our spouses we don't think planting a church is the right fit for us. We have the freedom to fail, to make mistakes, and also to succeed! Why? Because—finally—what we are living for and what we are basing our worth on isn't about succeeding in a task or even in a relationship. God isn't basing his acceptance of us on what we do or the choices we make, so why do we? Now, that is freeing!

Specific Call (Our Purpose and Naming)

The more we come to know the One who has called us, the more courage we have to look at our own stories and explore our individual purpose and naming. While our general calling doesn't change, it will probably express itself differently—sometimes radically so—from one season of life to the next. As we take risks, venture forward, and increasingly know the One who calls us (as well as the spouse who loves us), we come closer to knowing our purpose—the reason each of us is here on planet Earth at this particular moment in time and history.

But where do we begin in this process? A model used in church planting assessment looks at three areas of our lives: passion, ability (gifts), and opportunity.

Passion:

When in your life have you inwardly thought, "I was made for this!" What were you doing when you thought this? Look at your childhood, adolescence, and adulthood. Writing down these examples is usually the best way to examine this. What is it about each of these experiences that made you come alive? What do these experiences have in common and where are they unique? Where have you seen your passions used for the glory of God and the good of others?

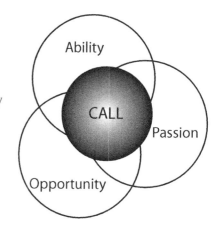

Don't discount what seems trivial. You may have experienced ridicule over areas of passion and in turn buried them deep. If this is true of your story, you may want to invite close friends to help you unpack more deeply.

Ability:

What are your resources, gifts, and talents? What may be unique to you that you haven't considered? How about your physical appearance, intelligence, personality, race, or the languages you speak? Have your abilities been affirmed by others? If you are unsure, get input from those who will be honest with you. What spiritual gifts have been recognized and affirmed? Have you had a chance to develop them? If not, what is stopping you? If you have gifts of teaching, leadership, or hospitality and you are caring for young children, how could these gifts still be used in your current stage of life? Is there a way they could be creatively expressed while your children are young?

Opportunity:

What life events have shaped and defined you? What experiences make you furious, sad, or propel you to stand up and fight? Which ones call out deep compassion? What experiences give you unique insight or ability? Your own fearful and mistaken reactions to the pain of life, as well as the times when love and redemption have rescued you, need to be remembered, honored, and reflected upon. As you come to see the Redeemer's hand in leading you through these events, a unique life purpose begins to emerge and you find you can and want to join with Christ to take back terrain ravaged by forces of evil. Do you have an idea of a specific place or setting where you want to join him to bring his light and justice to the world? Begin to pray for a divine opportunity to open to you. You may have the passion and the ability for a specific ministry but not the opportunity. Or you may have the ability and the opportunity but not the passion. In either case, pray for God to provide what is lacking. It would be wise, however, to not proceed without all three.

Spend some time looking at and thinking about the circles on your own and then as a couple.

As you look at different opportunities, you might want to go back to these three circles and ask the following questions to investigate if the opportunity presented is actually best for both of you, for your family, and if it is appropriate for your current season of life.

Passion:

Do you have a passion for this type of ministry? At this time in your life, do you feel that the option before you is the best way to express your calling? Do you sense this as a desire from God? Could you do something else and be satisfied?

                                                                           calling + identity

Ability:

Do you have the abilities needed for this ministry? Do you have a realistic idea of the abilities this ministry requires? Are both you and your spouse clear about what these are? Have these been affirmed by church leaders and others?

Opportunity:

Is there an opportunity that fits both you and your spouse? Are you in agreement on this? Do you and your spouse realize the implications of this ministry and believe that this opportunity is suited for both of you? One of you may be accepting a ministry offer which implies a change for the entire family; do you both see how this ministry is a place where you can each fit? Is it in a part of the world where both your callings can best be used? While asking these questions, it is important to remember that we live in a fallen world. We rarely find the perfect fit! Your answers to these questions may lead you to believe the opportunity before you is not the best fit for both of you. Yet, taking all things into consideration, one spouse may decide to give up what seems best for him or her as the opportunity before you as a couple seems best for the other spouse and ultimately God's kingdom at this stage of your lives.

RECENTLY JOHN AND I WERE FACING a major life decision. This encouraged us to take a deeper look at our callings. After we had rehearsed our passions, abilities, and the opportunities before us, we began to make lists of pros and cons for various options. We also began to pray about locations and jobs where both of us felt a right fit. We were at a stage in life where we did not have the limitations that would keep us from moving or traveling. It all sounded pretty great.

But I felt pressured for reasons I couldn't identify. I felt selfish if I kept John from taking a job others thought was ideal for him but might not be a good fit for me.

As a result, we invited some close friends to help us unpack our own stories and tell us what they really saw. I also began exploring my longings and not just acquiescing when I felt my longings were selfish. While I knew I loved beauty and color, I was surprised how tied I felt to my earthly possessions. But rather than quickly dismissing this as sin, I wanted to discover what was underneath the deep ties to my home and especially my new red kitchen that I loved. As I left my kitchen on the list of my top passions, I began to realize that I loved creating beautiful spaces where others were invited in to share their stories and where we could journey together. My kitchen had been a big part of that passion. Our kitchen had also been the place where our kids would bring their friends, and where I felt our outward-focused ministry best interfaced with our family.

My husband and our friends were wise to not dismiss this as 'materialistic' or 'unspiritual.' I began to realize that in the past, well-meaning Christians had convinced me that these longings were, if not wrong, then at least unimportant and 'worldly.' In my experience, an over-emphasis had wrongly been placed on Bible studies, prayer meetings, and church activities that seemed to be more spiritual than communing over food and drink. I had buried many of my passions to the point that I almost didn't even know what they were. As I was able to think through this, I realized that underneath the "hanging on" to my new kitchen was a glorious desire. Really, I was fighting for who God had made me to be. It wasn't about letting go of what I loved, but coming to agree with God. Eventually I came to have hope that I could watch how God might provide another space where this passion could be expressed if indeed we moved. I was able to ask God to release me—not from my desire for beauty—but from my desire to be in control of where I got that beauty and how I would be able to use it.

In the battle for my kitchen, we began to realize there was another, even deeper issue. Many of our past decisions had been based on what was best for the ministry. Again this goes back to my story and my life experience where it was modeled that everything needed to be sacrificed for the sake of the ministry. As John saw how this impacted me, he also began to see how our own decision-making process mirrored much of my upbringing. I watched as my husband went down a path of giving himself up for me and seeking what would ultimately be best for our marriage. He came to a firm conviction that in marriage, two people gifted, called, and created in God's image are joined together and that both their callings are equally valid and valued. He was not going to use the terms "ministry" or "God's call" as a trump card to do what he wanted and misuse headship and submission verses as proof texts that this was God's will for us.

In our marriage story, we have both fallen into the temptation of believing that John's calling trumps my calling; that if a decision is made in favor of the man and for ministry purposes then it must be more godly; that as a man he is somehow more gifted, more called, and therefore needs to be listened to more. We both began to see that though we may say we are all gifted and called, the actions of the church (and this varies radically between denominations and cultures!) often imply that only one gender and only one type of gifting is needed to do kingdom work. While few have used those literal words, over time we found we had come to accept this as the norm. We both began to enter into a season of repentance. My repentance took the form of seeing how I had used this thinking as a cop-out when I didn't feel like engaging in the fight anymore. It was perfectly acceptable in my circles to not work outside the home and to not be too involved in church ministry. I could easily say "you hired my husband, not me" and everyone would quickly be silenced. I could use the family and kids as my trump card and be praised for being a wise and godly woman, focusing my time where it should be. And, honestly, this was easier than bucking the system. I have tons of fun with my kids. Why should I go to all the work of teaching or preparing a seminar if others were going to question me about it? I could much more easily stay at home to relax or have fun.

In John's world, he appeared to be quite the fool to those who were moving ahead in their ministry careers. It looked like he was committing career suicide to take into consideration where my calling might best be lived out. Not only that, he often received counsel (from others who didn't know our marriage story) 'to just be a man and lead his wife.' But as John loved me well, I began to see that my husband was really giving himself up for me as Christ gave himself up for the church. He was living out Ephesians 5 with his hope in God, not in figuring out the next career move. John's repentance became a crucial key for me to understand God's love for me and who I am, and not for what I do for God. Yes, Christ has sacrificed everything for me. But it took John sacrificing his desires in order to win me, not just to himself, but also to the work Christ was calling us to,

We both began to see how the Author of history was writing our story into his and giving us an opportunity that uniquely fit us both. So what happened? To my surprise, God changed my heart. He began to give me hope that the ministry opportunity set before us was indeed a great opportunity for both of us to work out our calling. So, with hope (and fear and trepidation) we did what I thought I'd not be able to do again—pack up our stuff, leave our home and friends, and start over in a new city. And what joy we have found following Christ and mutually submitting to and hanging onto each other as we've taken these new steps to follow our call. It hasn't been perfect, or without hardship, but we've done it together and we can both testify: it's been a great walk forward.

calling + identity

Calling: Questions for Ministry Couples
by Shari Thomas

Why Use This Tool?
- to help couples explore their life calling
- to provide discussion questions to see if church planting fits with their life calling

1. Questions concerning your life call

Think through the decades of your life and ask God to bring significant experiences to mind where you felt, "I was made for this!"

Ask yourself: What do these experiences have in common? What talents or abilities was I using? What passions were demonstrated? How did others benefit and did they affirm this?

Age or Decade	Experience	Commonalities	Talent Exhibited	Passion Demonstrated	Affirmation from Others

Are common themes emerging?

2. Use the same questions for your spouse

Thinking through the decades of his/her life, ask God to bring significant experiences to mind where you thought, "He/She was made for this!"

Ask yourself: What do these experiences have in common? What talents or abilities was he/she using? What passions were demonstrated? How did others benefit and did they affirm this?

Age or Decade	Experience	Commonalities	Talent Exhibited	Passion Demonstrated	Affirmation from Others

Are common themes emerging?

Where does your spouse need your help in order to more fully express God's call on his/her life?

Where do you sense how you as a unique individual want to and could join Christ in bringing his kingdom more fully to this world?

How might you as a couple work better together than you do apart in order to more fully join Christ in bringing his kingdom to this world?

Continue to pray and ask the Spirit to guide you to resources and experiences that can help clarify God's calling on your lives.

3. Questions to discuss together

- Have both of you identified the competencies for church planting in yourselves, and do knowledgeable others affirm these in you?

- Do you have a consuming passion to see people brought to faith?

- Do you sense a divine intersection of both your life stories, your gifting, and the world's need in creating an opportunity that uniquely fits you both?

- Do you possess a growing belief in and a passion for God to use you, broken yet loved by Christ, to build his church?

4. Prayerfully ask and answer these questions on your own. Then consider discussing them together.
Let's be honest here; some of these questions may bring up old arguments. Would you consider discussing these questions with your spouse and a third party? Commit to asking for and honoring your spouse's answers.

- Do you desire to honor your spouse? Do you feel your spouse desires to honor you?

- Do you feel that either of you are so committed to pursuing your dreams that you have put God's stamp of approval on them by saying they are 'God's call'?

- As you look at possible ministry calls, have you invited your community (those who know you, as well as your church leaders) to speak honestly into your lives as to whether they think this is a right fit for both of you?

- Are you willing to follow their advice even if you disagree with it? Are you demanding that your spouse comply with what you are wanting?

- Do you believe that if God is leading one of you in a certain direction, and the other is not ready, that you can wait on God to bring your spouse along?

- Are you giving your spouse so much input about the decision that he/she is unable to listen for God?

- Are you using 'submission' or are you 'just being a good listener' as an excuse to not have to speak honestly if you disagree with your spouse?

- Are you using 'headship' or are you 'only giving my opinion' as an excuse to not listen to your spouse if he/she disagrees with you?

Answers to Often Asked Questions

Why can't church planting have less of an impact on the family unit?
Embracing a calling affects the whole family. A couple impacting their world through business may move to another country and in so doing will take the whole family. Their calling will affect their children and each other.

 calling + identity

Likewise, church planting affects the whole family. However, unlike the business world where there is a separate work space and community, in church planting, the community is the same for the planter as well as for the spouse and the children. Often the work space is an office in the couple's home or bedroom. This does not have to negatively impact the family, but there are implications for the entire family.

Can the spouse have a distinct career while planting a church?

If the ministry spouse is working in a career with typical work hours, she will usually have flexible time on weekends and nights just when the minister does not. Two intense careers will mean the couple will not have sufficient time to build their relationship.

A guideline from church planter/minister Tim Keller is that the church-planting spouse should be as involved and as competent as the most involved lay people and lay leaders in the church. Look at the most active deaconesses, small group coordinators, and other unpaid leaders. How many hours do they put in and how competent are they? The ministry spouse should be as active and competent as they. Of course the spouse can be more competent or more active, but she must at least be this committed.

Why?

Because the minister, spouse, and family will be spending time and energy and love on the church together. They will grow in their unity as a couple. Much of their social time will be spent in this way. If the spouse is largely uninvolved, say, only attending corporate worship, the couple will not be seeing enough of each other to maintain an intimate and healthy marriage.

The minister's spiritual credibility is also enhanced by the spouse's involvement. The church-planting spouse who is not passionate for the church's ministry will raise legitimate questions in many minds. If the church planter is asking the core group for commitment and involvement, then why wouldn't the planter's spouse be asked, also?

Can the spouse be involved in a high-powered intense job during the planting years?

Probably not. The couple will be too drained by two intense careers and have nothing left over for the family or the church.

Does this mean the spouse should not work outside of the home and church?

Absolutely not. Many spouses, especially in high-cost cities, have to work in order to allow the family to live where they are planting. Since the planter's hours are flexible during typical work week hours, this allows the planter time during the day with family that other professions do not allow. An option could be for the spouse to take a non-high-powered job during the planting years, one that allows flexibility so the couple can still have time to build into their marriage and the church.

Os Guinness On Calling: Book Review and A Chat

Why Use This Tool?
- To address our longing for purpose
- To articulate common fears regarding calling

Book Review: *The Call* by Os Guinness
by David W. Virtue

The Call: Finding and Fulfilling the Central Purpose of Your Life
by Os Guinness

"No book has burned within me longer or more fiercely than this one. The truth of calling has been as important to me in my journey of faith as any truth of the gospel of Jesus," writes Os Guinness at the start of his latest book, *The Call: Finding and Fulfilling the Central Purpose of Your Life*.

"Our passion," writes the China-born, Oxford-educated author, "is to know that we are fulfilling the purpose for which we are here on earth. All other standards of success—wealth, power, position, friendships—grow hollow if we do not satisfy this deepest longing." As Walker Percy wrote, "You can get all As and still flunk life."

Guinness writes that the core of our existence is the truth that God calls us to himself so decisively that everything we are, do, and have is invested with a special devotion, dynamism, and direction lived out as a response to his summons and service. Guiness unpacks four strands in the biblical notion of calling.

In the Old Testament, the Hebrew word translated "call" usually has the same meaning as our English word. Humans call to each other, to God, and to animals.

To call means to name, and to name means to call into being or to make. "God called the light 'day' and the darkness he called 'night.'" God calls Israel, thereby creating, naming, and constituting his people Israel.

In the New Testament, call is almost synonymous with salvation—God's calling people to himself as followers of Christ.

Calling also has a vital extended meaning in the New Testament. Jesus calls his followers to tasks: to peace, fellowship, suffering, service, and eternal life. But deeper than these is the call to discipleship.

Guinness makes a distinction between primary and secondary calling. "Our primary calling as followers of Christ is by him, to him, and for him. Our secondary calling, considering who God is as sovereign, is that everyone, everywhere, and in everything should think, speak, live, and act entirely for him." That is, our existence and work should be centered on him.

Guiness goes on to lay out the two grand distortions —Protestant and Catholic—that have crippled the truth of calling. The Catholic distortion, he says, elevates the spiritual at the expense of the secular. He traces this, the majority position in the Catholic tradition, back to Eusebius, who argued that Christ gave "two ways of life" to his church—"perfect" and "permitted." The perfect life is spiritual, dedicated to contemplation and reserved for

141

calling + identity

priests and the religious; the permitted life is secular, and open to tasks such as soldiering, governing, farming, trading, and raising families. It is higher vs. lower, sacred vs. secular, contemplation vs. action. Guinness says this view perversely narrows biblical teaching on calling to exclude most Christians.

It took Martin Luther's book, *The Babylonian Captivity of the Church*, to explode this view. Writing as an Augustinian monk, he recommended the abolition of all orders and abstinence from all vows, contending that the contemplative life has no warrant in the Scriptures, and reinforces hypocrisy and arrogance. The recovery of the holistic understanding of calling, Guinness contends, was dramatic for Luther. Bishop Thomas Bacon wrote, "Our Saviour Christ was a carpenter. His apostles were fishermen. St. Paul was a tent-maker." Abraham Kuyper, the great Dutch prime minister, once said: "There is not one square inch of the entire creation about which Jesus Christ does not cry out, 'This is mine! This belongs to me!'"

Guinness then faces the Protestant distortion, described as a secular form of dualism that grew out of Puritan thinking. This distortion elevates the secular at the expense of the spiritual, and is made more extreme by the pressure of the modern world. Vocation becomes another word for work, which "completely betrays the purpose of calling." The triumph of secondary callings over the primary calling meant that work was made sacred. Whereas the Bible is realistic about work, seeing it after the Fall as both creative and cursed, the late 19th and early 20th centuries lost the balance.

Guinness argues that the way back from the Protestant distortion is to debunk the notion of calling without a Caller, and to restore the priority of the primary calling. That involves restoring the worship that is its setting, and the dedication to Jesus that is its heart. We are not primarily called to do something or to go somewhere; we are called to Someone. We are not called first to special work, but to God. Guinness writes that God normally calls us along the line of our giftedness, but the purpose of giftedness is stewardship and service, not selfishness.

Guinness distinguishes between a later, special calling and our original, ordinary calling. Selfishness prefers the first, but stewardship respects both. A special calling refers to those tasks and mission laid on individuals through a particular supernatural communication from God. Ordinary calling, on the other hand, is the believer's sense of life-purpose and life-task in response to God's primary call, "follow me," even when there is no specific secondary calling from God. The importance of not equating calling with jobs becomes clearer when one becomes unemployed or retires, is depressed, or is found to be terminally ill. We may at times be unemployed, but no one ever becomes uncalled.

"Perhaps," Guinness concludes, "you are frustrated by the gap that still remains between your vision and your accomplishment. Or you may be depressed by the pages of your life that are blotched with compromises, failures, betrayals, and sin . . . But make no judgments and draw no conclusions until the scaffolding of history is stripped away and you see what it means for God to have had his say and made you what you are called to be." *The Call* is not only a welcome but a needed volume for any Christian's library. No one has written so perceptively and honestly about a theme that has plagued many of us for such a long time.

By David W. Virtue; virtueonline.org. Used by Permission of the author.

A Chat with Os Guinness

We recommend reading and discussing this article with your coach and/or spouse. Mark the paragraphs that especially strike you or that you want to explore further. Write a paragraph describing what you believe about calling—specifically, your calling. Is there an area (or areas) in your life you believe you need to change in order to more fully live out your calling?

Q: I'd like to have that sense of devotion and dynamism that you include in your definition of calling. But mostly I feel like I'm just trying to survive as a Christian and not be dominated by sin. I know I'm called to follow Christ and I'm doing that. How can a clearer sense of calling help me live a more dynamic Christian life?

Dr. Guinness: One of the characteristics of a human being is living with a sense of purpose, and the trouble with many people is that they take their sense of purpose from people and events and circumstances around them. But just as Archimedes looked for a leverage point from which to change the world, the great sense of calling is that it comes outside of the world, outside of ourselves. So if we start every day by asking how we are living for the Lord, we have something to give us the highest and deepest sense of purpose.

Q: If someone doesn't have any spiritual interest, but still believes that life should have meaning and purpose and is searching for that purpose, what would you say to him?

Dr. Guinness: There are three main families of faiths that attempt to give an answer. The desire for individual purpose is almost universal. There are billions of people born before us and billions will follow us. And billions are alive at the same time as us. And yet we each have a unique sense of destiny. Is it real? Or is it only a conceit and we are only dust in the wind? There are three big answers in the modern world. One is the eastern answer—Hinduism, Buddhism, and the New Age. And put simply, it says just forget it. The desire to have purpose is part of the fact that we are caught in the world of illusion. The second family of faith is the secularists. Its answer is yes, create your own meaning yourself. In other words, meaning is not there to be discovered. It is there for each one of us to create ourselves. And the third big family is Judaism and Christianity. It says that the deepest answer is to rise and answer the call of the God that created us. And there is no question that that third answer, by far, is the deepest answer in history. So I would say one of the big things about calling is that it is the very deepest answer to human longing, purpose, and fulfillment.

Q: You stated that there is no life without a Caller. What if a godless person feels called to sacrifice for a cause, such as the environment? She feels very fulfilled and passionate that she is doing something very valuable.

Dr. Guinness: I said in my book that there is no calling without a Caller. In other words, can there be any true meaning in that without God? The word calling has come out of the Bible and has been taken over by our modern, secular society and used without any real strong sense of purpose and passion. I guess another way to ask the question is, "Can God call an unbeliever to do His will?" But when secular people use the word calling, it is like a cut flower. They've borrowed the meaning but they have cut off the root. And that's really cheating. The word calling only comes into its own with depth and richness if there is a personal God who calls. The secular people have used the word, but they really don't have a right to it.

God can definitely call unbelievers. And the strongest biblical example of that is the way God called Cyrus, the pagan king, to be his servant and work on behalf of the Jews. And obviously, the reason is that the Creator can call his creatures even if the creatures don't acknowledge him. But calling comes into its own in the idea of relationship. When creatures come to know their Creator as they do in Jesus, the idea of calling is rooted in a deeply

calling + identity

intimate relationship. We not only follow our Caller, we follow knowing we love Him. I think even if human beings don't even acknowledge God or know God, they are still made in His image. So when they exercise the gifts that God has given them, there is tremendous satisfaction to them as well as service to others. But they don't have a higher fulfillment and joy of doing it for Him when they don't know Him.

Q: I'm a parent of teenagers. How can I help them in the process of discovering their call?

Dr. Guinness: That's a wonderful question. Because much of the confusion about calling comes from the fact that people aren't taught about it at the right age. For example, mid-life crisis comes when people come from a career in which they don't fit. And they would have been saved from the crisis if they had a sense of calling before they started their career. So the ideal time to teach a person about a sense of calling is between the ages of 12 and 25. I think it begins with parents pulling out of their children a sense of their unique individuality. For instance, from the age of 12, we began to encourage and affirm all the individual and unique gifts that my son has. And that's partly a matter of Christian teaching from the Bible, and partly a matter of affirmation and encouragement. And we stressed to him many, many times that he doesn't have to be like his mother and me. And so the ideal age for teaching and encouragement is before they go to college and face the challenge of choosing a career. So I think parents are the principal encouragers of calling. Although when parents don't do it, it can be done by a coach or youth minister or someone like that.

Q: I am happy as a process engineer but I often have the thought that I am not putting my life to best use for God. I just can't see how most of what I'm doing every day builds the kingdom of God. Do I need to consider a special calling?

Dr. Guinness: Your question touches the very heart problem of calling. Ever since the first century and a theologian called Eusbius, we've had this heretical idea that the spiritual is higher than the secular, and full-time ministry more valuable than secular work. And this is almost the universal, catholic position—a very common Protestant position. In contrast, Martin Luther stresses that calling applies to everyone, everywhere in everything. In other words, there is no higher or lower; there is no sacred or secular; there is no full-time or part-time. If you do what you do by faith, to the glory of God as a calling, it is just as valuable as being a minister or missionary. So I would say beware of the seminary trap that the idea of the spiritual is higher than the secular. On the other hand, always remember that your job—your paid job—is not necessarily the heart of your calling. For example, the famous French Christian lawyer, Jacques Ellul, used to say that the heart of his calling was not being a famous lawyer and professor. It was his work in his free time among the delinquent boys of Bordeaux.

Q: Did Jacques Ellul have a sense of frustration?

Dr. Guinness: Not at all, it was almost like Paul's. In other words, the paid work made him free to pursue his calling, which was unpaid.

Q: How does understanding my calling help me answer the question, "Who am I?"

Dr. Guinness: That's a very deep question. Because three deep questions come together. One is the search for meaning. One is the search for purpose. And the third is the search for identity. The biblical faith provides us with the answer to meaning. Calling provides the answer to purpose which is obviously very close to identity. Because God not only calls us to do something, he names us and therefore calls out our identity. It's important to remember that it would be an insult to define someone's identity in a sentence. It's far too intimate and deep. The same is true for calling. Sometimes we can talk about things we do. But the deepest part of it is God calling us out. That is our identity.

Q: Will God call me to do something I'm not gifted for or feel totally inadequate to accomplish?

Dr. Guinness: God usually calls us to employ the gifts that he has given us. And that's the clear teaching of Jesus, as shown in the parable of the talents and the pounds in Matthew. On the other hand, God sometimes—and this is his extraordinary call—calls us from what is typical and natural to something special. For example, Amos, who was a farmer, was called to be a prophet because the prophets of his time were so decadent and corrupt. But typically God calls us along the line of the gifts he has given us. The Puritans used to teach the great danger of focusing on the giftedness and forgetting the Giver. So we need to remember that if we are using God's gifts to us, we always have to be grateful to the Giver and use his gifts in clear dependence on him.

The mark of the great ventures we do for the Lord is that they are so much beyond us that they would never succeed without him. So the gifts come from him and the success depends absolutely on him. So everything we do, we do by faith.

Q: What is the place of career counseling and testing in determining God's call?

Dr. Guinness: I think there is a place, but a lower place, for career counseling. In other words, we shouldn't make the calling so spiritual that it doesn't touch the world. I would recommend the value not of things like Myers-Briggs, which is psychological testing, but of the best discernment of giftedness and aptitude. But the danger is if we focus on secular discernment of gifts, we lose touch with the Giver, the Caller, who is the source of the gifts and the power of the gifts. A superb book is Ralph Mattson's *The Truth About You*, which is published by Ten-Speed Press. Ralph is a Christian, but the publisher is secular. And it is all about how you discover your motivated abilities. There is a danger in some of the Christian gifts of discernment tests around today. Much of the Christian testing will only help you to discover your spiritual gifts, then they quickly put you to work in their churches. Whereas what we really need to discover is our natural as well as our spiritual gifts. And most of our gifts will be used in the world, not just in the church.

Q: I want to follow God and I want to feel like my life is special, but I don't want to be a hero. Everyone I have looked up to has disappointed me. I know if I am put on a pedestal I will fall and I don't want to disappoint others. I feel stuck between wanting to know my calling and afraid I can't live up to it. What should I do?

Dr. Guinness: That's a very deep question. Part of following God's call includes the Christian virtue of honesty and humility, so it would be wrong to avoid rising to God's highest just because we know we will trip up, just as the man in Jesus' story hid his talents in the napkin in the ground because of his view of the master. If we are a model to younger believers, part of our example is being honest about our failing. The calling should never be a matter of hypocrisy or pretense. And I would just challenge you to rise to the full height that God is calling you to rise to.

Q: I can relate to what you said about having too many choices. I feel paralyzed. I don't know which job to choose. I have several career options and I want God to make clear which I should choose, but He is silent. So am I really free to pick the job that seems best to me? I would feel better if there was some sense of divine confirmation.

Dr. Guinness: It is very important not to confuse calling with guidance. We need to remember the entrepreneurial part of calling. In the parable of the talents and pounds, the master never told them what to do. There was no micromanagement. They were simply given gifts, talents, and praised or blamed at the end according to what they

calling + identity

had done. When we confuse calling with guidance, we get paralyzed wondering if this is truly God's will and then we do nothing. Whereas calling is a venture and there is always risk. So I would not wait until you hear "it" from the Lord, but rather weigh up the talents of gifts and opportunities and figure out how best you can add fruit or value to the world. And recognize that there is always a process of trial and error.

Q: How realistic do you think it is for a student or someone right out of college to have a deep sense of God's calling?

Dr. Guinness: Because calling is so badly taught today and there is so much ignorance and confusion, it is a more lengthy process to discover it now than in the past. I came to Christ when I was 18 and it wasn't really until my late 20s when I came across the notion of calling, and even later still began to understand what my calling was. I came to Christ at 18, and at a time in England when if you were really spiritual you became a minister or missionary. My parents were missionaries, so I knew that wasn't my life. Though I went into the ministry, I wasn't ordained. I worked in a church for nine months, and to be honest, I absolutely hated it. I liked the pastor, I was pretty good at the things I did, but it simply wasn't me. It was in a time of very deep frustration that someone introduced me to the idea of biblical calling. And it was an incredible liberation for me. I was invited to consider becoming the minister in the church that Martin Lloyd Jones used to preach in. I sweated it for the whole weekend because I was horrified by the thought. When I had the freedom to say no because I knew it wasn't my calling, I never looked back and I had a tremendous sense of liberation and peace. Part of my calling is as an apologist, though I am always happier in the secular world. And it is a great relief to me to not be stuck in the Christian subculture. Whereas some people are the opposite. Their calling is to direct full-time ministry.

When I came to Christ, the present view of calling was almost absent. I came across it when someone gave me William Perkins' *A Treatise on Calling*. He was described as a Puritan C.S. Lewis. Today it is not very easy to read, but it is incredibly liberating when you understand it. I had to translate it to the 20th century and I've taught on it for nearly 30-odd years.

Q: If you could give any two pieces of advice to a young 20-something, what would it be?

Dr. Guinness: I would line up a number of very simple things in your life. First, be sure you have a deep intimate knowledge of the Lord. Second, develop a rich theology and know why you believe what you believe. Third, think through a very deep Christian world view so you understand the whole of life within the theological perspective. Fourth, think through and pray over your own sense of gifts and calling (so you know what you want). Fifth, cultivate a group of friends who can offer great encouragement and accountability to keep you going for life. And if you line up simple things like this, your life will start to surge forward in usefulness.

I have a new book coming out in September, *Long Journey Home*, on meaning, identity, and purpose. Meaning is the one that answers the other two. It is because of our faith that we know who we are in terms of identity. It is because of faith that we know our purpose in terms of calling.

Calling and identity are very close. In rising to answer the call, that call names us. In fact, George MacDonald argues that only when we see the Caller will we get our name. Because we've become who God called us to be—identity. So obviously if we call to each other by name, the calling, naming, and identity are very, very close. People can't wait around to discover their identity. They will discover their identity in following their calling.

Q: What do you mean by meaning?

Dr. Guinness: Human beings have a deep longing for meaning—meaning and belonging. The search for meaning is the search for making sense of the world. The search for belonging is the search for security in the world. Faith is the deepest answer to both of them. So meaning is that search, that hunt—how to make sense of our world.

What is humanist? What is right? What is wrong?

The postmodern world is characterized by a crisis of meaning. It doesn't fit into a larger whole. And it is only that larger whole that gives you that sense of meaning. Our modern world is very technological. We think of things as mechanisms, a machine assembled by its parts. What do you do with a car? You drive somewhere. The meaning is always the highest framework that makes sense of the whole. You go from the origin of the universe to the prospects of the human race after the end of this earth—all of this throws light on it. It gives meaning, too. We are suddenly born into a world as human beings and the world doesn't make sense of itself. So we have to make sense of the world by asking questions.

We always want meaning. The most awful things for us are pain and evil because we feel there is apparently no meaning. Beacher says that he who knows why only knows how. We can cope with the worst things we face if they have a sense of meaning. Of course the gospel is not only the deepest meaning, it is the true meaning. Everything else is just fiction.

The preceding conversation with Dr. Os Guinness was conducted via Instant Messenger on the evening of July 2, 2001. All efforts have been made to find the interviewer of this conversation. If you have any information about this conversation please notify the authors at www.parakaleo.us.

calling + identity

Summary on Calling
by John Smed

Why Use This Tool?
- To bring clarity to the complexity of calling
- To engage in the process of discerning our call

Calling is one way of looking at your whole life.
1. Given by God
2. Forged in prayer and the Word
3. Discovered in mission and service

Calling is specific and unique to each of us.
In general we all have the same calling and purpose in life: "to glorify God and enjoy him forever" (Westminster Shorter Catechism). Our mission is to make disciples of all nations. Calling is forged in the midst of our purpose and mission. This calling is applied and becomes as unique as each person.

Calling is comprehensive of our identity in Christ and our service to others.
- includes becoming a child of God: "Called to be saints"
- includes who you are: "I call you by name"
- includes what you do: "Called to be an apostle"
- includes your destiny and purpose in this life: "I will show him what he must suffer for my sake."

Calling is continually in process.
- includes assessing your key experiences, moments, and relationships that form your story of God's guiding presence in your life
- includes defining your biblical purpose and auditing your current behavior in light of God's reason for your existence in the context of his mandates for his people
- includes discovering the future and identifying/clarifying your personal vision
- includes intentionally living, growing, and ministering out of an increasing understanding of the life and ministry God has created you for

As calling matures it leads:
- to clarity in your life commitments and passions (core values) for what God wants to do in, through, and with you
- to a sense of life purpose
- to a vision or conception of what God might bring to pass in your life
- to a deeper understanding that vision comes in mission seasons
- to greater vision, which comes in prayer, providence, place, and service

Questions to Process Calling

For each question, start with personal reflection/prayer, then share your initial thoughts/insights/responses in small groups.

1. What is the difference between calling and occupation/career?

2. What is the relationship between calling and context?

3. What kinds of things move your mind and heart when you pray? For example:
   • healing the brokeness of souls and bodies
   • praying for missionaries/Christian workers/leaders
   • praying for those who do not know Christ, both near and far
   • praising God for his wonders in Creation and Redemption
   • praying about your work and workplace
   • prayer for your city, country, and its leaders

After prayer/reflection write a few sentences about your heart focus in prayer.

4. When you read scripture, or hear scripture read/preached, what passages, key teachings, commands and instructions seem most immediate and important to you – "as if God is talking right to me"? Include one or two.

For example:
   • a call to leadership
   • scripture encouragement to teachers/preachers/evangelists
   • passages about loving and caring for others/ social justice
   • teaching on holiness and consecration
   • encouragement to worship, praise and adoration
   • teachings about the importance of your work
   • scripture encouragement to creatively reflect your Maker
   • passages about family life, parenting, marriage

After prayer and reflection, write a few sentences about "what God is saying" to you.

5. A personal calling statement is your best understanding to date of your unique, personal direction and destiny. It is a holistic statement that integrates what you understand God is calling you to be and to do for his glory. After prayer and reflection, and write a few sentences about who God is leading you to be and what he is leading you to do.

Used by permission by John Smed, Pray for the City: Boot Camp for Urban Mission (info@prayerforthecity.com)

Identity: The Verdict Is In
by Ruth Ann Batstone and Tami Resch

Why Use This Tool?
- To hear again (and again) God's spoken verdict over us
- To use indicator questions to discover and name unbelief

As men and women in Christian ministry we are very good at doing, yet grapple endlessly with being. We often think of our value in terms of our roles, responsibilities, and reputations. But is that really who we are?

Who am I? Am I enough? These questions burn in our hearts. And they are good questions because we were created with a desire to be described, identified, and validated by our Creator. Stories throughout Scripture illustrate this truth. In the garden, Adam said of Eve, "She is now bone of my bone and flesh of my flesh." At Jesus' baptism the Father spoke over him, "This is my beloved Son, whom I love; in him I am well pleased!"

This deep yearning in our hearts has us poised on tiptoe waiting to discover if we are valuable, important, and loved. The problem is not our questions; the problem is where we go for answers. Too often we go not to God, but to everyone and everything else.

What does this look like? We compare ourselves to others to determine if we are more or less than those around us. We develop self-esteem resumes to prove to ourselves and others: "This is why I am ok!" We spend enormous amounts of energy prompting or waiting for the people in our lives to give us the right words: our spouses, our children, our parents, our bosses, our peers, and the members of our churches.

The result? When we give anyone or anything except God the power to define our value, we live at the mercy of someone or something. We give them the power to become our judge. Positive verbal strokes (the ones that make us feel worthy, valuable, and good) can sustain us for days, and these good words can give us a reason to get out of bed in the morning. But hard words (the ones that make us feel unlovable, worthless, and that we are never enough or too much) can make us want to hide for days under the covers.

God never intended for other judges to hand down the verdicts of our value. He had something completely other in mind:

"I care very little if I am judged by you or any human court: indeed I do not even judge myself. My conscience is clear, but that does not make me innocent. It is the Lord who judges me." I Corinthians 4:3-4 NIV

"What about me? Have I been faithful? Well, it matters very little what you or anyone else thinks. I don't even trust my own judgment on this point. My conscience is clear, but that isn't what matters. It is the Lord himself who will examine me and decide." I Corinthians 4:3-4 NLT

"It matters very little to me what you think of me, even less where I rank in popular opinion. I don't even rank myself. Comparisons in these matters are pointless. I am not aware of anything that would disqualify me from being a good guide for you, but that doesn't mean much. The Master makes that judgment." I Corinthians. 4:3-4 MSG

Paul states very clearly that his verdict comes from God. "It is the Lord who judges me." What makes Paul so eager to be judged by God? It is the good news of the gospel. This is the verdict that comes from the gospel:

- God loves me.
- God delights in me.
- I am seen in the courts of heaven as completely forgiven.
- I have been given righteousness that does not come from me; it comes from Christ.
- Christ's perfect record is mine, so no matter what I do, I can't add to or take away from my record.

This divine verdict is incredibly difficult to grasp, to believe, and to live out of as free men and women. We continually are drawn to the here and now verdict of our human judges. How do you know when you are being sucked back into the courtroom of man's judgment? Do you find yourself:

- Arguing?
- Spinning?
- Gathering evidence to prove or defend yourself?
- Judging others?

Hear the verdict the heavenly Father speaks over you: "Jesus received the verdict you deserved so you could have the verdict he deserved!"

Consider making a visual reminder for your mirror, your desk, or your wallet.

---

the VERDICT is IN!

"I care very little if I am judged by you or by any human court; indeed, I do not even judge myself. My conscience is clear, but that does not make me innocent. **It is the Lord who judges me**."

I Corinthians 4:3-4

Am I anxious?
Am I comparing myself to others?
Am I afraid of how I look?
Am I looking down on everyone else?
Am I devastated by my failures?

Jesus received the verdict we deserved so that we could have the verdict he deserved.

BUT I BELIEVE THE VERDICT IS IN, DON'T I?

It's so easy to think we fully and deeply believe the gospel, and yet areas of our lives remain untouched by its deep power and freedom, and we miss the glorious implications every day in our lives. The following questions are indicators of places where we may not fully believe.

- Do you feel bad about yourself if you haven't been productive?
- Are you unable to take vacations or a day off?
- Are you undone by failure?
- Are you often afraid of not looking good?
- Do you have activities in your life that you keep secret?
- Do you regularly despair?
- Do you feel as if you are unable to freely share with others?
- Do you find yourself being self-conscious?

When we recognize areas of disbelief we do not need to go to shame, rather, we can cry out, "Lord, I believe! Help my unbelief!" Our obvious need for the gospel points us to more freedom Christ has yet to bring to us— especially as church people.

calling + identity

LIFE CALLING *(known and/or inklings of) Living out your calling in the here & now with a vision of future expressions*

What never changes

IDENTITY

In Christ
Son or Daughter
Created & Formed
Image Bearer | DNA | Innate Gifts
Story | Family of Origin
Purposed* & Named

*To Glorify God & Enjoy Him Forever

Your truest identity. How God created, formed, and claimed you.

A

What changes some

UNIQUE YOU

Passions | Desires & Over-desires
Abilities | Talents
Experience | Lack Of
Personality | Dreams
Redeemed/Unredeemed Relating Styles

Your visible identity. How others experience and describe you.

B

What Influences You

VOICES

The Holy Spirit | The Word
Community of Faith
Other Key Voices:
Friends | Society
The Enemy | Your Past

The voices you listen to and how they
impact and form your identity and calling.

What always changes

CONTEXT

Age | Stage | Season of life | Culture
Limitations | Friends & Enemies
Resources & Health | Lack Of
Experience & Opportunities | Lack Of

Where you intersect your world. How God uses seasons
and circumstances to direct and invite you into his work.

C

What will need to change often

ROLES

Job | Occupation | Responsibilities
Serving | Volunteering
Long Term Roles That Morph:
[wife, mother, friend, neighbor, CPS]

The shape and structure of your work in this world.
The systems and categories of relationships
and responsibilities.

D

What you actually do

DAILY LIVING
In Creativity & Freedom

A thousand ways to live out *your* roles
in order to impact *your* world and
express *your* faith in love!

How the being you is manifested in the doing you.

E

LIFE CALLING *(known and/or inklings of)*

Living out your calling in the here & now with a vision of future expressions

Explanation of the Tool:
Interplay of Identity, Calling, and Roles
By Shari Thomas and Tami Resch

Why Use This Tool?
- To visualize the all-encompassing nature of calling
- To move toward expressing calling with creativity and freedom
- To consider how identity and calling are expressed in everyday living

The most common questions from women entering church planting are in regards to their role. *What does it mean to be a church planter spouse? What will be my roles? Will I have a say in what my roles will be? Can I have an outside career and still be effective in this new role? Is there something I need to give up? Can I say no to this role?* We firmly believe that the woman who is most successful in the role of church planting is the one who brings her true self and her calling to the plant. Not sure you understand your calling? You are not alone!

Often men and women alike report a deeper understanding of their life calling/life purpose somewhere in the fourth or fifth decade of life. If that is true, what benefit could be gleaned from grappling with this topic during the hectic and demanding season of church planting, especially if you are thirty-something? We've found it helpful because calling is an all-encompassing issue, and thus it will impact your marriage, the raising of your kids, and the responsibilities you take on in the church. Conversely, calling is often discerned through your marriage, the raising of your kids, and the responsibilities you take on in the church. Confused yet?

Throughout history, God has spoken forthrightly to his people, calling them *out of* a specific place and into specific roles or tasks (think Moses). God has also spoken through the community of faith, calling his people to wake up and see where and when they are been positioned for "such a time as this" (think Mordecai challenging Esther to beseech God). God calls through his Word. He can even call through a donkey. Do you have an inkling of how God has woven together the components of your life to impact this world to the glory of God and the welfare of others? You may have more than inklings. Regardless, your calling can be expressed today, in the here and now; and it will be expressed in the future as God continues to shape you and your context, inviting you to particpate further in kingdom work. Often our calling is in accordance with our God-given design, our affinities, dreams, desires, and contexts. Yet, God's call can intersect, trump, thwart, vex, eclipse, supersede, and transcend our plans (think Jonah, think Moses, think "Leave Ur, go to the land I will show you.")

Even while your calling remains unclear, it need not be weighty! The literal meaning of the word "glory" means weight/value/heavy. We have glory and value because we are image bearers and IN CHRIST, not because of the way we live out our callings. The weight is off! So enjoy discovering the interplay of calling, identity, context, roles, and daily living. To God be the glory—and the weight!

BOX A: Identity in Christ - *What Never Changes*
The most fundamental reality of your *identity* is that it never changes. While all humans bear God's image, if we are in Jesus Christ, we are beloved children. Identity (Box A) has the greatest potential of informing all the other areas (Boxes B-E) because it establishes our truest identity, the one that can never be destroyed or diminished. Each of us has been given a purpose that never changes: to glorify and enjoy God forever. Our internal sense of self also bears unique markings. God, who creatively designed 350,000 types of beetles, creatively designed and

calling + identity

formed us in our mother's womb. God providentially placed us in our family of origin, allowing select experiences to shape us. While our identity in Christ, our creation, and our forming will never change, our understanding of God's purposes in it can change and grow substantially.

BOX B: Unique You –*What Changes Some*

The most fundamental reality of the **unique you** (Box B) is that you are created to be the *unique* you. "Her impish grin." "Her infectious laughter." This is the described you, the experienced you. Think Facebook—what you show and tell about yourself. These are the attributes and aspects people note when introducing you to others, when writing you a job reference, when remembering their last encounter with you. The unique you can change some as new talents develop, as unredeemed relating styles are marked by redemption, and as your over-desires return to desires. The "all" of you, Boxes A and B, moves out and intersects with the world in Box C.

BOX C: Context -*What Always Changes*

The most fundamental thing about your **context** (Box C) is that it always changes! Each season of life brings new challenges, new opportunities, even new technology! Our finances give us options or limit our choices. Our state of health propels us, slows us down, or stops us. Our family grows larger or smaller. Our children require more or less of us. Our support systems help us or fail us. New opportunities require increased responsibility. We encounter new enemies. Church dynamics change. We move to a new region or country. The context of our life is never static. And into this vortex we find ourselves spinning and swirling and trying to make sense of it all.

BOX D*: Roles* – *What Will Need To Change Often*

The most fundamental thing about your roles (Box D) is that they change often. This is the place most of us get stuck. We look at our roles, jobs, and responsibilities and often confuse them with our identity and calling, when actually they may be the very thing inhibiting us from following our calling. As Box C constantly changes and as we keep in step with the Spirit, we are moved to work in this world in ever-changing ways. Even if one of your roles does not change from year to year—such as being a mom—how you live out that role will most definitely change as your context transitions. Our roles have tremendous potential for being lived out (Box E) boundlessly. There is so much freedom in the working out of the details! Boxes A, B, and C all inform Box D, rather than the other way around. Our roles must never be our truest identity or the place from which we derive our worth and value. However, we want to regularly assess Boxes A, B, and C in order to evaluate if and how our current roles need to change in order to align ourselves with God's purposes.

BOX E: Daily Living – *What You Actually Do*

The most fundamental thing about your **daily life** is that there are a thousand ways to live it out! Think *out of the box* and *into the boundless*! There are a thousand ways to be a wife, a mother, or a church planting spouse. There are a thousand ways to divide household labor. How you did it yesterday or last year does not constrain you to the same expression today. There is a beautiful interplay between living out of your true identity, living as to your unique design, and living where Christ has you or is taking you with creativity. Enjoy that freedom! You can express "faith working through love" in your life and work in ways that whisper, sing, or shout God's glory. His glory shines most through us when we are living aligned with his purposes for us.

Voices – *What Influences You*

There are so many voices that inform our understanding of our calling. What voices do you hear regarding your true identity and your unique design? How are the voices in your life speaking to you about your context, your roles, and your daily living? Do you recognize the voice of the Spirit? God's Word? How loud is society's voice in your ear? Does your past speak to you with a surround-sound quality that seems to drown out any other voice you hear? As we learn to distinguish the healthy from the harmful voices, we can increase our ability to tune in to those voices that bring us life and remind us of our true identity. And we can learn to turn down the volume on the voices that invite us to lies and death.

Examples of Interplay in Life Calling

A young church planter spouse had always enjoyed being surrounded by friends with different belief systems. After struggling with infertility, and having just found out that she and her husband would soon be receiving their adopted child, they found out she was pregnant. She gave birth when their oldest child was five months old. Their birth child was born with health problems that restricted exposure to other children. Naturally this woman's time was focused on caring for her babies to the point she was unable to attend church functions. Yet she found this did not limit her calling to friends outside her faith but rather enhanced it. Her focus, while on her children, also allowed her time with health care providers and young neighborhood teens whom she hired to help care for the babies.

I (Shari) was active in our church plant and became even more so as our children grew older. When a wise and trusted friend asked how I envisioned using my leadership gifts and passion in church planting for the broader kingdom, I was taken aback. She encouraged me toward a vision for the future. I spoke with our elders and prayed with trusted friends and eventually came to the decision to let go of current church roles. At first it was hard to not participate as actively as before. There were misunderstandings in relationships as some struggled to accept how these changes affected my role in the church and in their lives. Yet it was these changes that led me to come alongside women new to church planting, and eventually to start Parakaleo.

Example of a Life Calling Statement: *from a woman in church planting*
I am called to be a daughter of the King. I believe I have also been called to lead, teach, and train others to follow Christ. During this stage of my life, as a wife and young mother, I invest the majority of my time in teaching and leading our children. I live openly and vulnerably in our community, involving our children in local events and the public school system.

Example of a Life Calling Statement: *from that same woman later in life*
I am called to be a daughter of the King and to serve him in mission. However, nothing I do or don't do can add or take away from my standing in Christ. Together, my husband and I are called to live our lives openly and vulnerably before others, but especially before our children and church planters in order to encourage gospel living and ministry. I am called to lead, train, and pastor church planting couples. As a follower of Christ I am called to be involved in my local community, thus I place a high priority on involvement and activities with friends and acquaintances from other belief systems.

Example of a Life Calling Statement With a Vision for the Future: *from the same woman*
If God continues to lead and call as he has done so far, I envision our call to church planting will grow to the point that my husband and I will be traveling and ministering together on a broader basis. In order to be faithful to his call, there are issues I address in the here and now. I place a high priority on raising sufficient funds, exercising, eating nutritionally, and giving myself to prayer and study of the Word.

calling + identity

Diagnostic Questions
Interplay of Identity, Calling, and Roles
by Shari Thomas and Tami Resch

Why Use This Tool?
- To visualize the all-encompassing nature of calling
- To move toward expressing calling with creativity and freedom
- To consider how identity and calling are expressed in everyday living

Who Did God Create Me To Be? What Does He Have For Me To Do?
CALLING
- Spend time in prayer and the Word.
- Where have others said they see God's glory because of you?
- What common theme(s) have emerged through the decades of your life?
- Where do you willingly and joyfully sacrifice?
- From where do you derive enjoyment?
- Do you have an inkling of the name God may be giving you?

What Never Changes
IDENTITY
- Spend time in prayer and the Word.
- What does it mean for you to be in Christ?
- How does your childhood impact you today?
- What passages of scripture particularly attract your attention?
- Do you sense a common life theme that may be from the Holy Spirit?

What Changes Some
UNIQUE YOU
- Spend time in prayer and the Word.
- What gifts/abilities do others recognize in you?
- What are your current passions?
- If known, what have been your lifelong passions?
- What personality or relating style traits stand out to you and to others?
- What are you both good at and love to do?

What Always Changes
CONTEXT
- Spend time in prayer and the Word.
- Is there a current opportunity you are drawn to?
- Is there an opportunity to hone your skills?
- What family responsibilities are currently yours?
- What limitations do you have on your time or health?

• What about your current context energizes and fits you?
• What about your current context discourages and does not fit you?

What Will Need To Change Often
ROLES
• Spend time in prayer and the Word.
• How do you glorify God and enjoy him in your current roles?
• Assess boxes A-C. What current roles and jobs might need to be adjusted in light of your growing awareness of God's purpose and mandates for you?

What You Actually Do
DAILY LIVING
• Spend time in prayer and the Word.
• Ask God to help you think creatively and live out of the freedom won for you in Christ Jesus. There are a thousand ways to fulfill a role or task.
• What are you free to do? How can you creatively express your faith in love right here, right now?
• CONSIDER THE NOW: How might you intentionally live and minister out of the purpose God has called you to in the here and now?
• How might you do this more fully in the future?

Who You Listen To
VOICES
• Spend time in prayer and the Word.
• To what voices have you given authority and power in your life?
• What are the loudest voices speaking to you about your roles and daily living?
• What voices conflict with one another?
• Zephaniah 3:17 says God rejoices over you with singing. What might the words of his chorus be for you?
• Do you refuse to hear God's truth about you? Do you know why?
• How does your community of faith, the Enemy, and other key voices inform your understanding of each box (your identity, the unique you, your context, your roles, and your daily living)?
• Ask God to help you tune your heart to the voices he would have you follow.

Ministry Can Be Dangerous to Your Spiritual Health
By Timothy Keller

Why Use This Tool?
- To explore how to survive a life of ministry
- To consider how spiritual gifts could be a liability in ministry
- To look at our prayer life

Ministry places enormous pressures on one's integrity and character, pressures which require extra vigilance and a deeper understanding of one's need for God.

It is always gratifying to see Christians become active in church ministry rather than remain mere consumers of spiritual services. There is nothing so fulfilling as to see lives touched and changed through your service, whether you are a volunteer, lay leader, church officer, or staff member.

But the Bible sounds a cautionary note. By its very nature, Christian leadership involves extolling the glory and beauty of God above all else. It means pointing others to God's worth and beauty even when your own heart is numb to any sense of divine love and glory. As someone who ministers to others, how will you survive when that happens? Following are two things to remember.

The right thing to do. The first—and right—thing to do is to watch your heart with far more diligence than you would have otherwise, and to be very disciplined in observing regular times of daily prayer. In these times you may find your heart warming to God's reality. Prayer can fan the flame of that reality, allowing you to speak to others out of your daily sustenance from God.

Even so, your heart may continue to feel spiritually dry or dead for an extended period. Such a condition requires that you keep your regular times of prayer even more diligently. Humbly acknowledge your dryness to God and set your heart to trust him and seek him despite it and during it. This deliberate act is itself a great step of spiritual growth and maturity. When you speak to God about your dryness, rather than avoiding prayer times, it reminds you of your weakness and dependence upon his grace for absolutely everything. It drives home the importance and preciousness of your standing in Christ.

The wrong thing to do. The second—and wrong—thing is to rely not on prayer and your relationship with God but on the excitement of ministry activity and effectiveness. In this way you can begin to lean more on your spiritual gifts than on spiritual grace. In fact, you may mistake the operation of spiritual gifts for the operation of spiritual grace in your life. Gifts are abilities God gives us to meet the needs of others in Christ's name—speaking, encouraging, serving, evangelizing, teaching, leading, administering, counseling, discipling, organizing. Graces, often called spiritual fruit, are beauties of character—love, joy, peace, humility, gentleness, self-control. Spiritual gifts are what we do; spiritual fruit is what we are. Unless you understand the greater importance of grace and gospel-character for ministry effectiveness, the discernment and use of spiritual gifts may actually become a liability in your ministry. The terrible danger is that we can look to our ministry activity as evidence that God is with us or as a way to earn God's favor and prove ourselves.

If our hearts remember the gospel and are rejoicing in our justification and adoption, then our ministry is done as a sacrifice of thanksgiving—and the result will be that our ministry is done in love, humility, patience, and tenderness. But if our hearts are seeking self-justification and desiring to control God and others by proving our worth through our ministry performance, we will identify too closely with our ministry and make it an extension of ourselves. The telltale signs of impatience, irritability, pride, hurt feelings, jealousy, and boasting will appear. We will be driven, scared, and either too timid or too brash. And perhaps, away from the public glare, we will indulge in secret sins. These signs reveal that ministry as a performance is exhausting us and serves as a cover for pride in either one of its two forms, self-aggrandizement or self-hatred.

Here's how this danger can begin. Your prayer life may be nonexistent, or you may have an unforgiving spirit toward someone, or sexual desires may be out of control. But you get involved in some ministry activity, which draws out your spiritual gifts. You begin to serve and help others, and soon you are affirmed by others and told what great things you are doing. You see the effects of your ministry and conclude that God is with you. But actually God was helping someone through your gifts even though your heart was far from him. Eventually, if you don't do something about your lack of spiritual fruit and instead build your identity on your spiritual gifts and ministry activity, there will be some kind of collapse. You will blow up at someone or lapse into some sin that destroys your credibility. And everyone, including you, will be surprised. But you should not be. Spiritual gifts without spiritual fruit is like a tire slowly losing air.

So let's examine ourselves. Is our prayer life dead even though we're effective in ministry? Do we struggle with feeling slighted? Are our feelings always being hurt? Do we experience anxiety and joylessness in our work? Do we find ourselves being highly critical of other churches or ministers or coworkers? Do we engage in self-pity? If these things are true, then our ministry may be skillful and successful, but it is hollow, and we are probably either headed for a breakdown or doomed to produce superficial results. Abraham Kuyper wrote that Phariseeism is like a shadow—it can be deepest and sharpest closest to the light.

Christian ministry changes people. It can make us far better or far worse Christians than we would have been otherwise, but it will not leave us unchanged.

Calling & Identity Resources

Beyond Identity: Finding Yourself in the Image and Character of God, Dick Keyes
The Call, Os Guinness
Counsel for Pastor's Wives, Diane Langberg
From Fear to Freedom: Living as Sons and Daughters of God, Rose Marie Miller
The Heart Of A Servant Leader, C. John (Jack) Miller
The Inner Voice of Love, Henri Nouwen
The Journey of Desire, John Eldridge
LifeKeys: Discover Who You Are, Jane Kise, David Stark, and Sandra Krebs Hirsch
A Praying Life, Paul Miller

SERMONS:
"Blessed Self-Forgetfulness" by Tim Keller; www.redeemer.com

COMMUNITY

IS IT CRUCIAL ?

IS IT POSSIBLE

FOR LEADERS ?

Life is meant to be wild and tragic. The nature
of love is being in a dance with others that spins
us to the face of God.   DAN ALLENDER

Myths of Community
By Shari Thomas

"My church community should treat me like any other member, not as the pastor's spouse."

"The needs of my community are more important than my personal needs."

"Couples in the pastorate can't have personal friends in their church community."

"As leaders at the top, we don't expect others to be able to understand what we experience, nor do we think they should know about our struggles."

"Since this is my spiritual community too, I should be able to talk about my issues as openly as others do."

"My personal needs are more important than the needs of my community."

"My needs should be met by my church community."

WE LIVE IN A FRAGMENTED culture. On any given day, I talk face to face with the guys who work in the bodega below my apartment, the women in my gym class, and my neighbors on the street. And I also communicate with friends and co-workers scattered throughout fifty states, five countries, and three continents. This would have been shocking fifty years ago, but my life is not unusual for today. What will fragmentation look like for ensuing generations?

Rarely have we experienced such a pluralistic culture as the one in which we live in today. Most of us inhabit worlds where work, home, school, family, and friends occupy separate spheres and a variety of geographical locations. And often these spheres have little or no overlap with one another.

> *Now, mind you, it was never easy at the Pretty's.... If it was hard times, they shared, they helped their neighbor. No, they didn't have any money, the sea was dangerous and men were lost, but it was a satisfying life in a way people today do not understand. There was a joinery of lives all worked together, smooth in places, or lumpy, but joined.*
>
> *—E. Annie Proulx,*
> The Shipping News

Christians may join a church or a plant with the expectation—if not the demand—that the church carry the weight of and solve the deeper cultural issue of fragmentation.

Without identifying their deeper longings, people may join a core group expecting that here at last is a group that will meet their every need for community. Unnamed and unrealistic expectations are often placed on the planting couple who also desire to create a loving community. Often, the lead couple find that the very ones they thought would be sharing the burden of ministry are actually creating a greater drain on their energy and time. Those who join the team may be disappointed that they have not developed the life-long friendship they thought they would have with the planting couple.

Lead couples wrestle with the demands placed on them for meaningful relationships with a vast number of people. In many cultures, pockets of North America included, there is an expectation that the pastor's wife is supposed to fulfill a list of responsibilities that automatically attach to her role. Because friendship is often one of those expectations, women in ministry often question the meaning of friendship and wonder if it is even possible in ministry. How can we be striving to create community, but so often feel we aren't even able to have our own friends within that community?

Often, myths about community develop because our focus is too small

community

> *He works on us in all sorts of ways. But above all, he works on us through each other.*
>
> —*C.S. Lewis,* Mere Christianity

or we vow we won't be hurt again. Yet, as we begin to understand God's purpose for community we increasingly will risk trusting God with the pain that living in community brings.

Whatever we create in our churches, one thing we can guarantee is that no one on this side of eternity will create the perfect model of community. We aren't living in the future yet! Oh, we will see redemption break through and surprise us in amazing ways. We will experience seasons of support where we bear each other's burdens well. We may even find those with whom we can share our deepest fears and longings! There will be many times when we put aside our individual needs for the sake of the community. And there will be times when we need to put aside the needs of the community for the sake of our families, marriages, and ourselves. Certainly, community can be a beautiful thing. And it can be a painful thing.

We won't cover all that needs addressing on this topic. Our main focus in this section is to define biblical community, address some of the challenges we face as leaders of these communities, and to more deeply understand and embrace our need to walk in forgiveness within our communities.

> *Over time, I have learned two things about my religious quest: First of all, that it is God who is seeking me, and who has myriad ways of finding me. Second, that my most substantial changes, in terms of religious conversion, come through other people. Even when I become convinced that God is absent from my life, others have a way of suddenly revealing God's presence.*
>
> —*Kathleen Norris,* Amazing Grace: A Vocabulary of Faith

A Time to Grieve

by Carrie Ott

It was in the rented space in the early months of my father's's fledgling church plant that I first laid eyes on the teenage boy who would one day become my husband. I was fifteen. Russ and I would spend the next twenty years as part of this community we had entered as the daughter of a pastor and the son of an elder. Here we would grow up, marry, have and raise our kids. Here is where we would give of ourselves as volunteers, and here is where we would later weld our careers as paid staff to what had become a large and thriving church. Our family, our closest friends, our kids' school, our kids' friends, our jobs—all of it was contained in this one church community.

As the church prepared to celebrate its twentieth anniversary, life and community as we knew it broke apart. The place that had been the center and hub of our social, professional, familial, and communal world somehow spun out of orbit. Unexpected changes in leadership, staff, and the pastorate left us to wander in a foreign place that had once been as familiar as our own home. The sense of clarity, joy, and belonging we had always known was replaced with confusion, sadness, and feelings of betrayal. We lived in this new and sad place for some time, not wanting to abandon what felt like a faltering—but surely not a sinking—ship. Did we belong here anymore? Was our presence bringing health or harm? How long should we wait for the healing we hoped would come? How would we know if and when it was okay to walk away? It was many, many months before we felt God gently leading us away from all we and our preteen children had known.

I resigned my staff position. Russ continued to wrestle and find his way in his. And suddenly we were the visitors walking into various sanctuaries and auditoriums looking for a new church home. For the first time our children stood on the outside looking in, wondering if there was a place for them. At the end of one particular church visit we sat quietly in our seats until our middle child sadly whispered, "No one knows us here." We spent months grieving all we had known, all we had lost, and all we had assumed would remain ours.

In time we found a new church community, and now, many years later, I can say it became as great a blessing as our old one. We found healing and grace and friendships we can't imagine not having known. But a few years in one place doesn't replace twenty years in another. Time had to pass and new experiences had to be shared. Rarely is one instantly wrapped into the deep folds of a new community. I knew what life in the deep folds felt like and I missed it more than ever. The new place brought honest joy, but it also reminded me of all we had lost.

In our case, because of Russ' job and many dear friends, we still had deep ties to our old community. We still lived seven miles from the church we loved so dearly. Each Sunday we drove past the old church on our way to the new. And the grief continued.

I often spent hours sifting through the rubble of what had been and what had happened, hoping to find one clue, one piece of something that would finally free me to shovel all the debris into the back of a dump truck and let it drive off, leaving me to stand in a clear space. Sensing my growing urgency to be done with my grief, our

community

counselor told me, "How you grieve this church is part of your relationship with the church. Don't cut the grieving short. Grieving well allows you to come full circle in your relationship with this community."

Something about her words gave me the courage to sit with the pain and not run from the grief. We had spent many joyous and significant years at our old church, and sweeping up my pain prematurely meant I would be loading up the good, the bad, the ugly, *and* the beautiful all at once into the back of that dump truck. I didn't want to do that. I wanted to grieve well.

But continuing in grief was painful. And it meant wrestling with the strange scenario that God had chosen to use something awful to give us something good; that he had exiled us from one place to introduce us to another. Over time there was no doubt we were exactly where we should be in our new church home, but why did the circumstances have to be so miserable to get us there? Couldn't God have lured and enticed us to this new place minus the chaos and pain? Why did we have to feel utterly misplaced and lost in the desert before we found our new home?

Recently, I spoke with a woman in the process of entering a new community of believers. She and her husband had been deeply involved in the inception, establishment, and growth of their previous church. Yet a series of confusing, hurtful, and bizarre events (and then much prayer and seeking) led them to follow God's nudge to a new place. Our hearts resonated with the shared experience of how often God uses painful circumstances to move us to the next place he has for us.

When this kind of pain and hurt accompanies the leaving of any community, we are tempted to avoid further and future pain by any means possible. Often, we are tempted to remove ourselves from community altogether. "Who needs it?" we tell ourselves. "I will not enter the possibility of that kind of pain again!" But what happens when you are the wife of a pastor or a planter? You rarely have that option. So we show up, but we show up dressed head to toe in our shiny new and recently-reinforced armor. "Yes, I am here," we say, "but I will protect myself from future pain." Not only do we try to keep pain away, we even brace ourselves against possible joy that might one day lead to pain.

In this new place, I longed for a few guarantees regarding future community. Guarantee One: that I'd never have to go through that (what we had gone through) again. Guarantee Two: that the sense of belonging we were experiencing in our new church would always be ours.

But there are no such guarantees. We live in a fallen world and community on this earth is as fallen as we are. It is impossible to protect ourselves from future pain, and our acts of self-protection guarantee even greater losses.

The first thing we lose is our heart. A hardened and self-protecting heart is a heart that withers. Another loss: the giving of ourselves that invites deep community from others. Do we think others can't feel our self-protection and aren't profoundly affected by it? Tragically, we also lose the ability to watch redemption unfold—in our present and in the past that brought such pain. I wanted to see redemption unfold in the here, and the back then, and in the what was yet to come. And thank God he showed us that! Not only did God give us joy in our new community, over the years, he granted us bits and pieces and washes of healing in regard to the old one as well. The healing I've tasted makes me long even more for the full healing of community that is yet to come in eternity.

There's another loss we suffer in our self-protection, and it's a big one. We lose that *particular* presence of Jesus that he promises will come to us when we mourn—not avoid—pain. *Blessed are those who mourn*, Jesus says. Blessed? Yes, blessed. How often I sat in the pew of our new church feeling as if it were just me and Jesus sitting there. Only he knew exactly where I had come from, exactly what I had lost, and exactly what I was grieving and longing for most in that moment. Sunday after Sunday our family sat in our new church and Sunday after Sunday Jesus comforted me as only he could. I felt as if I was sitting in that pew, literally leaning my heart and all its sorrow on Jesus' shoulder, just like my youngest child sat, quietly and full of loss and sadness, leaning his head on me.

Recently we attended a memorial service at our former church for a man we've known since its earliest days. It's been many years since we left, yet walking down those halls, sitting in that sanctuary, even walking into the restroom, I was overwhelmed with the familiarity of the place—as if I'd never left and no time had passed at all. I was stunned again by the sense of displacement—that I *had* belonged here, but belonged no more. Home, but not home. Visiting, yet already having left. A remembered friend to some, a stranger to many.

As gracious as God is to us in our experiences of community suffering, we never become immune to the pain and loss. As we celebrated this man's sudden home-going to Jesus, the longing I had for heaven, and community as it should be—as it will finally be, filled me with a deep ache for all things to be made right and whole once and for all with Christ's Bride.

Our children are mostly grown and beginning their own journeys in their own church communities. If we make a community change again, we imagine it will look quite different from the last time. But what will be the same— what will feel entirely familiar—is that *we will suffer loss*. We will endure the earthly breaking of community bonds. We will say goodbye to many relationships and be forced to hold loosely those we hope will remain, even as they are altered. We will feel displaced again, no matter how sure or clear the path to the next community seems to be, because leaving a community—no matter the reasons or circumstances—requires that we walk, one step at a time, across that wide space between one church door and another.

If God asks us to do make that walk again, I'll have an advantage I didn't have the first time: I've done this before. And I have found God to be faithful and true and full of tender mercy. I have found him to be near to the brokenhearted. I have found him to be near to me.

TOOLS on COMMUNITY

community

170

Implications of a Christian Community
by Shari Thomas

Why Use This Tool?
- To answer the question, "How does the gospel impact a leader's life in a Christian community?"
- To explore practical helps for ministry leaders

The influence our fragmented society has on community is profound and deeply impacts the planting couple. Why? People come to our congregations lonely, yearning for a spiritual home, and seeking friendship. And we are desperately looking for warm bodies to fill empty pews. We embrace these newcomers like long lost friends. We need them. They need us. We feel great. Yet all too soon we are exposed as the tick on the lean dog that we are, wondering what went wrong. We become so concerned about growing our church that we've neglected to understand the community that Christ has come to provide through his church.

What is Christian Community?
Christian community is defined by three theological terms as seen in scripture: the "people of God, the "body of Christ," and the "fellowship of the Spirit."

The "people of God" are those who have believed the gospel, the message of grace. The gospel not only gives us a personal identity, but a corporate one as well. In this book we've focused mainly on how the gospel of grace impacts us individually. As this gospel of grace seeps into the community, it forms an incredible corporate identity. It leads to inclusion, humility, and vulnerability. The relationships in this type of community are atypical and rare.

The "body of Christ" in a local setting (as opposed to the universal church) is comprised of people who have consciously decided to throw their lot in with one another. They are members of one another in Christ. This commitment means they have deliberately chosen to be in relationship with, and available to, one another. The "body of Christ" includes those who are in him and those who will be in him when he makes all things new. Thus we can't choose to be only with other Christians. Our community must also include those who do not yet know Christ.

The "fellowship of the Spirit" shows us how a Christian community should operate and also gives us the power to do so. We have an opportunity to live together in the here and now in such a way that points to the future of how we will live when God fully heals and brings all under the lordship of Jesus Christ. One of my seminary professors used to say we are mini-models of redemption showing the world what a society under the reign of Christ will look like (Eph. 3:10-12).

You may only get a taste of true community on this side, but when you do, savor it. Delight in it! Thank God for it! Let it be a reminder that it truly exists and that you have been given a great privilege and calling to show others the beauty of gospel community.

The implications of this short summary are expansive. I'll highlight just a few:

In the first years of the plant, expectations for the planting couple to be the hub of the community will be high. Obviously, how we relate to others impacts the growth of our churches. However, allowing ourselves to remain the hub for an extended period can actually damage community. Christian community implies members are committed to one another in *Christ*, not just us. Naturally strong and winsome couples will draw others. Wise leaders will connect others to one another as soon as possible.

community

It is key to let people know that the relationship formed with you during the initial stages of the plant *will* change with time. All relationships change. Our intimacy level and commitment to the person we are training for leadership at the beginning of the church plant will be different than the one we will have when the church becomes mature. This does not mean the relationship ends, but that it shifts. This doesn't have to be negative but we often feel it is unless it's talked about. *"I've enjoyed our relationship this past year and it's hard to see this phase come to a close. I'm going to greatly miss seeing you every week in a small group setting. I'll look forward to hearing how God continues to grow you and use you in the life of others."*

When we are working on a highly focused task team it's hard to tell if we are actually good friends, if we just work well together, or if it is both. It's likely that without the task the friendship may disintegrate. Discussing this process of change is especially important for those who join a launch team or ministry team. Again, talk about it! *"Several of you will more than likely form deep relationships during this season. Others will struggle with chaos and staying committed to the process when conflict is faced. Some will be surprised how hard it is to work together. When it's over and we disband this group—for we **will** disband as the church grows—we will probably wrestle with the inevitable changes that come in our relationships. Yet all of this is part of growth as we develop a community."*

Holding a leadership position or being married to a person high up in leadership means people will look to you. Whether you like it or not, it is what it is. Recognizing this sooner than later and naming it will be helpful to all.

Friendship has been described as two people who choose one another. Quite frankly, it's hard to tell if we've even had the opportunity to choose when we are the planter or the spouse. Our time is so limited and focused we may be drawn to people mostly because they move the vision forward. Or they may be drawn to us because of our position of authority. This is more common than we want to admit and quite painful when either party becomes aware of it. Recognizing and naming this, rather than pretending or leaving the other person to think there actually is a deep relationship, carries more possibility for building true community in the long run.

A pastor's wife or a woman in a leadership position has the potential of more relationships than the average woman. While we may not be able to explore the depths of those friendships in the present, we will have all eternity to continue them. Often I tell women that if we had more time I could see us being good friends. The truth is we do not have the time in the here and now for all the relationships we could possibly have. But what is begun now can deepen and grow throughout eternity.

When a person expresses desire for relationship with you or disappointment in the lack of it, ask for further clarification. *"How do you picture the relationship if it were to come about?"* Their desire could range from friendly acknowledgment to sharing family vacations. Knowing how you come across to others while understanding their desires goes a long way in helping us clarify realistic and unrealistic expectations. Remember, knowing the expectation, *even if it's realistic*, does not mean you have to meet it.

Our experience of community now will not fulfill us as it will in that future society where we will all be under the reign of Christ. Our desire for deep community stems from our God-given design. *We are created for it.* However, just like all desires, it can become an over-consuming desire. We can try and crush the desire by refusing to have deep relationships in the church or we can demand our need for relationship be met in a specific way, such as insisting on respect or silencing people in order to control them. Gospel relationships will require the hard work of repentance, forgiveness, and holding out hope for each other even in the face of our brokenness. But it is well worth it!

Building A Community Of Personal Support
by Tami Resch

Why Use This Tool?
- To answer the question, "Who pastors the pastor's spouse?"
- To identify gospel friends and mentors

We believe that a community of personal support is vital to every believer, but especially so to the church planting spouse who lives day in and day out with the intensity of a planting ministry. A community of personal support can be "Jesus in skin" when you need physical, emotional, and spiritual care. This community is made up of individuals: family, friends, neighbors, co-workers, mentors, coaches, and counselors.

A Community of Personal Support

Church planting spouses and their families live and battle on the front lines of kingdom advancement. For Paul, church planting was a place where he was hard pressed, perplexed, persecuted, struck down, and outwardly wasting away. Yet, he declared that in the midst of church planting life, he was not crushed, nor in despair, nor abandoned, nor destroyed, and he was inwardly being renewed day by day. Fixing his eyes on Christ, Paul did not lose heart and could see his troubles as light and momentary. He was able to renounce his secret and shameful ways, preach the gospel without deception or distortion, and remain confident that his competence was from God.

How do we find and maintain this perspective in the middle of the battle? Is it just us and the Holy Spirit? Can we look to others? What part does community play? Dick Kaufmann, pastor of Harbor Church in San Diego, asked "Who pastors the pastor?" His answer for pastors is the same for us all.

You are the primary pastor of your own heart—preaching the gospel to yourself. Whether we happen to be alone in our house or driving with a car full of small children or in a prolonged season of aloneness and isolation, we often find ourselves with no one present to discuss the onslaught of fear or self-condemnation screaming in our heads. It is in these moments that we need to know how to pastor our own heart.

The Holy Spirit has promised to transform us into the image of Christ. We have the same God that Jacob, from his death bed, speaks of in Genesis 48:15, "…The God who has been my shepherd all my life to this day…" God will be our shepherd all our lives to this day—and to our death. Jesus promised to not leave us as orphans (John 14). He has promised to never leave us or forsake us. What he began, he will complete (Phil. 1: 6).

So we partner with the Holy Spirit to mentor, shepherd, and pastor our hearts. And, at other times, the Spirit works on our behalf in the hearts of those who are in relationship with us. He gives us what Dick Kaufman calls gospel friends and gospel mentors.

Gospel Friends are people who literally come alongside you and point you to Christ. They know your tendencies, your fears, and your battles of faith. They know how to tell you what is true and they never laugh or yawn.

Are there people in your life who point you to Jesus? Who ask you the hard questions? Who remind you of your identity in Christ? Gospel friends don't often tell you what to do or how to do it; rather, they ask, "How are you preaching the gospel to your heart?" "How would things change if in this moment you truly believed that God loves you?... or that you didn't need man's approval?... or that you are forgiven?"

community

We cannot go it alone. And God never intended that we look only to ourselves for the care of our hearts.

Gospel Mentors are those people who literally and figuratively come alongside us. They are counselors, coaches, authors, sermons, books, etc. Do you have mentors and counselors and coaches that point you to Jesus? Do they challenge you to find your identity in Christ, rather than in your performance? Do they point you to the cross, rather than touting the latest set of rules or programs to live by?

It is important to be aware of the cultural mentors we let influence us. To which voices do you give credence? Do they point you to the gospel or to your own goodness? Do they encourage you to trust in God's mercy or your merit? Do they invite you to believe in God's power or tempt you to believe in man's effort?

When We Are Metaphorically Lame

The Holy Spirit is in and alongside us. Some days in solitude and in partnership with the Spirit, we have the strength and the presence of mind to take our restless and broken hearts to the Father. We can sit in his presence and be quieted by his love. We find his kindness draws us back to repentance and we are restored.

But other days, we are lame—physically, emotionally, and spiritually. It is then that we need a community of support (husband, friends, co-workers, neighbors, mentors, coaches, and counselors) to take us to Christ. Getting to Jesus on our own is unrealistic.

Some men came carrying a paralytic on a mat and tried to take him into the house to lay him before Jesus. When they could not find a way to do this because of the crowd, they went up on the roof and lowered him on his mat through the tiles into the middle of the crowd, right in front of Jesus.
—Luke 5:18

Only because of the love of his friends was the paralytic on his mat before Jesus.

Ask Yourself

* What symptoms or cues let you know you are physically, emotionally, and spiritually on the mat and in need of through-the-roof friends to take you to Christ?
* Who are your gospel mentors?
* How could you pursue more or other gospel mentors?
* Who are your gospel friends?
* How could you pursue gospel friends?
* What does gospel friendship look like in your marriage?
* How could you be a more intentional gospel friend to your spouse?
* Do you pastor your heart? How well?
* What steps will you take to grow in taking truth to your own heart?

This article is excerpted from the Parakaleo Leader Handbook.

Why Church Planters Need A Theology of Suffering
by Shari Thomas

Why Use This Tool?
• To address and ponder our aversion to suffering
• To consider three of the dangers of an absence of a theology of suffering

Dear friends, don't be surprised at the fiery trials you are going through, as if something strange were happening to you. Instead, be very glad—for these trials make you partners with Christ in his suffering, so that you will have the wonderful joy of seeing his glory when it is revealed to all the world.
—1 Peter 4:12-13 (NLT)

Earlier we explored the importance of examining our childhood stories and identifying our idols. We are promised that we will suffer for the sake of the gospel. But our sin patterns will also cause and complicate suffering. Situations where we have been made to feel powerless in childhood may trigger us as adults. Abandonment in the past may tempt us to keep emotional distance from congregants in the hope that we can avoid further pain. Betrayal may trigger suspicion and hypervigilance. Knowing our stories of wounding and our particular idols may help identify the role our sin plays in suffering, but it will not eliminate it.

Living in community with others in a fallen world guarantees suffering. Because suffering is most often viewed as negative, and because it just feels awful, we'll do almost everything in our power to escape it. Often in our churches we don't leave room for relational pain. People don't like to get uncomfortably close and frustrated with each other. Conflicts arise and we find ourselves surprised and bothered. Even though we know entering conflict in relationship has the potential to ultimately draw us more deeply to each other, we avoid it at all costs. We don't like pain!

The biggest fear many of us face in ministry is wondering how big of a toll suffering will take on us and our families. How much will we suffer? In 1 Peter we are told to be glad about our trials. Quite frankly, that's hard for me. I don't like to suffer. I am not a happy camper when I'm in pain, and especially when I'm in relational pain.

Yet, scripture teaches us that joy and suffering are inexorably linked. 1 Peter 4 implies that because we live in the "now, but not yet" time period of history, we will experience both the "now" and the "not yet." In other words, we will suffer (the "not yet") and we will also see glimpses of his glory (the "now"). Almost all the passages about suffering are linked to joy. In some inexplicable way suffering links us to Jesus.

I believe we need a strong theology of suffering because without one we suffer more, we may reject God's call on our lives, and we often forgo the deep joy and partnership with Christ that come only through suffering.

We suffer more without a theology of suffering

We are often surprised when we face suffering, but especially so when we face it in the context of ministry. We wonder what we, our husbands, or others did wrong for there to be such pain in our lives. We point fingers. We blame. We want to find the cause and above all else fix it so it won't happen again. We suffer on account of our own sin. We suffer on account of the sin of others. And we also suffer on account of the gospel. Those who bring the gospel of Jesus Christ to a community will suffer (note Stephen in Acts 7). We often forget that in church

175

planting this is what we are doing! Colossians 1:24 says we will suffer for the sake of Christ's church. 2 Corinthians 4:8-11 seems to be saying that through our suffering as church leaders, the body experiences life.

Because as spouses of church planters/pastors we do not have official job titles and clear boundaries, we often don't consider ourselves to be in positions of leadership. Our roles, identities, and calling feel fluid. Thus, we can fail to read verses written to church leaders as applying to us. Often the passages of scripture that could offer the greatest comfort are ignored because we don't realize they address us!

We may reject a hard life calling

I often participate in the assessment process before a couple is released to plant a church. Among other things, we ask about their experience with suffering. Why?

The American church often has a blind spot when it comes to a theology of suffering. If the planting couple doesn't understand that suffering is normal to the Christian life, not only will they be tempted to quit when the going gets rough, but they will most likely cultivate the idea that church is supposed to be a comfortable place.

Most of us share the experience of rolling over in bed sometime during our planting years and telling our spouse we think we missed God's call. Our failures loom before us. We don't see fruit. We hear complaints and even threats. We are exhausted and we wonder what we have gotten ourselves into. Without a proper theology of suffering, every one of us would run for cover or beat a hasty retreat. Surely we would seek other employment. The calling to bring the gospel to a community is hard work! We will be resisted, often by other Christians, the very ones we thought would be there to support us. Because everyone comes to a church with mixed motives and preconceived notions of what "church" should look like, those joining you come with unspoken desires and expectations of you. And you have desires and expectations of them. Yes, it's a perfect recipe for conflict. But, rather than trying to do everything possible to avoid conflict and the suffering that ensues, how about entering it? Oh, it will be painful. You say you are not good at conflict management? Maybe planting a church is what God will use to grow you, too.

We miss out on joy

One thing I love about the Old Testament is that it oozes with joy. It's full of celebrations, festivities, beauty, and rejoicing. Even the description of creation is written in the form of a poem. When God talks about creating mankind, the Hebrew word used implies he poem-ed us. Talk about art at its best! As the story of God points toward the consummation, again the description is one of rejoicing and beauty beyond anything we can wrap our minds around.

Yet as we study further, we see joy is linked closely to suffering.

If we settle only for gratification or satisfaction in life, we miss out on joy. Not only can seeking gratification lead to addictions, it's also an easy substitute in ministry for real joy. I am so easily satisfied when everything works well, when people like us, when my kids feel settled and comfortable. And I can work hard to make that happen.

Yet embracing a call to ministry means embracing a call to suffering. People will misunderstand us. We will get knocked down, we will be pressed with troubles on every side. Through this suffering, we continue to share in the death of Jesus so the life of Jesus may be seen through our bodies (II Corinthians 4:8-11). One of the purposes of suffering is so that others will see Jesus.

When I first conducted research among church planting spouses, the overwhelming commonality that made church planting a joy was seeing lives changed. I didn't find anyone so bold as to say, "that person is finding Jesus because of my suffering." But really this is what's happening.

The analogy of birth fits the church planting description perfectly. There is something about that phase of gathering a core group, designing the vision, and planning for what the church will be that is similar to carrying a child in the womb for nine months. We spend time preparing for the child as well as for the birth experience and the pain it will inevitably bring. Why aren't we preparing ourselves for the suffering we will endure in bringing the gospel to a community? Genesis 3 speaks specifically to women about pain in childbirth and also implies that the relationships we birth will also be painful. 1 Peter 4 12-13 says we should not be surprised by the fiery trials we go through as though something strange were happening to us, and that this suffering makes us partners with Christ in his suffering. And it is here where we will also experience the joy of seeing his glory when it is revealed to all the world.

When my husband came home today, I told him I was writing on the theology of suffering. I got a strange look. I'm not known for suffering graciously. To be perfectly honest, I'll do just about anything to avoid it. When I'm sick, my family is not happy. They know I will audibly moan and groan and insist I'm dying. When things go wrong in the church, I'm not much different. Yet part of the calling on our life as a couple is entering difficult situations. Listening to arguments, entering pain, and walking with people when they are in darkness is not easy. While I hate to put this in writing, I really wouldn't trade it for the world. We are sharing in the sufferings of Christ on behalf of others and on behalf of his church. In this, we share in his glory! The joy that comes from this is beyond anything I can describe.

1. In your own words, what is your view of suffering?
2. How confident are you in the biblical soundness of your answer?
3. What might you do to grow in a Biblical understanding of suffering?
4. If you believed God's Word regarding suffering, how might your response to your current suffering be different?

community

Serving Each Other Through Forgiveness and Reconciliation
by Timothy Keller

Why Use This Tool?
- To identify subtle ways we attempt to exact payment rather than forgive
- To explore the emotional humility and wealth needed to forgive
- To learn practical skills for reconciliation

On both a theological and a practical level, forgiveness is at the very heart of what it means to be a Christian. True forgiveness comes at a cost and is pursued intentionally within a community of believers.

The new human community that the Bible requires cuts across all cultures and temperaments. Put another way, it doesn't fit any culture but challenges them all at some point. Christians from more individualistic cultures love the Bible's emphasis on affirming one another and sharing hurts and problems—but hate the idea of accountability and discipline. Christians from more traditional communal cultures love the emphasis on accountability for morals and beliefs but often chafe at the emphasis on racial reconciliation and being open about one's personal hurts and financial needs.

But one could argue that the biblical teaching on forgiveness and reconciliation is so radical that there are no cultures or societies that are in accord with it. It may be here most of all that we see the truth of Bonhoeffer's statement, "Our community with one another [in Christ] consists solely in what Christ has done to both of us. Christian brotherhood is a spiritual and not a human reality. In this it differs from all other communities."[1]

In its most basic and simple form, this teaching is that *Christians in community are to never give up on one another, never give up on a relationship, and never write off another believer.* We must never tire of forgiving (and repenting!) and seeking to repair our relationships. Matthew 5:23–26 tells us we should go to someone if we know they have something against us. Matthew 18:15–20 says we should approach someone if we have something against *them.* In short, if any relationship has cooled off or has weakened in any way, *it is always your move.* It doesn't matter "who started it." God always holds you responsible to reach out to repair a tattered relationship. A Christian is responsible to begin the process of reconciliation, regardless of how the distance or the alienation began.

WHAT FORGIVENESS IS
When speaking of forgiveness, Jesus uses the image of *debts* to describe the nature of sins (Matt. 6:12; 18:21–35). When someone seriously wrongs you, there is an absolutely unavoidable sense that the wrongdoer *owes* you. The wrong has incurred an obligation, a liability, a debt. Anyone who has been wronged feels a compulsion to make the other person pay down that debt. We do that by hurting them, yelling at them, making them feel bad in some way, or just waiting and watching and hoping that something bad happens to them. Only after we see them suffer in some commensurate way do we sense that the debt has been paid and the sense of obligation is gone. This sense of debt/liability and obligation is impossible to escape. Anyone who denies it exists has simply not been wronged or sinned against in any serious way.

What then is forgiveness? Forgiveness means giving up the right to seek repayment from the one who harmed you. But it must be recognized that forgiveness is a *form of voluntary suffering.* What does that mean?

178

Think about how monetary debts work. If a friend breaks my lamp, and if the lamp costs fifty dollars to replace, then the act of lamp-breaking incurs a debt of fifty dollars. If I let him pay for and replace the lamp, I get my lamp back and he's out fifty dollars. But if I *forgive him* for what he did, the debt does not somehow vanish into thin air. When I forgive him, I absorb the cost and payment for the lamp: either I will pay the fifty dollars to replace it or I will lose the lighting in that room. To forgive is to cancel a debt by paying it or absorbing it yourself. Someone always pays every debt.

This is the case in all situations of wrongdoing, even when no money is involved. When you are sinned against, you lose some thing—perhaps happiness, reputation, peace of mind, a relationship, or an opportunity. There are two things to do about a sin. Imagine for example that someone has hurt your reputation. You can try to restore it by paying the other person back, voicing public criticisms and ruining *his or her* reputation. Or you can forgive the one who wronged you, refuse payback, and absorb the damage to your reputation. (You will have to restore it over time.)

In all cases when wrong is done there is a debt, and there is no way to deal with it without suffering: either you make the perpetrator suffer for it or you forgive and suffer for it yourself.

Forgiveness is always extremely costly. It is emotionally very expensive—it takes much blood, sweat, and tears. When you forgive, you pay the debt yourself in several ways.

First, you refuse to hurt the person directly; you refuse vengeance, payback, or the infliction of pain. Instead, you are as cordial as possible. When forgiving you must beware of subtle ways to try to exact payment while assuring yourself that you aren't. Here are specific things to avoid:
+   making cutting remarks and dragging out past injuries repeatedly
+   being far more demanding and controlling with the person than you are with others, all because you feel deep down that they still owe you
+   punishing them with self-righteous "mercy" that is really a way to make them feel small and to justify your-self
+   avoiding them or being cold toward them

Second, you refuse to employ innuendo or "spin" or hint or gossip or direct slander to diminish those who have hurt you in the eyes of others. You don't run them down under the guise of warning people about them or under the guise of seeking sympathy and support and sharing your hurt.

Third, when forgiving you refuse to indulge in ill will in your heart. That is, don't continually replay the tapes of the wrong in your imagination in order to keep the sense of loss and hurt fresh so you can stay actively hostile toward the person and feel virtuous by contrast. Don't vilify or demonize the offender in your imagination. Rather, recognize the common sinful humanity you share with him or her. Don't root for them to fail, don't hope for their pain. Instead, pray positively for their growth.

Forgiveness, then, is granted before it is felt. It is a promise to refrain from the three things above and pray for the perpetrator as you remind yourself of God's grace to you. Though it is extremely difficult and painful (you are bearing the cost of the sin yourself!), forgiveness will deepen your character, free you to talk to and help the person, and lead to love and peace rather than bitterness.

Further, by bearing the cost of the sin, you are walking in the path of your Master (Matt. 18:21–35; Col. 3:13). It is typical for non-Christians today to say that the cross of Christ makes no sense. "Why did Jesus have to die?

Why couldn't God just forgive us?" Actually *no one* who has been deeply wronged "*just* forgives"! If someone wrongs you, there are only two options: (1) you make them suffer, or (2) you refuse revenge and forgive them and then you suffer. And if we can't forgive without suffering, how much more must God suffer in order to forgive us? If we unavoidably sense the obligation and debt and injustice of sin in our soul, how much more does God know it? On the cross we see God forgiving us, and that was possible only if God suffered. On the cross God's love satisfied his own justice by suffering, bearing the penalty for sin. There is never forgiveness without suffering, nails, thorns, sweat, blood. Never.

WHAT WE NEED TO FORGIVE

The experience of the gospel gives us the two prerequisites for a life of forgiveness: emotional humility and emotional wealth.

You can remain bitter toward someone only if you feel superior, if you are sure that you "would never do anything like that!" To remain unforgiving means you are unaware of your own sinfulness and need for forgiveness. When Paul says he is the worst among sinners (1 Tim. 1:15), he is not exaggerating. He is saying that he is as capable of sin as the worst criminals are. The gospel has equipped him with emotional humility.

At the same time, you can't be gracious to someone if you are too needy and insecure. If you know God's love and forgiveness, then there is a limit to how deeply another person can hurt you. He or she can't touch your real identity, wealth, and significance. The more you rejoice in your own forgiveness, the quicker you will be able to forgive others. You are rooted in emotional wealth.

> *Forgiveness founders because I exclude the enemy from the community of humans even as I exclude myself from the community of sinners. But no one can be in the presence of the God of the crucified Messiah for long without overcoming this double exclusion—without transposing the enemy from the sphere of monstrous inhumanity into the sphere of shared humanity and herself from the sphere of proud innocence into the sphere of common sinfulness. When one knows that the torturer will not eternally triumph over the victim, one is free to rediscover that person's humanity and imitate God's love for him. And when one knows that God's love is greater than all sin, one is free to see oneself... and so rediscover one's own sinfulness. [2]*

Jesus says, "If you do not forgive men their sins, your heavenly Father will not forgive your sins" (Matt. 6:15). This does not mean we can earn God's forgiveness through our own forgiving but that we can disqualify ourselves from it. No heart that is truly repentant toward God could be unforgiving toward others. A lack of forgiveness toward others is the direct result of a lack of repentance toward God. And as we know, you must repent in order to be saved (Acts 2:38).

GOD'S FORGIVENESS AND OURS

When God reveals his glory to Moses, he says he forgives wickedness yet "does not leave the guilty unpunished" (Exod. 34:6–7). Not until the coming of Jesus do we see how God can be both completely just and forgiving through his atonement (1 John 1:7–9). In the cross God satisfies both justice and love. God was so just and desirous to judge sin that Jesus had to die, but he was so loving and desirous of our salvation that Jesus was glad to die.

We too are *commanded* to forgive ("bear with each other and forgive whatever grievances you may have against one another," Col 3:13–14) on the basis of Jesus' atonement for our sins ("Forgive us our debts, as we also have forgiven our debtors... If you do not forgive men their sins, your heavenly Father will not forgive your sins," Matt. 6:14–15; cf. Luke 6:37). But we are also required to forgive in a way that honors justice, just as God's forgiveness does. "If your brother sins, rebuke him, and if he repents, forgive him" (Luke 17:3). "Christians are called to abandon bitterness, to be forbearing, to have a forgiving stance even where the repentance of the offending party is conspicuous by its absence; on the other hand, their God-centered passion for justice, their concern for God's glory, ensure that the awful odium of sin is not glossed over."[3]

PURSUING TRUTH, LOVE, AND RELATIONSHIP

The gospel calls us, then, to keep an equal concern (a) to speak the truth and honor what is right, yet (b) to be endlessly forgiving as we do so and (c) to never give up on the goal of a reconciled, warm relationship.

First, God requires forgiveness whether or not the offender has repented and has asked for forgiveness. "And when you stand praying, if you hold anything against anyone, forgive him" (Mark 11:25). This does not say "forgive him *if he repents*" but rather "forgive him right there—as you are praying."

Second, God requires speaking the truth. That is why Jesus tells his disciples in Luke 17:3 to "rebuke" the wrongdoer and "if he repents, forgive him." Is Jesus saying that we can hold a grudge if the person doesn't repent? No, we must not read Luke 17 to contradict Mark 11. Jesus is calling us here *both* to practice inner forgiveness *and* to rebuke and correct. We must completely surrender the right to pay back or get even, yet at the same time we must never overlook injustice and must require serious wrongdoings to be redressed.

This is almost the very opposite of how we ordinarily operate. Ordinarily we do not seek justice on the outside (we don't confront or call people to change and make restitution), but we stay hateful and bitter on the inside. The Bible calls us to turn this completely around. We are to deeply forgive on the inside so as to have no desire for vengeance, but then we are to speak openly about what has happened with a desire to help the person see what was done wrong.

In reality, inner forgiveness and outward correction work well together. Only if you have forgiven inside can you correct unabusively—without trying to make the person feel terrible. Only if you have forgiven already can your motive be to correct the person for God's sake, for justice's sake, for the community's sake, and for the person's sake. And only if you forgive on the inside will your words have any hope of changing the perpetrator's heart. Otherwise your speech will be so filled with disdain and hostility that he or she will not listen to you.

Ultimately, to forgive on the inside and to rebuke/correct on the outside are not incompatible, because they are both acts of love. It is never loving to let a person just get away with sin. It is not loving to the perpetrator, who continues in the grip of the habit, nor to those who will be wronged in the future, nor to God, who is grieved. This is difficult, for the line is very thin between a moral outrage for God's sake and a self-righteous outrage because of hurt pride. Still, to refuse to confront is not loving but just selfish.

Third, as we "speak the truth in love" (Eph. 4:15), we are to pursue justice gently and humbly, in order to redress wrongs and yet maintain or restore the relationship (Gal. 6:1–5). There is a great deal of tension between these three things! Almost always one is much more easily attained if you simply drop any concern for the other two. For example, it is easy to "speak the truth" if you've given up on any desire to maintain a warm relationship. But if you want both, you will have to be extremely careful with how you speak the truth! Another example: it is possible to convince yourself that you have forgiven someone, but if afterward you still want nothing to do with them (you don't pursue an ongoing relationship), then that is a sign that you spoke the truth without truly forgiving.

Of course it is possible that you do keep these three things together in your heart and mind but the other person simply cannot. There is no culture or personality type that holds these together. People tend to believe that if you

community

are confronting me you don't forgive or love me, or if you really loved me you wouldn't be rebuking me. God recognizes that many people simply won't let you pursue all these things together, and so tells us, "As far as it depends on you, live at peace with everyone" (Rom. 12:18). That is, do your part and have as good and peaceful a relationship with people as they will let you have.

WHEN DO WE NEED TO CONFRONT AND RECONCILE?
Jesus tells us that if we have been sinned against we may need to go and speak to the offender. "If your brother sins, rebuke him, and if he repents, forgive him" (Luke 17:3). But *when* do we "rebuke"—every time anyone wrongs us? First Peter 4:8 says famously that "love covers over a multitude of sins," and Proverbs 10:12 backs this up. This means we are not to be thin-skinned, and it would be wrong to bring up every matter every time we have been treated unjustly or insensitively. Still, passages like Matthew 18 and Luke 17 say there are some times in which we should make a complaint. When do we do so?

This is where Galatians 6 gives us guidance. "Brothers, if someone is caught in a sin, you who are spiritual should restore him gently. But watch yourself, or you also may be tempted" (6:1). We should give correction under two conditions.

First, we should correct when the sin is serious enough to cool off or rupture the relationship. Matthew 18:15 indicates that the purpose of a rebuke is to "win your brother over"—that is, to rescue the relationship. That is implied when Galatians 6:2 tells us that correcting someone is a way of "carrying each other's burdens;" it is an expression of an interdependent relationship.

Second, we should correct when the sin against us is evidently part of a pattern of behavior that the other person is seriously stuck in. "If someone is *caught in* a sin, you who are spiritual should restore him" (Gal. 6:1): the image is of being trapped in a pattern of behavior that will be harmful to the person and to others. In love this should be pointed out. So we rebuke for the person's sake—to "restore him." Our concern is his or her growth.

And how do we do it? "You who are spiritual should restore him *gently*" (Gal. 6:1). This is essential. If the motive of the correction is helping the other to grow, then we will be loving and gentle. Verses 2–3 indicate that we should do this very humbly. We are making ourselves servants by doing the correction.

Ultimately, any love that is afraid to confront the beloved is really not love but a selfish desire to *be* loved. Cowardice is always selfish, putting your own needs ahead of the needs of the other. A love that says, "I'll do *anything* to keep him or her loving and approving of me!" is not real love at all. It is not loving the person; it is loving the love you get from the person. True love is willing to confront, even to "lose" the beloved in the short run if there is a chance to help him or her.

Nevertheless, it is clear that there are plenty of times we should not correct and not seek an apology even when one is owed. The stronger a Christian you are, the less sensitive and easily hurt you will be. When people "zing" you, snub you, ignore you, or let you down in some way, it should not immediately cool you to them. As a mature Christian, you immediately remember (a) times you did the same thing to others or (b) times that people who did this to you were later revealed to have a lot on their mind and heart. If you find that any wrongdoing immediately cools you to another and you want to insist on your right to an apology, do some self-examination regarding the level of your emotional humility and emotional wealth in Christ. Love should cover a multitude of sins (that is, most of them!) You should be able to warmly treat people who by rights owe you an apology but whom you haven't corrected because the slights were rather minor, or the time isn't right to speak about it, or you don't know them well enough to be sure it is a major pattern in their life.

HOW DO WE RECONCILE?
Here are some basics.

What Are The Marks Of An Unreconciled Relationship?

An unreconciled relationship is marked by avoidance, coldness, and irritability (that is, the same action performed by another person does not disturb you as much as it does when *this* person does it!) If you find yourself avoiding, being cold toward, or being very irritated with someone (or if you can tell that someone is cold or irritable toward you or avoiding you), then you probably have an unreconciled relationship.

On the other hand, "I forgive you" does *not* mean "I trust you." Some people think they haven't reconciled until they can completely trust the person who did the wrong. That is not the case. Forgiveness means a willingness to try to reestablish trust, but that reestablishment is always a process. The speed and degree of this restoration entail the re-creation of trust, and that takes time, depending on the nature and severity of the offenses involved. Until a person shows evidence of true change, we should *not trust* him or her. To immediately give one's trust to a person with sinful habits could actually be enabling him to sin. Trust must be restored, and the speed at which this occurs depends on the behavior.

This also applies to the people who owe you an apology but whose sins have been "covered" (see above). A person who has let you down but whom you don't correct has damaged your trust, albeit in minor ways. If he or she comes to apologize, it will restore the level of trust and respect you had before, but until that happens you can still have a civil and cordial relationship with them.

How Can You Reconcile With Someone?

We can look at Matthew 5 and Matthew 18 as two different approaches: Matthew 5 lays out what you do when you believe you have wronged someone else, while Matthew 18 is what you do when you believe someone has wronged you. But it is also possible to also look at these passages as giving us two stages of the normal reconciliation process, because seldom does just one party bear all the blame for a frayed relationship. Almost always reconciliation involves *both* repenting *and* forgiving—both admitting your own wrong and pointing out the wrong of the other. If we put these two approaches together, we can create a practical outline like the one that follows.

Stage 1

Begin by confessing anything you may have done wrong (this might be called the "Matthew 5:24 phase"). Begin with yourself. Even if you believe that your own behavior is no more than five percent of the problem, start with your five percent! Look for what you have done wrong, and collect the criticism.

List whatever you think you have done wrong and ask the other person to add to the list of things you have done wrong or ways you have contributed to the breakdown in the relationship. Example: "I'm here because I don't like what has happened to our relationship [or—*if the term applies*—our friendship]. It appears to me that there is a problem between us; am I wrong?" Then, "Here is what I believe I have contributed to the problem between us—where I've wronged you.... But where else have I wronged you or contributed to the relationship problem, in your estimation?"

If you are almost totally in the dark about what went wrong, you may have to simply offer to listen. Example: "It appears to me that there is trouble between us and I have offended you. Am I right? Please tell me specific ways I have wronged you. I am ready to listen—honest."

Then listen well to the criticism you've invited. Seek to distill this criticism into something clear and specific. To do so too quickly may seem defensive, but eventually ask for as many specific examples as possible. If the other says, "You are bullying," you need to find out what actual words or actions or tones of voice strike the other person as bullying.

Here is a practical checklist:
+ Pray silently, asking God to give you wisdom and allow you to sense his love for you.
+ Assume that God is speaking to you through this painful situation and is showing you ways you should be more careful or change.
+ Assume that God is speaking to you even through a very flawed person.
+ Beware of being defensive. Don't explain yourself too quickly, even if you have a good answer or can show the person that he or she was mistaken. Be sure you don't interrupt or keep the other from expressing frustration.
+ Show sympathy even if you were misunderstood.
+ Always ask, "Is there anything else? I really want to know!" In a stressful situation it is natural for the other to hold back some complaints or concerns. Get them all out on the table, or you'll have to do this again!
+ Make it safe to criticize you: support individual criticisms with, "That must have been hard; I see why you were concerned."
+ Look for needs in the critic that may underlie the criticism.
+ Now respond to the criticism, by doing either or both of the following:
  1. "Please, forgive me for...." This is your repentance, your confession of sin.
  • Admit your wrong without excuses and without blaming the circumstances. Even if the criticism included exaggerations, extract the real fault and confess it. Even if only ten percent of the relationship problem is you, admit it.
  • Don't just apologize; ask for forgiveness.
  • If you can think of a plan for changing your behavior, say, "Here is what I will do to make sure I don't do such a thing again in the future." Ask if there is anything you can do to restore trust. If you really cannot see any validity in any of the criticism, ask whether you can get back to the person later, after checking with others.
  • Avoid overstatements—"How terrible I feel over what I've done!" Such confessions may be mainly a painful catharsis designed to relieve one of guilt feelings through a kind of atonement/punishment, or to get others to provide lots of sympathy.
  • On the other hand, avoid being deadpan, lighthearted, or even flip. Such confessions may aim to preserve pride, merely to fulfill a requirement, to force the other person to let you off the hook but without showing any real contrition or emotional regret at all.
  • Most of all, do not make a confession that is really an attack. "If I upset you, I am sorry" falls in this category. It means, "If you were a normal person, you would not have been upset by what I did." Do not repent to the person of something that you are not going to repent to God for nor take concrete steps to change.
  • Real repentance has three aspects: confession to God, confession to the person wronged, and offering a concrete plan for change so as to avoid the sin in the future (see Luke 3:7–14).

  2. After you have repented, then turn to those issues that involve no sin on your part (as far as you can tell) and about which you have to say, "Please, accept my explanation for...."
  • "Here's how I see it. Can you see my motive or meaning was very different from what you inferred?"
  • "Can you understand my point of view? Can you accept that I could have perceived this very differently and had the motives I am describing?"
  • "Is there a way, though we see this issue differently, that we can avoid hurting each other like this again?"

Stage #2

Now (if necessary) address any ways that the other person has wronged you ("Matthew 18 phase"). If you have done all of the above, you may well find that this approach elicits a confession from the other without your having to ask for it! This is far and away the best way to get reconciliation.

However, if the other person is not forthcoming, begin with: "From my point of view, it looks as if you did _____. It affected me this way: _____. I think it would be far better for all concerned if instead you did this: _____. But my understanding may be inaccurate or distorted. Correct me if I am wrong. Could you explain what happened?" Be sure your list of things the other person has done is specific, not vague.

If the other person offers an apology, grant forgiveness—but avoid using the term unless forgiveness is asked for! Otherwise to say "I forgive you" may sound tremendously humiliating. Alternative ways to express forgiveness might be "Well, I won't hold this against you," "Let's put that in the past now," or "Think no more of it."

Here are some general guidelines for this part of the process:

- Maintain a loving and humble tone. Tone of voice is extremely important. Overly controlled, nice, and calm may sound patronizing and be infuriating. Don't resort to flattery or fawning syrupiness or fall into abusive or angry tones.
- Attack the problem, not the person. For example, don't say, "You are so thoughtless"; rather, you might say, "You have forgotten this after making repeated promises that you would not."
- Suggest solutions and alternative courses of action or behavior. Make sure all criticism is specific and constructive. Never say, "Don't do this" without saying, "Instead do this."
- In the heart of the discussion, you may discover some other underlying goal or need that the other person is trying to meet that could be met in more constructive ways.
- Keep in mind differences in culture. A person from a different culture may consider your approach incredibly disrespectful and demeaning when you think you are being respectful.

What if the other person won't be reconciled to you?

First, some thoughts on failed reconciliation with a non-Christian. Christians are commanded to seek peace and reconciliation with all people (Rom. 12:18; Heb. 12:14), not just Christians. However, non-Christians may not feel the same responsibility to live in reconciled relationships. In general, you will find that non-Christians will not feel compelled to respond with forgiveness and repentance.

If that occurs, you must take what you are given. Romans 12:18–21 provides guidelines on how to stay gracious, kind, open, and cordial to persons who are being standoffish.[4]

What if a Christian from your church is resisting reconciliation? Matthew 18 indicates that if a fellow believer will not reconcile after repeated intentional efforts on your part, you should go to stage B—getting some other Christian friends (preferably including someone who is respected by the other person) to go along with you to reconcile the relationship. If that does not work, at stage C you "tell it to the church" and ask the elders to speak to the person.

If the person with whom you are seeking reconciliation is a Christian but lives in another region or attends another church, you should take the Matthew 18:15–20 process as far as you can. However, if you are not members of the same church it may not be possible to go to the final step of "telling it to the church." Again, you may have to take what you are given and deal as cordially and as graciously as possible with someone who is not reconciled to you.

community

More generally, learn to accept the apologies and repentances you get without demanding that people admit more than they honestly believe. If they repent nearly as extensively as you feel they should, then the relationship can be almost what it was before. If they only go halfway, then you are still better off, though the relationship is weakened because you don't fully trust their wisdom and self-knowledge.

It is usually hardest to forgive someone who will not admit any wrong and who stays haughty. Internal forgiveness may be a longer process. Use all the spiritual resources we have in our faith:

+ Look at God's commands to forgive—it is our obligation.
+ Remember God's forgiveness of us. We have no right to be bitter.
+ Remember that God's omniscience is necessary to be a just judge. We have insufficient knowledge to know what others deserve.
+ Remember that when we allow the evil to keep us in bondage through bitterness, we are being defeated by evil! Romans 12 tells us to "overcome" or *defeat* evil with forgiveness.
+ Remember that we undermine the glory of the gospel in the world's eyes when we fail to forgive.

WATCHING FROM THE SIDELINES

When two people within the church are in conflict with each other, it can wreak a lot of havoc in the hearts and lives of the Christians around them who are not immediately involved in the dispute. The worst thing (but the common thing!) that happens is that rather than suspending judgment, praying, and encouraging the parties toward reconciliation, people take sides in the dispute in a very world-typical way. It is hard not to sympathize with the party you know best. It is also hard for that person not to "share" his or her hurt with you in a way that does not vilify the other party in the conflict.

As a result, we can have second- and third-order unreconciled relationships. That is, we feel alienated from people who are friends of the person our friend is alienated from! The problem with this is obvious—there is no direct way to heal such breaches. If someone is avoiding you because your friend is mad at his or her friend, there is no "wrong" that you can confess or repent for. It is a spiritually poisonous situation. The problem is not that you have sinned or have been sinned against, but you have heard a bad report about another Christian and you let it come into your own heart and take root as distrust and hostility.

What should we do? First, see what James says about passing along bad reports: "Humble yourselves before the Lord. Brothers, don't slander or attack one another" (James 4:10–11). The verb *slander* simply means to "speak against" *(kata-lalein)*. It is not necessarily a false report, just an "against-report"—one that undermines the listener's respect and love for the person being spoken about. "As a north wind brings rain, so a sly tongue brings angry looks" (Prov. 25:23). James's linking of slander with pride (4:10) shows that slander is not a humble evaluation of error or fault, which we must constantly be doing. Rather, the slandering person speaks as if he or she never would do the same thing himself. Nonslanderous evaluation is gentle and guarded, and it's always evident that the speaker is aware of sharing the same frailty, humanity, and sinful nature with the one being criticized. It involves a profound awareness of one's own sin. It is never "against-speaking."

"Don't grumble [literally, don't groan and roll your eyes] against each other" (James 5:9). Here James refers to a kind of against-speaking that is less specific than a focused slander or attack. It is hinting with not only words but also body language—shaking one's head, rolling eyes, and reinforcing an erosion of love and respect for someone else ("You know how they do things around here!") But it accomplishes the same thing. It brings "angry looks;" it undermines love and respect.

Second, see what the book of Proverbs says about receiving bad reports: "He who covers over an offense promotes love, but whoever repeats the matter separates close friends" (Prov. 17:9). The first thing to do when hearing or seeing something negative is to seek to "cover" the offense rather than speak about it to others. That is, rather than letting it in, you should seek to keep the matter from destroying your love and regard for a person. How?

+ *Remember your own sinfulness.* "All a man's ways seem innocent to him, but motives are weighed by the LORD" (Prov. 16:2). Your motives are never as pure as you think they are. To know your sinfulness automatically keeps you from being too sure of your position and from speaking too strongly against people on the other side of a conflict. You realize that you may not be seeing things well.

+ *Remember that there is always another side.* "The first to present his case seems right, till another comes forward and questions him" (Prov. 18:17). You never have all the facts. You are never in a position to have the whole picture, and therefore when you hear the first negative report, you should assume that you have far too little information to draw a conclusion.

What if the injustice seems too great or grievous for you to ignore? In Derek Kidner's commentary on Proverbs 25:8–10, he writes that when we think someone has done wrong, we should remember that "one seldom knows the full facts, or interprets them perfectly (v. 8); and one's motives in spreading a story are seldom as pure as one pretends (v. 10). To run to the law or to the neighbors is usually to run away from the duty of personal relationship—see Christ's clinching comment in Matthew 18:15b."[5] In short, if you feel the problem is so great that it threatens to destroy your regard for the person, you must go to him or her personally before you go to anyone else.

When might this be necessary? Galatians 6:1 says we are to go to someone if they are "caught in a sin." That means some pattern of negative behavior is involved. Don't go the first time you see or hear of someone doing wrong. When you do go, remember the principles of gentleness and persistence from Galatians 6 and Matthew 18. The purpose is restoration of relationship.

If you hear a bad report about another Christian, you must *either cover it with love or go to him or her directly before speaking of it to any others.* The first thing to do is to simply suspend judgment. The second thing to do is "cover" it in love. The last thing to do is go and speak to the reported offender personally. What you should never do is withdraw from them or pass the negative report on to others.

CONCLUSION

Unreconciled relationships within the church are inevitable *because* the church is such a wonderful, supernaturally created community!

> *The reason there are so many exhortations in the New Testament for Christians to love other Christians is because... the church itself is not made up of natural "friends." It is made up of natural enemies. What binds us together is not common education, common race, common income levels, common politics, common nationality, common accents, common jobs, or anything else of that sort [that bind most other groups of people together]. Christians come together not because they form a natural collocation, but because they have all been saved by Jesus Christ and owe him a common allegiance. In this light we are a band of natural enemies who love one another for Jesus' sake. That is the only reason why John 13:34–35 makes sense when Jesus says: "A new command I give you—Love one another as I have loved you." ...Christian love will stand out and bear witness to Jesus because it is a display, for Jesus' sake, of mutual love among social incompatibles.[6]*

The reason we will *have* to hold ourselves accountable for our relationships is that mutual love in Christian community is super-hard. Jesus has brought incompatibles together! But the reason we will want to hold ourselves accountable for our relationships is that mutual love in Christian community is one of the main ways the world will see who Jesus is. So we must never give up on each other. So we must pursue each other in love.

1. Dietrich Bonhoeffer, *Life Together* (New York: Harper, 1954), 23, 25–26.

2. Miroslav Volf, *Exclusion and Embrace* (Nashville: Abingdon, 1996), p. 124.

3. D. A. Carson, *Love in Hard Places* (Wheaton, Ill.: Crossway, 2002), p. 83.

4. A great book on relating to people who are cold or even hostile is *Bold Love* by Dan Allender and Tremper Longman (Colorado Springs: NavPress, 1992). Don't miss it.

5. Derek Kidner, *Proverbs: An Introduction and Commentary*, Tyndale Old Testament Commentary Series (Downers Grove, Ill.: InterVarsity Press, 1981), p. 157.

6. Carson, p. 61.

Diagnostic Tool On Forgiveness
by Shari Thomas

Why use this tool?
- To diagnose where you may struggle with forgiveness
- To take steps towards living a lifestyle of forgiveness

We suggest writing out your answers and sharing them with a like-minded group or friend.

What new insights, if any, did you gain from Keller's article?

What ideas, if any, did you disagree with from Keller's article?

Define emotional humility and emotional wealth in Christ.

How might emotional humility and emotional wealth in Christ be exhibited in you (particularly and specifically)?

What are the marks of an unreconciled relationship?

What are the two approaches to reconciliation from the book of Matthew?

What are the two conditions Keller states for when we should give correction?

List practical steps for listening to and receiving criticism.

What lies from your childhood story are you tempted to believe that make it difficult for you to receive criticism?

List several tips regarding second and third-party conflict.

What are some hallmarks of non-slanderous evaluation?

What are your primary ways of exacting payment instead of offering forgiveness?

Consider asking a family member to describe to you how you exact payment rather than forgive.

Has a name or face come to mind as you have used this tool?

With the help of your group or a friend, outline steps you could take to begin the process of forgiveness. *Remember the crucial need for prayer and belief in Christ's finished work on the cross on your behalf in this process.*

If you are ready, with whom and how will you journey through these steps of forgiveness? *Consider how often you'd like to have or need contact with the person helping you. Consider what is helpful and harmful to you in this process.* **If you are not ready**, how might your group continue to walk with you in this process?

NOTE: If you are dealing with deeply abusive situations in your own life or the life of another we highly recommend getting the help of a professional.

community

Community Resources

A Sword Will Pierce Your Soul: A Journey of Healing and Restoration, Caroline Julihn

The Church, Edmund P. Clowney

The Connecting Church, Randy Frazee

The Cross and Christian Ministry, D.A. Carson

The Death of Character, J.D. Hunter

Exclusion and Embrace: A Theological Exploration of Identity, Otherness, and Reconciliation, Miroslav Volf

Holy Listening, Margaret Guenther

The Household of God, Lesslie Newbigin

Idols of the Heart, Elyse Fitzpatrick

Liberating Ministry from the Success Syndrome, Kent and Barbara Hughes

Life Together, Dietrich Bonhoeffer

Living Faithfully in a Fragmented World, Jonathan R. Wilson

The Peacemaker (revised), Ken Sande

Peacemaking for Women, Judy Dabler and Tara Barthel

Practicing the Presence of People, Mike Mason.

Repentance: The First Word of the Gospel, Richard Owen

Total Forgiveness, R.T. Kendall

The Unnecessary Pastor, Eugene Peterson

Worship, Community & the Triune God of Grace, James Torrance

Bibliography

Allender, Dan. *Sabbath*. Nashville: Thomas Nelson, 2009.

Allender, Dan. *The Wounded Heart: Hope for Adult Victims of Childhood Sexual Abuse*. Colorado Springs: NavPress, 2008.

Allender, Dan. *To Be Told*. Colorado Springs: WaterBrook Press, 2006.

Bearce, Kathy. Roswell, GA. www.careofsouls.net.

Bonar, Horatius. *God's Way of Peace*. Oxford: Benediction Classics, 2010.

Brown, Stephen. *A Scandalous Freedom: The Radical Nature of the Gospel*. New York: Simon and Schuster/Howard Books, 2004.

Buechner, Frederick. *Telling Secrets*. New York: Harper One, 1992.

Chapman, Stephen Curtis and Scotty Smith. *Restoring Broken Things*. Nashville: Thomas Nelson, 2005.

Crabb, Larry. *Inside Out*. Colorado Springs: NavPress, 2007.

Doherty, Catherine de Hueck. *Poustinia: Encountering God in Silence, Solitude and Prayer*. Washington, D.C.: Madonna House Publishers, 2000.

Dorsey, Jenny. "Obvious and Hidden Idols." Indianapolis, Indiana. Unpublished document.

Frankena, William. *A Model of Ananlyzing a Philosophy of Education*. Ann Arbor: University of Michigan Press, 1966.

Guinness, Os. *The Call: Finding and Fulfilling the Central Purpose of Your Life*. Nashville: Word Publishing, 1998.

Keller, Timothy. "Christ's Confession." Redeemer Presbyterian Church. New York City. 25 Feb. 2007. www.redeemer.com

------. "A Paraphrase of Martin Luther's Preface to the Galatians" Redeemer Presbyterian Church. New York City.

------. "How the Gospel Changes Us." Redeemer Presbyterian Church. New York City. 12 Sept. 2003.

------. "Ministry Can Be Dangerous to your Spiritual Health." Redeemer Report. Redeemer Presbyterian Church. New York City. March 2007.

------. "Mortification Through Joy." Redeemer Presbyterian Church. New York City. www.redeemer.com

------. "Serving Each other Through Forgiveness and Reconciliation." Redeemer Presbyterian Church. New York City. October 2009. www.redeemercitytocity.com.

------. "Spiritual Warfare." Redeemer Presbyterian Church. New York City. 3 August 1998.

Lundgaard, Kris. *The Enemy Within: Straight Talk About the Power and Defeat of Sin*. New Jersey: Presbyterian and Reformed Publishing Co. 1998.

MacDonald, George. *A Book of Strife in the Form of the Diary of an Old Soul*. Whitefish, MT: Kessinger Publishing, 2010.

Oliver, Mary. "The Summer Day." *New and Selected Poems*. Boston: Beacon Press, 1992.

Ott, Carrie. "How To Discover Your Story." Woodstock, Georgia. Unpublished document.

------. "Story Discovery: Helps and Prompts." Woodstock, Georgia. Unpublished document.

------. "A Time To Grieve." Woodstock, Georgia. Unpublished document.

Rohr, Richard. *Things Hidden: Scripture as Spirituality*. Cincinnati: St. Anthony Messenger Press, 2008.

Sauls, Scott. "What is the Gospel?" New York City. Unpublished document.

Smed, John. "Prayer Walking the City." October 2009. www.prayerforthecity.com.

Smith, Scotty. "The Narrative of God's Story" Nashville, Tenn. Unpublished document.

Sonship. World Harvest Mission. Jenkintown, Pennsylvania. www.whm.org

Taylor, Daniel. *The Healing Power of Stories*. New York: Doubleday, 1996.

Thomas, John. "The Gospel for Everyone But Pastors." New York City. Unpublished document.

Thomas, Shari. *The Primary Sources of Stress and Satisfaction Among PCA Church Planting Spouses*. Atlanta: Mission to North America, 2005.

Tournier, Paul. *Reflections*. Philadelphia: Westminster Press, 1982.

Virtue, David. "Book Review: The Call by Os Guinness." October 2009. www.virtueonline.org.

Acknowledgements

Now we understand why acknowledgment pages can be so long. There is no way we could have accomplished this feat on our own!

Thank you, **John** (Shari's husband), for giving me the courage, the time, and the research skills for this project. More importantly, you have relentlessly pursued my heart, refusing to let me give up on finding and following my calling regardless of the difficulty it has caused.

Steve (Tami's husband), you believed in me long before I believed in myself. In your 'gospelicious' way, you invite me to strength and to faith. You live what you preach in and out of the pulpit!

To our children, **Michaelanne, Corey, Becca, Steve, Emily, and Katherine** who grew up in the weird and wacky world of church planting—while you've experienced pressures, expectations, and ambiguity most kids never know, you turned out to be amazing people! You are among our greatest delights. Thank you for loving us so well.

Without the skills, persistence, and patience of **Carrie Ott** we could not fathom accomplishing this project. Carrie, you were able to get inside our thoughts and put into words what we were unable to express. You not only honored and valued our unique styles but with your gifted writing skills, you make us look way better than we really are. But more than this project, you have walked with me (Shari) during my darkest hours. Words are not sufficient.

Our Parakaleo staff, **Cristina Caires** and **Maria Garriott**, you have been amazingly gracious to join us when there hasn't been pay and have walked with us into the unknown of creating a ministry for church planting spouses. Thank you, Maria, for giving the insight and editing skills to this project that only a published author could give.

Thank you, **Jim Bland** and **Ted Powers** with Mission to North America, for being risk-takers and bringing us on staff before we even knew what we were doing!

Susie Quillin, once again, you freely gave your artistic talents to yet another Parakaleo project knowing we could never afford someone with your ability. Thank you for rescuing us so many times during this project.

Chris Rank, you've been a giver as long as I've (Shari) known you. Thank you for still answering my texts after all these years and willingly doing our photo ops. Thank you, **Clara Lee** at Redeemer City to City, for locating and making it possible to use Tim Keller's articles. **Melanie Ponchot**, thank you for creating the original art for our Right Turn/left Turn chart. **Lois Swaggerty**, your love of words, wit, and whimsical writing was a most appreciated gift.

We are indebted to **David Arms, Steve Brown, Stu and Ruth Ann Batstone, Jenny Dorsey, Tim Keller, Carrie Ott, Scott Sauls, Scotty Smith, John Thomas, and David Virtue** for allowing us so graciously to use their work in this book.

Thank you, **Walnut Creek Church** family, for making my (Tami's) church planting years some of the best years of my life! Thank you for loving us so well and for releasing Steve to care for the family when I'm away. The buoyancy I experience is largely in part to your friendship, generosity, prayers, and gospel CPR.

Dad (Shari's), long ago you opened doors for me I didn't know were shut. You taught me to look for the third way, to question, to challenge the status quo—all with a grain of humor and that twinkle in your eye.

Finally, to you wonderful women who freely shared your stories, struggles, fears, and joys with us: without you, this book would never have been written. Thank you for allowing us the honor and privilege of walking with you in this wild and exhilarating roller coaster life of church planting.

Deserts, silence, solitudes are not necessarily

places but states of mind and heart. They will be

small solitudes, little deserts, tiny pools of silence,

but the experience they will bring, if we are

disposed to them, may be as exultant and as holy

as all the deserts of the world. For it is God who

makes solitude, deserts, and silences holy.

—Catherine de Hueck Doherty, Poustinia

Parakaleo, a ministry that comes alongside church planting spouses and couples, serves under the auspices of Mission to North America, an agency of the Presbyterian Church in America (PCA).
Parakaleo develops networks of coaching, caring, connecting, and celebrating both within and beyond the PCA.
You can find them at **parakaleo.us** or **pcamna.org**.

Made in the USA
Coppell, TX
27 September 2020

38715798R00109